Before the Mast

Boys from H.M.S. *St. Vincent* working aloft.

BEFORE THE MAST

Naval Ratings
of the Nineteenth Century

Henry Baynham

HUTCHINSON OF LONDON

HUTCHINSON & CO (*Publishers*) LTD
178-202 Great Portland Street, London W1

London Melbourne Sydney Auckland
Wellington Johannesburg Cape Town
and agencies throughout the world

First published 1971

*This book has been set in Garamond type, printed in Great Britain
on antique wove paper by Ebenezer Baylis and Son Ltd.
The Trinity Press, Worcester, and London
and bound by Wm. Brendon, Tiptree, Essex*

ISBN 0 09 107170 4

CONTENTS

ILLUSTRATIONS

Frontispiece. Boys from H.M.S. *St. Vincent* working aloft.

The illustrations are reproduced by courtesy of the Trustees of the National Maritime Museum.

INTRODUCTION AND NOTES ON SOURCES

This book is a sequel to *From the Lower Deck* and again attempts to give a picture of a period of the Royal Navy's history as far as possible in the words of the men themselves. It is, though, complete in itself and indeed there is a certain overlap in time between the two books. In the previous book the idea was to present a picture of the Old Navy, that of Nelson and the Great War against France. It was a time of stirring deeds worth recording for one's grandchildren, and many sailors of that period left memoirs and letters behind them telling the story of 'battles of long ago'. Not that all their memoirs recorded stirring deeds; many of them spent a great deal of ink deploring the conditions under which they lived, worked and fought, and not least the manner in which they had been forced to join—the infernal 'Press Gang'. The emphasis lay, though, in their memoirs and consequently in the book, on the fighting, and even after the end of the Great War itself, a seaman author, Charles M'Pherson, at Navarino, carried on under the great Nelson tradition: 'No Captain can do very wrong if he places his ship alongside that of an enemy.' But the role and practice of the Navy was changing.

The previous book ended with a description of the changes being brought about in the science of gunnery and with a letter from a young seaman who had just joined H.M.S. *Excellent*, the new naval gunnery school. In this sequel the emphasis lies more in the changing conditions themselves and on the new roles that the navy was called upon to play.

> When the balls whistle free,
> O'er the bright blue sea,
> We stand to our guns all day.

wrote W. S. Gilbert in the 1870s, but the times when it was normal practice to 'Stand to our guns all day' had passed and it was shells, not cannon balls that emerged from the new guns. Not that the Navy's guns were never fired in anger—indeed, time and again the Navy played an important role by bombardment or other violent action. Yet, as late as 1900 live ammunition provided for practice shoots was thrown overboard to avoid dirtying the guns! By the late nineteenth century, in every corner of the globe, the guns of the Royal Navy brought respect, if not obedience, and this was frequently achieved without their even being fired.

This, then, is a story of the Navy, if not at peace, at least the Navy of the *Pax Britannica*. The military actions are described, the V.C.s won by the sailors of the Royal Navy are recorded, but the interest lies primarily in how the sailors adapted themselves to the changing conditions, and many were the changes.

The material of this later period is far less well worked over than that of the Napoleonic Wars, and many of the most interesting accounts have not merely never been published, but are entirely unknown even to students of the period. For helping me to uncover this information I have to thank the *Daily Express* who published a letter 'Any Old Tars?' which brought in a rich haul of material. I am also most grateful to all those who took the trouble to reply to my appeal, and particularly those who lent me journals and letters, some of which I have used directly, but there are others, to whom my thanks are also due, whose documents have helped to form the background of the story. In particular I would like to thank Mr. Frederick Humphreys, who loaned me the manuscript of Charles Humphreys' Recollections, to Miss Relph for J. J. Stratton's diary and letter, to Mrs. Ivy Thomson for John Tilling's journal, to Mr. A. J. Franks for John Franks' letter, and to Mr. H. D. Thomas for Michael Toman's diary. Two other manuscripts, those of William Simpson and Daniel Harley, are in the National Maritime Museum.

Of the printed material, William Richardson's autobiography *A Mariner of England* (published by John Murray to whom due acknowledgement is made), John Bechervaise's two works *Thirty-six Years of Seafaring by an Old Quartermaster* and *Farwell* and Patrick Riley's *Memoirs of a Blue Jacket* (published by Samson Low and Marston to whom also due acknowledgement is made) are all fairly well known; Sam Noble's autobiography and Tom Holman's *Life in the Royal Navy* which he published anonymously, less so. The pamphlet which forms the basis for Chapter Eleven *Seamen of the Royal Navy, A View from the Lower Deck by One who Knows* was also published anonymously as was the series of letters from the Crimea written by a soldier in the Rifle Brigade.

Concerning other books on the period, there are numerous accounts of Arctic voyages written by the officers who took part in them. In particular I have used Beechey's own description of his voyage in the *Blossom* and Nares' account of his exploration in the Arctic. The famous Captain Marryat's son was on board the *Samarang* and his account supplements that of Joseph Stratton, as also does Sir Edward Belcher's own narrative. Miss Agnes Weston's autobiography *My Life Among the Blue Jackets* gives her view of the actions taken to improve the conditions *Afloat and Ashore*, and I have used Captain Verney's *Last Four Days of H.M.S. Eurydice* as a basis for the description of the loss of that ship. More generally, the only book on the social life of the Navy during the period is Michael Lewis' *The Navy in Transition* but this only covers the time up to 1864. On particular topics Christopher Lloyd's *The Slave Trade* is still the best work on the subject, as is Cyriax on the Franklin expedition, though L. P. Kirwan's *History of Arctic Exploration* gives a very lucid description of developments in polar research. There are numerous books on the winners of the Victoria Cross, but none of them are really more than an explanation of the official citations.

On general conditions there are numerous pamphlets issued by officers who had an axe to grind, but probably the most significant collection of articles is in the *United Services Journal* which throughout the nineteenth century carried a steady stream of articles on life on the lower deck, viewed through the officers' eyes.

Here I must again acknowledge my gratitude to the Headmaster and Governors of Canford School and to the Master and Fellows of Balliol College, Oxford.

Finally, a few further words of thanks: to Mr. Pearsall and all the staff of the National Maritime Museum in Greenwich for their help; To Mrs. Hazel Jarvis for typing the manuscript, a thankless task as anyone who has tried to read my writing knows. Several pupils of mine have helped, especially Geoffrey Calvert who compiled the index and Peter Lyle who read the proofs. Naturally any errors or omissions are my responsibility.

A NAVAL CHRONOLOGY 1815-1887

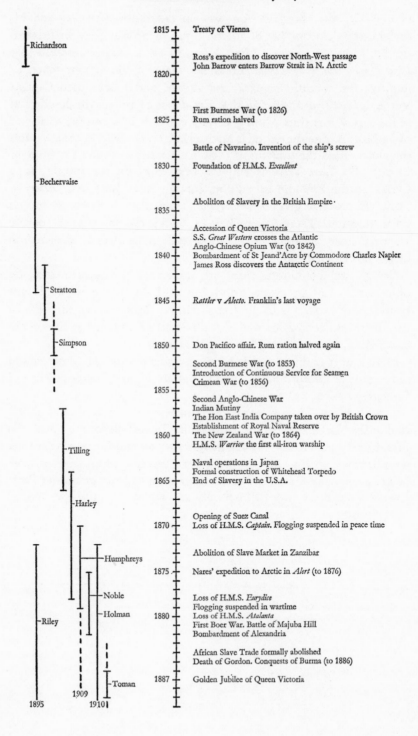

1815	Treaty of Vienna
	Ross's expedition to discover North-West passage
	John Barrow enters Barrow Strait in N. Arctic
1820	
1825	First Burmese War (to 1826)
	Rum ration halved
	Battle of Navarino. Invention of the ship's screw
1830	Foundation of H.M.S. *Excellent*
1835	Abolition of Slavery in the British Empire ·
	Accession of Queen Victoria
	S.S. *Great Western* crosses the Atlantic
	Anglo-Chinese Opium War (to 1842)
1840	Bombardment of St Jeand'Acre by Commodore Charles Napier
	James Ross discovers the Antarctic Continent
1845	*Rattler* v *Alecto*. Franklin's last voyage
1850	Don Pacifico affair. Rum ration halved again
	Second Burmese War (to 1853)
	Introduction of Continuous Service for Seamen
	Crimean War (to 1856)
1855	
	Second Anglo-Chinese War
	Indian Mutiny
	The Hon East India Company taken over by British Crown
	Establishment of Royal Naval Reserve
1860	The New Zealand War (to 1864)
	H.M.S. *Warrior* the first all-iron warship
	Naval operations in Japan
	Formal construction of Whitehead Torpedo
1865	End of Slavery in the U.S.A.
	Opening of Suez Canal
1870	Loss of H.M.S. *Captain*. Flogging suspended in peace time
	Abolition of Slave Market in Zanzibar
1875	Nares' expedition to Arctic in *Alert* (to 1876)
	Loss of H.M.S. *Eurydice*
	Flogging suspended in wartime
1880	Loss of H.M.S. *Atalanta*
	First Boer War. Battle of Majuba Hill
	Bombardment of Alexandria
	African Slave Trade formally abolished
	Death of Gordon. Conquests of Burma (to 1886)
1887	Golden Jubilee of Queen Victoria

Richardson

Bechervaise

Stratton

Simpson

Tilling

Harley

Humphreys

Noble

Holman

Riley

Toman

1895

1909

1910

I

The Old and the New

When, finally, in 1815, H.M.S. *Bellerophon* set sail for St. Helena, bearing Napoleon to exile and death, the sigh of relief that echoed round the country undoubtedly originated from over a hundred thousand seamen in the Royal Navy who at last hoped to be free from the terribly harsh conditions under which they laboured. Within three years, the manpower of the Navy was reduced from 145,000 men to 19,000. For the last time, the infernal Press Gang had roamed the streets of England's seaports. Never again would the merchant seaman, homeward bound, tremble with fear as he saw a Royal Naval vessel bear up towards his ship, and he be forced into serving His Majesty without even seeing wife or family.

The ending of the Press Gang introduced a fundamental change in the conditions of service. The Royal Navy became almost entirely a volunteer force, but not quite—as this extract from the *Portsmouth Herald* of 29th January, 1832 shows:

> Edward Burnett and William Burnett, brothers, natives of Portsmouth, have been convicted to serve five years in the Navy, having been taken, on Friday last, at Spithead, with contraband spirits in an open boat, by Mr. Martell, Officer of customs.

Clearly, the problem of recruiting the sailors for the Royal Navy was by no means yet solved. One legacy of the Great War had been to imbue the merchant seaman with a fear and loathing of His Majesty's Service. When one by one the old wooden walls of Nelson's navy were decommissioned after the war most seamen were only too glad to 'swallow the anchor'. But one group of seamen was not immediately freed; this was the boys, often from the Marine Society or some other charitable institution, who had been bred to the Navy. Many of them orphans, they had nowhere else to go. These formed the basis for manning the new volunteer navy, a nucleus of continuous service men.

A second group was later formed by the 'Seamen Gunners' of H.M.S. *Excellent* who signed on for a number of years. Indeed, one of the major differences between the old and the new navies was this change from service for one commission only to service for a period of years— not that this came about at once. John Bechervaise, one of the sailors whose memoirs are given here was in a sense a permanent naval seaman and eventually he went to H.M.S. *Excellent* but at one point in 1824 he had considerable difficulty in obtaining a ship in spite of a good record of conduct. This was because the ships for which he applied had already taken their quota of men of his ability or 'rating'. While looking for another berth, Bechervaise received no pay and had to support his wife and children from his previous earnings; hence his great relief that his son was at the Naval school at Greenwich. If the Navy then was to be assured of a satisfactory supply of seamen, it somehow had to hold on to them between berths, but this was not achieved until the 1850s. Until then the majority of seamen continued to serve for one commission only. Generally there were not enough seamen, and ships would not wait, sometimes for months, whilst the Captain desperately tried to man his ship, for until the 1850s this remained a Captain's responsibility. The senior rates might all be filled, as in Bechervaise's case, and yet there might not be sufficient Able Seamen to man her, and the ship would have to wait.

The problem was not really under the Admiralty's control. It was a jealously guarded right of a seaman that he could choose which ship he wished to join. Continuous service meant the end of this right and many officers feared that there was more to be lost than gained by enforcing it. Certainly H.M.S. *Excellent* the naval gunnery school did provide a nucleus of seamen gunners who were further encouraged by a higher rate of pay and this became the rule in the end, but H.M.S. *Excellent* was not founded until 1830 and it was another twenty-five years before continuous service became general, encouraged by a higher rate of pay. However, by the 1850s most sailors were signed on, not just for the commission but for a period of years and at the end of twenty-one years were offered pensions. The Royal Navy thus became not just an alternative to the merchant service, but a career in its own right. In addition, nearly all the ratings joined as boys, and thereby acquired a sense of belonging to, and a pride in the Service of the Queen.

The process of training these boys forms an important element in the New Navy which is treated in detail later in the book, largely in the boys' own words. Things became very different from the time when Jack Nastyface was thrown into the hold of a receiving ship, though there were many problems and terrible accidents occurred, as the loss of H.M.S. *Eurydice* shows.

These changes took place in a navy that was also being revolutionised in its material aspect in three distinct ways. Steam took the place of sail, iron hulls took the place of the wooden walls and turret guns replaced the broadside.

The role of the Navy, too, was more varied. One of the major activities now became exploration and three of the seamen here took part in voyages into the Arctic Circle. John Bechervaise, an Old Quartermaster as he styles himself, sailed with Captain Beechey into the Pacific and so north through the Bering Strait: William Simpson, a Sergeant of Marines was involved in the search for the famous Franklin expedition; a third, Daniel Harley, at the end of the period sailed in the *Alert* on an expedition that reached further north than any of its predecessors, though it failed to reach the North Pole.

Combined with these voyages of exploration was an important, if rather less exciting role, the monotonous work of surveying and charting the oceans of the world. Indeed Bechervaise, under Beechey, helped to chart many an unknown or little known Pacific island, including the unique Pitcairn, home of the *Bounty* mutineers. During the century the oceans of the world were surveyed by the ships and men of the Royal Navy, making the seas safer for shipping, and the charts they produced were available from the Admiralty to all at home or abroad who wished to purchase them—a generous action quite out of line with previous maritime tradition as nations in the past had generally jealously guarded their navigational discoveries.

These surveying voyages were a trying and even dangerous business.* Joseph Stratton, a first class petty officer served in the *Samarang* and, under Captain Sir Edward Belcher, surveyed various islands in the North Pacific Ocean and China seas. An account of his surveying voyages appears in chapter 6.

Another vital and generous task which the Navy performed was the suppression of the Slave Trade. England had formerly been one of the major participants in this lucrative trade, and the Royal Navy helped to expiate the offences previously committed, by releasing, wherever possible, these wretched human cargoes, and capturing the slaving ships themselves; but it was at a terrible price:

> Beware and take care of the Bight of Benin:
> There's one comes out for forty goes in!

An exaggeration, yet in 1829 a quarter of the whole West African squadron died of disease. We have no Lower Deck accounts of this terrible task; all too often the seamen never returned from the West Coast of Africa—the White Man's Grave. However, slaving was not

* See the picture of the *Samarang* (p. 80).

confined to the West Coast and an important and almost as lucrative trade was carried on in the Persian Gulf. Death from disease there was not quite so common as off the African coast and among others, Charles Humphreys survived to write an account of his experiences in the struggle against the slavers. There were, of course differences, but both the dangers and the monotony were similar to those faced by Humphreys' forbears off the West African Coast. Another seaman, Thomas Holman, gives a further description of a duel with slavers in the Persian Gulf.

However, the slave trade was only one aspect of the Royal Navy's role as a peace keeping force. The African slave trade was largely eliminated by 1865 (though Sam Noble was involved in a slave chase in 1876) and by 1883 the trade in the Persian Gulf had virtually ceased. Throughout the century the navy was commissioned to police the seas and act as 'a safeguard unto our most gracious sovereign Lady Queen Victoria and her Dominions and a security for such as pass on the seas upon their lawful occasions'.

Aside from the suppression of the Slave Trade, there is surprisingly little in surviving memoirs about the 'military' history of the Royal Navy. Descriptions of various incidents certainly form part of these narratives, and are included in the sailors' accounts here, yet they seem almost incidental to the main purpose of the memoirs themselves— not as in previous examples largely the justification of writing down their memoirs at all. This may be because the campaigns in which they were involved, though forming a continuous framework as we view them now, must frequently have seemed isolated and not very significant incidents. On the one hand in the 'Great War', John Nicol and even Jack Nastyface with the rest of their countrymen recognised the importance of the Battle of Trafalgar. An isolated gun-boat action somewhere up the Irawadi, even though it did much to bring peace to Burma, can hardly be viewed in the same light. Even in the only major war of the period fought against Russia and generally known as the Crimean War, the Navy's role was of no obvious significance. The Navy was engaged in four different areas—in the Black Sea, the Baltic, the Arctic and in the Far East and yet not one decisive engagement was fought.

But the Navy did play an important part in the land campaigns of the Crimean War. As the 'Naval Brigade' they manhandled their guns on shore and used them with conspicuous courage as heavy artillery. Unfortunately no first-hand lower deck account of their achievement seems to have survived and consequently I have included here extracts from an account by a soldier who served with the army. I feel that this gives a better inside picture of what the sailor's life was like ashore than any quarter-deck account. Aside from this, the Navy's military role was enormous in scope, yet small in detail. Some glimpses of this are seen in this book in accounts of seamen who won the Victoria Cross.

The changes in the ships did not necessarily mean an improvement for the men who served in them. A gunnery officer in 1867 wrote: 'The warships of the present are not so comfortable to live in as the old wooden vessels, and are not so attractive to the eye, however much they may excel them in fighting properties and sailors like to belong to a handsome ship in which they can take pride.' However, the seamen themselves, possibly because their time in the Navy tended to be short made little of this. They seem to have simply accepted the ships as they found them.

This is not to say that the seamen were content with their conditions; one of them, John Tilling, is more outspoken against the officers even than his predecessor, Jack Nastyface, though Tilling's opinions were never published. In contrast, Michael Toman, a successful and enterprising Engine Room Artificer views the Navy from a very different angle. Spanning the century, though, are two Gunners, both promoted from the Lower Deck to Warrant Rank, yet utterly unalike, and it is with the first of these that this history begins.

A sailor's life in the 'Old Navy' was by no means simply 'Rum, sodomy and the lash'. As the previous volume has shown, these elements were certainly present to no small extent but things were improving, the mutinies of 1797 were not entirely in vain. Some correction of the pessimistic view is all the more necessary since Stanley Bennett in a recent book, *The Price of Admiralty*, has castigated the Navy's record over the last 156 years. 'Generally', he writes of a flogging, 'the last few hundred strokes were inflicted on a corpse.' The picture immediately springs to mind of rows of blood-thirsty Tory admirals delightedly licking their sadistic lips as the body of poor Jack is mercilessly flogged. That flogging round the fleet took place we know only too well 'for those were crude and cruel days and human flesh was cheap'. But it hardly occurred after 1815. The press gang was a vile institution but there is not much to be said in favour of any form of conscription, and no press went out after 1815. Of course many things were wrong with the Old Navy, but the very people who criticise the parsimony of the Admiralty then, also claim that defence costs today should be cut. Britain has always wanted her Navy on the cheap and sometimes she has got it, but there is always a price to pay, and often the sailors have paid it with their lives. Of course there was muddled thinking, of course there were stick-in-the-muds who dragged their feet, who said that flogging was necessary for discipline. In an element such as the sea where experience teaches what no man or book

2

can, the old sea-dog is liable to be arrogant and opinionated and to regard innovation as dangerous and progress as undesirable.

I have made here no attempt at special pleading. I am not out to castigate the Admiralty for its incompetence or its conservativeness. Equally I have not tried to glamorise 'our boys in blue' and glory in the days when Britannia really ruled the waves and Britons not merely were not slaves but did their best to see that no one else was either. This is the navy as the sailors saw it and I have deliberately started again with the 'Old Navy' if only to show how far they had to come. It did take many years for the sailor to get a fair deal—but then this was true for most people from the coal miner to the crossing sweeper. There was much to put right, much to condemn but we will be fairer both to them and to ourselves if we first listen to what the seamen themselves had to say. William Richardson tried not to criticise or condemn—but let him speak for himself.

2

A Mariner of England—William Richardson

In 1817 the *Bedford* was broken up, and I became a supernumerary for six months, and then was appointed to the *Pitt*, a new 74-gun ship at this place, and remained with her until March 1819, at which time so many ships had been broken up, and others sold out of the service, that almost each ship that remained had a double set of warrant-officers on board. The Admiralty, therefore, thought proper to make reduction by superannuation, and being all examined at Haslar Hospital, upwards of a hundred were put down for super-annuation, and I among the rest.

As I had not expected this, I could hardly believe it true that I should have my liberty so soon again. I could hardly describe my agreeable feelings, and thought sometimes it was only a dream; but, thanks be to God, it was true, and I hope I shall ever be thankful for such mercies in being delivered from so many dangers and hardships, and hope to pass, please God, the remainder of my days in comfort and peace.

Indeed I had no cause to regret being superannuated, as I con-sidered myself much neglected in promotion, after being so often recommended by my superiors. My name had been more than twelve years on the Admiralty list for promotion. Sir Richard Strachan had written personally to the Admiralty for a warrant to appoint me to a new three-decker building at Plymouth; but another person got her through Parliamentary interest, and one who had seen little sea service during the war. I had followed the sea service up to this time near thirty-nine years in the King's and merchant service.

According to the scale of superannuation, which jumps every five years, this entitled me to £65 per annum, and for which I am satisfied; had I remained twenty-five years I should have got £75. However, thank God, I am contented, and would not change for a commission in the Navy.

So wrote William Richardson, a gunner, at the end of his career in the Navy. Another gunner, Thomas Holman, who joined the Navy forty years later wrote:

I now have to answer the question as to whether we should send our boys to the Navy. I say 'Yes', emphatically 'Yes'—after a period of twenty years in its lower ranks. My school contemporaries may now be a bit ahead of me, but I doubt if many of them have extracted so much fun and enjoyment out of the last twenty years of life as I have done; I am quite certain none of them have been happier or are more in love with their profession.

Besides, I hope and believe, in fact feel absolutely certain, that the authorities are on the eve of opening up opportunities for the Ranker in the Navy that will make it a popular public service in which ability can rise to responsible and remunerative positions equal to those to be obtained in the Army, Church, Law, Civil Service, Mercantile Houses and Marine. In fact making it what it should be, a service that will attract all the best of the youths among the masses of the nation.

Let us endeavour to keep up the glorious tradition of our Navy, and still maintain the prestige of the flag that shall, in the future, as in the past, command respect from every nation, as its graceful folds travel slowly every morning to the peaks of our War Ships to the strain of God Save the Queen.

Possibly nothing could emphasise more clearly the changing attitude towards the Navy than these two passages written by men so alike and yet so different. Both were able, more able than most of their contemporaries in the service. Both received rapid promotion to Warrant Rank having started at the bottom of the ladder; both were gunners, but the similarity almost stops there. Holman will be allowed to speak for himself at the end of the book and it is with Richardson that we must start.

William Richardson, of course, belonged to the 'Old Navy'. And will serve well to introduce the harsh conditions that were to be changed in the next seventy years.

His early career was very similar to many of the sailors of the 'Great War'. Born in 1768, he first went to sea with his father and after a period as an apprentice was promoted to second mate. In 1790 he joined a slaver, and though he did not particularly like the way the captain treated the slaves he found the situation 'comfortable'. This was to change greatly as later accounts of the slave trade will show. Richardson later joined another slaver, but two days after his return to England he was taken by the press gang. Surprisingly he did not mind this too much. 'I was young and had the world before me, did not fret much and was willing to go to any part of the world.' This may well have been because he had just had news of his father's death. He was sent on board the *London* of 98-guns.

It was on June 4 (the birthday of George III) that I went on board, and was stationed in the maintop. Her lofty masts and square yards appeared wonderful to me, and I wondered how they were able to manage them; but I soon got accustomed to that, for we had plenty of exercise with them and the great guns almost daily.

Not that he liked everything about his new life:

Although the usage was good in general on board the *London*, yet I did not altogether like their manner of discipline, for soon after I got on board we had to cat the anchor, and in running along with the foul, boatswains' mates were placed on each side, who kept thrashing away with their rattans on our backs, making no difference between those that pulled hard and those that did not.

This system of 'starting' was soon to disappear.

Richardson quickly showed himself to be above the normal run of pressed men.

One day a man fell overboard when not a boat was alongside; he could not swim, and went down twice, but came up again. I had heard that if a man goes down the third time he rises no more, therefore without waiting to pull my clothes off I jumped overboard and caught hold of him, but before I could recover myself he had got on my back and clung to me like a leech; I tried to shake him off, to hold him by one arm and swim with the other, but could not. A heavy rope was thrown, which I caught hold of, but there was so much slack I let it go again: it is strange that no one threw a grating or a stool overboard to us; and in this manner we kept drifting astern, it blowing fresh and a rough swell on, and I very nearly suffocated; and in this near fatal affair we should certainly both have been drowned had not a dockyard launch coming along taken us up. To mend the matter, when we got on board I did not receive the least pity, for the man I had saved had a tail the size of a short pipe-stem; and an old boatswain's mate swore that it was no wonder the man fell overboard—'only look at his tail!' said he; 'was it not enough to drag him overboard?' and set them all a-laughing.

Richardson's first period of service was a short one.

The first three months I had been here, no seamen got liberty on shore except those that had entered into the service (and I had not);

but it being now reported that the fleet would soon be paid off, liberty was given to all, so I with near fifty more got leave for forty-eight hours, as they did not care now whether we deserted or not. This was the first time I had ever been at Portsmouth, and the first place that brought us up was, of course, a public-house; but as I was not partial to strong liquors I went to see the town, and in the evening met one of my brother top-men, who (knowing his failings) begged me to take care of his watch until the morning. Next morning I met him again, and with a woeful countenance he told me he had lost his watch. I asked him where, but he could give no account of it whatever. 'Now,' says I, 'this is the result of drinking too much, and you ought to know better and be more careful.' He promised he would for the future, so I gave him his watch which surprised him greatly!

Soon after this we sailed for Plymouth, where the ship was paid off with many others—this was September 24—and I received £4 10s. four months' duty at the rate of three and ninepence per day as Paddy called it (that is three farthings and ninepence a day); we subscribed two shillings apiece to buy Mr. Cooper, the boatswain, a silver call with chain and plate, with a suitable inscription on it for his kindness to the ship's company, and a silver pint pot for his wife; then several of us went on board the *Quebec* frigate for a passage to Portsmouth, she being ordered for that purpose, and soon after landed there.

Already, Richardson has underlined three aspects of lower deck life in the 'Old Navy'. The discipline was unbelievably harsh. Starting as described above was officially abolished in 1809 but continued to be used for some years, though the practice more or less ceased after the war; it was indeed more suitable for 'pressed' criminals than for volunteers—but flogging, on which there is more to be said, went on. Drunkenness remained a continual scourge and the fact that Richardson 'was not partial to strong liquors' accounts, to a certain extent, for his later success, and in this he differed from all the seamen in the previous volume and even from many of his successors here; unlike starting, drunkenness could not be easily eliminated. Third, Richardson frequently refers to the extraordinary generosity of the seamen; later writers were to deplore a decline in this quality, though how truly it is hard to say.

Richardson's next contact with the Press Gang resulted in a rather longer term of service. After being shipwrecked at Ostend in another slaver, he served in a number of merchant vessels in India, but in the last of them, the *Elizabeth*, he was shipwrecked and spent several days in a leaky open boat with no compass. Fortunately they were picked up and eventually got back to Calcutta, but this was not the most fortunate berth for him.

As I was sitting near the door, and it open, and smoking a cheroot while brooding over my hard fate, a guard of soldiers came along, and the serjeant seeing me, came and said that I was to go along with him. I asked him what for: that I was no deserter from an Indiaman, which I supposed he was looking after. He replied that his orders were to take every English seaman he could meet with, and at this time he had upwards of twenty that he had taken, and one of them was the chief mate of a country ship which I knew, and said it was best to submit, as the serjeant must obey his orders.

The reason of this pressing, a thing seldom known here, was that the *Woodcot* Indiaman was lying here in want of seamen, having on board stores and ammunition and 150 artillerymen to sail for Pondicherry, a French place our army was besieging; so we were all taken to Fort William and put into prison for the night, and after that sent on board the *Woodcot*, and put under the charge of Mr. Cole, a Master's mate of the *Minerva* frigate, who had been here with a prize and was returning to his ship again in the *Woodcot*.

Shipwreck and the loss of all our clothes is distressing enough, but to be pressed into the bargain is really shocking; and I began to despond even to tears at my hard fate.

His previous experience in the Royal Navy had not enamoured him of the service and he had no desire to serve again. To show how greatly hated was the royal service these were Richardson's final words on parting the merchant service:

We pressed men (to the number of twenty-three) were sent on board the *Minerva*, and being arranged along the quarter-deck, were examined by the admiral and the captain. I told them I had been only three years at sea and had no clothes but the shabby ones on my back, and tried all I could to get clear; but it would not do, and out of twenty-three only three of us were kept; the other twenty were sent on shore at Madras to shift as well as they could. And thus ended my services of near thirteen years in the merchant's employ, a period of poverty, hardships, dangers, and disappointments such as few, I believe, have experienced during that time.

Richardson seems to have considered that he had been thrown out of the frying pan into the fire. However, until he was actually on board the *Minerva* he did not give up all hope of escaping.

Hope, now, was my only comfort, for I knew the ship must anchor several times before she got to sea, as the south-west monsoons were against us; so I made up my mind, should an opportunity offer while at anchor in the night, to swim on shore in defiance of tigers, alligators, or anything else, and run my chance; and the following evening after leaving Calcutta, we came to anchor a few miles above Fulta, where we had been so merry the other day. After the watch was set, the people being much fatigued with hard duty all day, soon fell asleep, but the artillerymen were stationed all round the ship as sentinels.

Although I was fatigued as much as others, my mind would not allow me to go to sleep, for I kept watching and hoping some of the sentinels would soon go into a doze; and at last one of them on the poop began nodding, and lay with his head over the rails as if asleep. Now is the time, thinks I; so passing silently along the quarter-deck to the poop and taffrail, I was in the act of getting over to slip down the boat's painter into the water when the sentinel awoke and asked what I was doing there. I had just presence of mind to answer that I was going to bail the boat out. He said I should not go there without leave of the officer of the watch, who was sitting asleep in a chair on the quarter-deck; and he, hearing the noise, awoke and said, 'Damn the boat! never mind her,' and went to sleep again; so I thought it best to retreat in time, went forward and then below, where I slept on a chest lid until the morning.

We got under way from here, and the next place we came to anchor at was Cudgeree, where they make the pots. Here we lay farther from the land than before, but a country brig laden with rice came alongside to deliver. Her captain and crew were all natives, and I began to hope I might conceal myself in her hold; so when the hatches were taken off, none was more ready than I to jump down and begin to sling the bags of rice as they were hoisted up, and thus I continued until it was all out; then I stole forward to the fore-peak, lay down and covered myself with some mats lying there, hoping every minute the brig would put off and I escape, for the wind and tide were running strong up the river; but while I was thinking of this the black captain came into the hold and began taking up the mats and shaking the loose rice together, and discovered me, but I have thought since the black rascal had watched me.

He seemed much surprised, and I, being prepared, got up and told him I had been mate of a ship at Calcutta; how they had pressed me, and brought me away against my inclination. Seeing he hesitated, I offered him my watch to say nothing, but he would not take it, and going silently away I was in hopes that all was right; but very soon after I heard the rough voice of Mr. Edgar Hay, the chief mate of the *Woodcot*, hailing us to know who was there, so I answered it was me, and that I was waiting for an empty bag to put loose rice into. 'Damn the loose rice!' said he; 'if you don't make haste and jump on board you will lose your passage' (God grant it! thought I—nothing would please me better); but he had no suspicion of my intentions, and this was the last prospect I had of escaping.

He was stationed to do duty in the Maintop of the *Minerva* and he was, indeed, in adverse circumstances.

All my clothes were on my back, and with an old silver watch and one rupee, which constituted my all, I had now, as it were, the world to begin again; and a poor prospect I had before me. I had no bed, neither did I care for any, for my bones had got so hardened since I came to sea that I could sleep as comfortable on a chest lid or on the deck as on the best bed on the ship; and having only one shirt, I went without when I had to wash and dry it.

Unfortunately there is not room here to follow Richardson's career in detail through his 27 years of service. He served for a year in the *Minerva* and was then drafted into the *Prompt*, a smaller frigate. He served in her until 1799 and while in her he was promoted and later confirmed as Gunner, a warrant-officer—no H.M.S. *Excellent* then. There were qualifying examinations but he had not passed them. Most of this time was spent in the West Indies, though during a brief spell in England he did get married: he then served in several different ships until joining the *Caesar* in which he stayed until the end of the war. Leaving her, in 1815, he served for another four years and then gladly 'swallowed the anchor' as has already been recounted.

Richardson came from a background well above that of the normal lower deck sailor. He received a boarding school education and also a special course in Navigation, as did his other brothers, but although, or more truly because they all 'followed the sea', they were not a close knit family and saw little of one another. Richardson records this in 1789.

This winter died my youngest sister Ann, aged ten years. Her funeral was the only one in our family that I ever remember attending, and the rest of us were distributed as follows: My father commanding a ship abroad; my elder sister at home; my brother John, apprentice in the *Mary*; my brother Robert, apprentice in the *Golden Grove*, with the expedition to New Holland; my brother James, in the Greenland fishery trade; my brother George, at home with his sister; so that we were pretty well separated from each other.

The fact that they all served at sea did not mean that they often met and of only one of his brothers—James—was William ever to see much. This was first in 1795 when a new captain was appointed to the *Prompt*—the Hon. Edward Leveson-Gower, who brought several of his former officers with him.

To my surprise and joy, who should be among them but my brother James, then a Master's mate, whom I had not seen or heard of for six years, and of course we were glad to meet each other again. From him I learnt that my brother John was in the *Assurance*, Robert in the *Seahorse*, and George in the *Espiègle*; so that we were all five in H.M. Royal Navy.

William and James served together for a time, but, inevitably, the exigencies of the service soon took them apart, and it was not until the 12th September, 1810 when,

Arrived the *Scylla*, a 20-gun ship; and to my great surprise I found my brother James to be gunner of her and of course we were glad to see each other again, this being the third time in twenty-one years (and all seven year intervals) since we had left Shields; but neither of us knew where our other brothers were (John, Robert, George).

The fact that the brothers only met so rarely is not altogether surprising given the situation of wartime service. Their entire lack of knowledge of one another may indicate a lack of interest, but it is also a comment on the almost complete lack of communication between men in the Navy unless they happened to be on the same station. The ships themselves were very close knit units but outside the ship itself personal contacts seem to have been few. The sailors were indeed virtually married to the ship—even if the union was frequently inharmonious. The absence of outside contacts brought the men closer together and there was a close bond between them which is surprising to modern eyes. The following extract is an example. This took place in the *Minerva* and they had obtained a small prize, though Richardson's share was only 3¼ rupees.

My little prize money was soon expended, together with my watch, which I sold to pay my part of the expenses of the mess; and most of it went for gin, though I was averse to ardent spirits. But some of them were as wild as March hares, and among them a little Welshman named Emmet, whom we had sometimes to lay on a chest and tie his hands and feet to the handles till he was sober. One day when he was on shore on liberty, and of course tipsy, in passing a shop in Bombay he saw a large glass globe hanging in it, with goldfish swimming and live birds in it; he stopped and stared at it with astonishment, and muttered to himself, 'What, birds swimming and fish flying—impossible'; and in order to be satisfied, he threw a stone which hit the globe and knocked it all to pieces about the shop.

He was soon arrested and sent to jail, and a report was sent on board next morning that one of our people was there. An officer was sent to see who it was, and there found poor Tom Emmet very much cast down in the mouth. He was released and brought on board, but the globe was to be paid for; therefore the ship's company subscribed eight hundred rupees (a great sum for the value of the globe), and paid the owner for it.

There are later examples of generosity, but the close comradeship of the seamen under adversity during the Great War was not equalled by their successors. The sailors were certainly drunkards and in many respects utterly irresponsible. Perhaps the very posting of sentinels encouraged the men to try to break ship, but they soon became a necessity. This is shown by the following account of an incident when Richardson was in the *Prompt*. They were visiting Guernsey, and in order to get at the ship's bottom to scrape and clean it, the ship was lashed alongside the pier, and sentinels placed on the pier to prevent the men from leaving the ship. However:

Our officers had not considered that the end of the pier was dry at low water, and our people soon availed themselves of that opportunity, and when the ship floated again there was hardly anyone on board to warp her into the roads again.

The captain was of course very angry, so he, with some more officers, went into the town, and found most of them half-seas-over in gin-shops, and the sentinels on the pier not much better. It was laughable to see them staggering along and hastening on board except one, who by accident fell into the water and was drowned, and the ship was soon anchored in the roads. As our captain knew what sailors were, none were punished, but it is a great pity that sailors should be so fond of strong drink; it is the only thing that disgraces them.

It was not even as though they had a harsh disciplinarian as a captain. The Hon. Leveson-Gower treated the men as well as any captain (as indeed his action in this incident indicates). Only very shortly before it they had been given leave.

We left the Downs and arrived at Spithead, where ten of us at a time were allowed twenty-four hours' liberty on shore, Captain Leveson-Gower having said that his ship should never be called a prison ship. I had the luck to be among the first ten, and glad was I to get my foot on English ground again, being the first time since I left it to go to the West Indies. When we left the ship in the liberty boat some of our officers seemed to signify that they did not expect to see us again, and among the rest our old rip of a boatswain, who had been a deserter himself; but they were all mistaken, for we returned to our proper time (and so did the others that went after us), for we thought it would be very ungrateful now to desert, when we had got a captain who would give us liberty.

I think it only fair and just, that when seamen are pressed in coming home from a long voyage, they should be allowed a few weeks' liberty on shore to spend their money among their friends and relations; when that was gone, they would soon be tired of the shore, return more contented to their ships, and by such means there would not be half so much desertion.

Richardson's comments were very fair, but they become irrelevant after 1815 when the Press was suspended. After the war, men may not have been easy to obtain at times, but at least they were all volunteers and the dangers of granting leave became far less. What Richardson quite correctly seizes on is that the problem was caused by the Press itself. Some form of conscription in wartime and even in peacetime has often been regarded as necessary, be it to fight against Napoleon or Hitler, or indeed as a safeguard against any aggression. The real fault lay in the conditions of service. The oppression and brutality of the law only encouraged brutality and irresponsibility among the sailors, as Richardson repeatedly shows.

After he had served in the *Minerva* for over a year the ship went into Portsmouth to be paid off.

After being a week in there (the ship stripped and nearly cleared of her stores), without having a moment's liberty on shore, after being so long abroad in unhealthy climates, thirty-seven of us were drafted on board the *Royal William* at Spithead, and the same day drafted again into the *Prompt*, a frigate of twenty-eight guns (Captain Taylor), and ready for sea. Here was encouragement for seamen to fight for their King and Country. A coolie in India was better off.

Richardson gives a large number of examples of complaints against the conditions in the Navy. In the *Prompt*, under Leveson-Gower's predecessor, no leave was given, with the inevitable result. There is little doubt that a less harsh discipline and a greater respect for the seamen would have been more successful but then the really successful officers, such as Nelson and Collingwood, did generally treat their men better. Even at a lower level there were humane officers, as Richardson records:

> One of these evenings, as I was sitting on the coamings of the after-hatchway pondering my hard fate, Mr. Robinson, our first lieutenant, a worthy and good man, observed me, and sent for me to his cabin; and then, taking a sheet from off his bed, gave it to me and told me to get some clothes made from it, and said that when his dabash (a gentoo agent) came on board he would give me a good rig-out of clothing; but the ship sailed before he came, and so disappointed us. However, I got a light jacket and two pairs of trousers made from the sheet, and was very thankful for his kindness to me, a stranger.

This sort of action took tragically long to become common practice. In the 1860s a later seaman, Tilling, behaved and was treated as though the Great War was still being waged.

A few changes did come quickly. The abolition of impressment in 1815 has already been mentioned, and for the next hundred years the Navy was manned entirely by volunteers. But the old customs lingered. Richardson describes Flogging Round the Fleet in the following passage when he was in the *Caesar*. One of their seamen, Samuel Morgan, had been recaptured after deserting and was sent to the *Barfleur* for trial.

> He and two men belonging to the *Kent* (likewise for desertion) were tried by a court-martial and each sentenced to three hundred lashes. Poor Morgan was much pittied, being a good and mild creature, and almost fainted when the sentence was pronounced. By the kind interference of the humane Lady Hardy poor Morgan afterwards got reprieved, but the two other poor fellows were punished round the fleet; but did not receive their number of lashes because they could not bear it, so they were sent on board the flag-ship until they recovered to receive the remainder.
>
> Horrid work, could anyone bear to see a beast used so, let alone a fellow creature? People may talk of negro slavery and the whip, but let them look nearer home, and see a poor sailor arrived from a long voyage, exulting in the pleasure of soon being among his dearest friends and relations. Behold him just entering the door, when a press gang seizes him like a felon, drags him away and puts him into the tender's hold, and from thence he is sent on board a man-of-war, perhaps ready to sail to some foreign station, without seeing either his wife, friends, or relations; if he complains he is likely to be seized up and flogged with a cat, much more severe

than the negro driver's whip, and if he deserts he is flogged round
the fleet nearly to death. Surely they had better shoot a man at once:
it would be greater lenity.

It may be said that England cannot do without pressing. Be it so;
but then let it be done in a more equitable manner, and let sailors
arriving from long voyages have liberty a month or more to spend
their money and enjoy themselves with their friends; then I will be
bound to say they will endure pressing with more patience, be
better satisfied, and not so ready to desert.

In the course of the century disease became less of a scourge, though
not everywhere. The death-rate from illness on the West Africa
station during the struggle against the slavers was probably as high as
at any previous time, but some improvement was made immediately.
In particular, scurvy, long the scourge of mariners, was largely
contained—though not always on the Arctic voyages. As we know
now, scurvy is caused by a lack of vitamin C, the vitamin found in
fresh vegetables which were almost entirely absent after the first week
or two at sea. The supply of lemon juice which the Admiralty were
persuaded in 1795 to issue to the whole crew and not just to the sick
greatly helped to solve this problem—though by no means completely,
as Richardson records:

> I now began to weigh matters and ponder on my situation, and found
> that since I had left England the balance was much against me: then
> I had a chest of clothes and bedding, and my liberty; now I have
> little clothing, no shoes or stockings, and no liberty, and much
> decayed in my condition; my gums were swelled over my teeth by
> the scurvy so that I could not chew my victuals without them
> being covered with blood. I and several others ought to have been
> sent to the hospital, but instead of that we were not allowed to set our
> feet on the land.
>
> However, by getting good, fresh provisions the scurvy began to
> abate, thank God, and my gums broke away bit by bit at a time, and
> without any pain as the new ones came.

This was at the end of the voyage. But again, at the end of his time
in the *Prompt*:

> Many of our people were bad with the scurvy, and if you only made
> a dent with your finger on the flesh it would remain a considerable
> time before it filled up again. From a small pimple that broke out
> on a man's thigh (and which the doctor could not stop) it increased
> until all the flesh on the thigh was consumed, and this was by the

scurvy; but being now in the land of plenty the rest of them soon recovered.

More terrible still were the events on board the *Tromp*, though Richardson's account of the causes of the disease might not be accepted by modern medical opinion. At Martinique:

There was an agent of transports here named Whittaker, who always took care to be first on board to tell the Admiral the news; and being asked how the *Tromp* got on in delivering her stores, he told him rather slowly; and when our captain went on board the *Leviathan* to pay his respects to the Admiral (who was none of the best-tempered men) he told our captain that we were dilatory in getting the stores out, which hurt our captain's feelings much, as the story was untrue.

The consequence was (and let this be known to tale-bearers) the death of many brave men; for after this reprimand, when a boat-load of stores or raft of spars were ready to put off from the ship, they were ordered away directly, rain or shine, and the people getting wet with rain and letting their clothes dry on their back with the hot sun when the shower was over, brought a dangerous fever on them which affected the whole ship, and we thought one time that no one would survive it.

Whatever we may think of Richardson's diagnosis of the cause of the disease, the results were apparent to all.

Every day for some time we were sending people to the hospital, and few returned. The captain and purser with their wives left the ship to live on shore; the doctor went to the hospital and got invalided; the first lieutenant, Mr. Pine, and the clerk, his brother (whom by-the-bye he had much neglected, though a very decent man), both died; next the master with his wife (large in a family way) both died; then the marine officer; and the wardroom was cleared of all its officers except the sick second lieutenant, Mr. Frankland.

Next died Mr. Campbell, the boatswain, leaving a wife and son and daughter on board; next went Mr. Hogan, the surgeon-assistant, a funny little fellow who pretended to tell by their constitutions who would die and who would not, little thinking he was to go so soon himself; next followed near all our fine young midshipmen who had come out for promotion; then the master-at-arms, the armourer, gunner's mate (a fine stout fellow), the captain's steward, cook and tailor, then the captain's lady's maid, and many brave men. Mr. Jury, the carpenter, got the fever too, but would not go to the hospital, as so many were dying there every day; he went on shore to sick quarters at his own expense, and partially recovered.

A somewhat surprising list, both in number and content, but then Richardson had his wife with him, and she also caught the fever. He did not allow her to go to hospital and she was treated privately. She recovered, but it was a long process:

> When her appetite came, she was at first permitted to eat only a little at a time, and by degrees recovered, but very weak; the skin on her hands and feet came off like peelings of onions.

Bit by bit the disease subsided:

> The few hands left were now set to work to wash their blankets and bed-ticks, and the flocks sent on shore by the Admiral's order to be dried in ovens. A Mr. Hearn from the *Leviathan* came on board as acting master, and promised to do great things in bringing the ship into a healthy state. In two or three days he caught the fever, but would not believe it, and when requested to go to the hospital refused; however, he was soon compelled to go, but not before his hands and feet were dead, and he died that night, having been only a week on board.
>
> By the ship lying with her stern to the wind, and the sea breeze blowing through her fore and aft, she began to be more healthy, and some black mechanics came off from the dockyard and cut scuttleholes through her sides on the orlop deck for the admission of air, which made her more so.

Disease was to remain a scourge for the Navy particularly on unhealthy stations as among the West African Squadron where so many seamen died. The problem was only really solved with the advances in medical science of the present century. But great improvements had been achieved by 1815, and one Naval medical authority wrote that but for these improvements:

> the whole stock of seamen would have been exhausted ... For there would have died annually 6,674 men, which in twenty years, would have amounted to 133,480, a number which very nearly equals the whole number of seamen and marines employed in the last year of the war.

A major change which had also begun, but far less dramatically, was the rising standard of education among the sailors. Not much could be achieved in a Navy drawn too often from the sweepings of society:

> Having been told that a French frigate and brig were lying there, and as it was thought there might be an occasion for landing, 150

H.M.S. *Blossom*'s barge passing an Esquimeaux village.

The barge beset in the ice.

Tracking the barge round Cape Smyth.

H.M.S. *Plover*

of our crew were picked out to be trained to the use of small arms, and I was one of the number. Nothing could be more diverting than to see the blunders we made at the first beginning: we were arranged in two lines along the quarter-deck, with the captain and fugleman in our front, and the booms full of people laughing and grinning at us; some put their muskets on the wrong shoulder, some let the butt fall on their neighbour's toes, some could not stand with their backs straight up, and were threatened in having a cross-bar lashed to it, and some had their shoulders chalked by the captain, that they might know the right from the left, which only bothered them the more; in short, there was nothing but blunders for a week or two, and then we began to mend.

This exercise was performed twice every day, and for our encouragement when over we were marched, with drum and fife playing before us, round the quarter-deck gangway and forecastle, and in the evening had an extra pint of grog each; but the awkward squad had to stand on one side with their muskets presented to us as we marched past them, and not allowed extra grog. We improved so in the course of a few weeks that it was said we fired a better volley than the marines.

Diverting as the early stages may have been for other members of the crew, the fact that at least some of the sailors could not tell their right from their left is a comment on the standard of education, if not the intelligence, of the naval ratings. This certainly was not true of the naval brigade in the Crimean war fifty years later.

One surprising aspect of life on the *Minerva*, was the absence of any supply of clothing or slops:

There were no slops at this time on board the *Minerva*; the purser at stated periods served out to the ship's company so many yards of dungaree as were required to each man for jackets, shirts and trousers, with needles and thread for them; and my messmates, being a set of good fellows and accustomed to the work, soon taught me to cut out and make them, by which means I soon got a good rig-out and a new straw hat, which I made by their instructions; as for shoes and stockings, they were not worn by sailors in this hot country.

It was probably in the power and authority of the Captain, that the Navy of 1815 differed most markedly from what was to follow. The question of promotion brings this out particularly clearly. Here, though challenged at times by the Admiralty, the Captain considered that he had absolute power. Warrant-officers were promoted simply at the Captain's whim, as Richardson's own promotion shows:

3

On our arrival at Spithead, Mr. Taw, our gunner, got an appointment to a higher rate, and Captain Leveson-Gower, who had been very kind to me, ordered me to take charge of the gunner's stores, and said he would soon get me a gunner's warrant; but I begged him to excuse me, as I knew little of gunnery, and, indeed, I had never been so much as in a gunner's crew. But he was a man that would not be contradicted, and he ordered me to go to the gunner's cabin and take charge of the stores immediately, and next day he got me an acting-warrant from Sir Peter Parker, the Commander-in-Chief on this station (dated September 3, 1795); moreover, I was sent on shore to pass my examination before the passing gunners and a mathematical master: very inconsiderate was this for me to be sent to pass without any preparation! However, I was fortunately relieved from my anxiety by meeting one of the passing gunners, who informed me that they could not pass anyone who had not been four years in H.M. Service; and as at this time I had only been about two years and a half, I returned on board and continued acting-gunner, and when at leisure began to study the art of gunnery from books my brother James bought for me. I soon improved much, and my brother officers taught me how to keep my books and make up my accounts of stores.

A better educated recruit, less harsh discipline, greater liberty for the man ashore, less drunkenness and no women on board (even if things did not change when they got ashore!): these were the most obvious changes which came into effect in the next seventy years. But if the powers of the Captain were reduced, the relations between the officers and men greatly improved. This is especially obvious in the desperate and daring expeditions which were launched in the period— not this time against the French but against the dangers and hardships of the Arctic wastes.

3

Arctic Exploration—John Bechervaise

Let anyone who reads these words, pause for one moment ere he undertake a discovery voyage. In these dismal regions, where eternal snows cover the face of nature, where the voice of soothing pity was never yet heard, or the foot of a European ever before trod; there, even there, the indefatigable Englishman has found his way, and after experiencing toils and hardships almost unequalled, he returns to his native country, and sometimes reaps that reward his exertions have merited from his superiors, or if forgotten, returns on a second mission to support himself and a numerous family.

So wrote John Bechervaise—an 'Old Quartermaster' as he styled himself following his voyage with Captain (later Admiral) Beechey into the Arctic in H.M.S. *Blossom*. Yet unlike so many of his predecessors he was by no means dissatisfied with the naval service itself.

For my part, I never in any one instance had cause of complaint. Sobriety and a desire to fulfil the duties imposed on me carried me through with comfort, and I look back with a degree of pleasure to the day on which I first stood on a ship of war's boards.

Service in the Arctic was especially arduous. On this particular voyage the privations suffered were very considerable but, they were shared by officers and men alike. At one point the crew was reduced to 'eight on four'—that is eight men on the rations for four, one ration consisting of 8 oz. of soft bread (baked on board, daily) six ounces of salt beef or pork on alternate days, six ounces of flour for dinner one day and one gill of peas the next. In every respect the crew suffered severe hardships:

It has been my lot during the vicissitudes of a seafaring life, to have suffered hunger and thirst to excess, and although it is impossible to express the corporeal agony it causes, yet some notion may be conceived of it from the effect it had on the mind: it seems to a person oppressed with hunger as if he hated the whole world, but that would be a virtue if committed to procure food, and no effort is thought too great to get it.

Such is the case that a person going to sleep overcome with hunger or thirst, is always sure to dream of it. It was to be my watch below; a few minutes before night the order was given for the watch to turn in with their boots on, or in other words to lay down with their clothes on.

He then dreamed of being ordered a mutton dinner by a former Captain.

The tureen was well filled with the said mutton stew and dumplings (vulgarly called doughboys) gracefully floating on the top, and shewing their white tops in beautiful brown liquid. Oh! the happiness, the delight of such a moment; but mark the change; just as I was about to grasp the ladle, first a gentle twit twit arrested my attention, and presently the horrid pipe of 'All hands save ship', sounded in my ears. In a moment the gay vision vanished, my hopes were shattered, the ship was on shore. Oh, the horror of such a dismal pipe! None but those who have heard it can tell; it was said that no such order had been given, and that the Captain never knew anything of it; indeed with such a multiplicity of duty on his mind, it would have been wonderful if he could have attended to all. The ship had stuck on a mud bank, but it was with the most powerful exertion that she was got off, nor was this accomplished till after 2 o'clock in the morning.

This accident took place north of the Bering Strait in August 1826, and the voyage was indeed full of incident. A great naval historian, Laird Clowes, wrote, 'The objects of the Arctic voyages of the nine-teenth century were not the discovery of routes for commerce, but the attainment of valuable scientific results.' This probably oversimplifies the case. Following the Napoleonic Wars Britain was unquestionably supreme at sea. In addition, Free Trade led to the belief that the seas themselves should be free and this, coupled with an interest in the advance of science, gave a very real impetus to exploration. Yet the choice of the Arctic was not altogether altruistic. Trade was not a primary consideration, but fear of Russia certainly played a part. At this time Russia had totally occupied Alaska and by 1820 had spread her trading posts as far south as San Francisco. In 1818 an Act of Parliament offered substantial rewards for the discovery of a North

West passage, or for the farthest passage north towards the Pole if a route westward to the Bering Strait could not be found. This prize was eventually won by Sir Edward Parry. Before them, a number of expeditions were dispatched into the Arctic, mostly with this end in view.

In spite of many previous voyages, surprisingly little was known about the far north—for example, no one was certain that Greenland was an island. In consequence, much was learnt, but the men went for a variety of reasons. Bechervaise himself joined the *Blossom* not out of any particular desire to take part in an Arctic voyage but because 'Just then, ships of war were scarce, I had no alternative.'

Success in the search for the northern seaway was not achieved until the twentieth century. It was, though, in connection with one of Edward Parry's attempts that the *Blossom* under Captain Beechey sailed with Bechervaise on board in May 1825. Early in 1819 Parry, sailing from the East, had reached a longitude of 110 W. (nearly half-way across, and therefore entitling him to a reward of £5,000 under the 1818 Act of Parliament); but he had then been held up by a barrier of ice. His second voyage achieved little and in 1824 a third expedition was proposed to search for a passage further south than Melville Sound where he had previously been held up. Linked with this, John Franklin was to make a second expedition to explore the north coast of Canada by land. It was unlikely that either of these expeditions could arrive at the open sea in the Bering Strait without having nearly exhausted their resources, and the *Blossom* under Captain Beechey was therefore sent there to await the possible arrival of one of the expeditions.

Captain Frederick William Beechey himself had already achieved considerable distinction in exploration and everything possible was done to make the voyage a success.

The greatest care was bestowed on her outfit; no pains, no expense was neglected to render her safe and comfortable to officers and men. Men were easily to be got, but none were entered but such as produced good characters as thorough seamen, or were well recommended. Her boats were the very best, particularly her barge. Our supply of provisions (as far as the general opinion forward ran) liberal in the extreme; although plenty of old were in store, our salt provisions had been got ready for the ship and were barely corned. Besides the usual allowance of provisions, there was a great quantity of pickled cabbage, sour crout, pippins, portable soup, preserved meats in tin cases, air beds, swimming jackets etc. rifle pieces and articles of traffic.

Nevertheless, Bechervaise was very pessimistic about the voyage.

May 14th. Anchored at Spithead; here I had again the melancholy pleasure of seeing my family; melancholy it was, for considering the nature of the voyage we were about to commence, there seemed but little prospect of again meeting. Happy it is that the page of futurity is shut from our eyes, for if one half of the suffering I had to go through then had been exposed to my view I should have declined; but the ways of providence are inscrutable.

They sailed from Portsmouth on May 17th for South America and in spite of the fact that all the men were volunteers they were soon discontented with their lot. When they were in Rio de Janeiro, about a week before they left:

Fourteen of our men left us. Four of them had taken away the jolly-boat and got safe on shore and another of them had run from the beef-boat.

In order to get them back the Captain adopted the following ruse:

As men were not to be got easily, it was necessary to get them back on any terms; application was made to the authorities but without success, at last the Captain himself thought of a scheme, by which all those we wanted were safely got back. He gave out that he positively would sail on a certain day; on the appointed day the ship got under weigh in the afternoon, and just at dusk, came to at the mouth of the harbour. After dusk a boat, well manned and armed, was sent up to the place, and the men supposing the ship on her way southward had come into the town, and thus became easy prey to the police and to our boat; six of them were taken in one room, enjoying themselves after the privations of a week's residence in the woods; all were brought on board except two lads who were of little use.

Sailing from Rio de Janeiro, they rounded Cape Horn without any particular incident and then visited various South Sea Islands.

The most interesting was Pitcairn, refuge of the *Bounty* mutineers, and Adams the last survivor of the mutiny, came on board the *Blossom*.

It was the first ship of war's side he had ever ascended since the fatal occurences that had made him an alien and a criminal, and even then he was uncertain how far his life was safe; but the gentlemanlike and kind reception of Captain Beechey soon dispelled his fears, and perfectly restored his assurance. Methinks I see him just now, a venerable old man, fair as possible, locks short and thin, white as the driven snow and a countenance a perfect model of benevolence. As I stood with my eyes rivetted on the object before me, so calculated to inspire respect, I said to myself, and is it possible that the being before me is a mutineer; so it is, but who can tell the cause of the mutiny, or how small his share in it has been? From Adam's own lips, as we sat at the table in his home I got the whole account of the fatal mutiny which forever blasted the prospects of Mr. Christian and his companions, and at first intended to have inserted it in this little volume, but fearful of giving the slightest offence, or wounding the feelings of any one by recalling to their minds scenes long past, and which we may justly hope from the present pleasing regulations of our navy will never occur again, I shall draw a veil over all the unfortunate affair and only tell the reader that I saw the *Bounty*, or at least as much of her as had not been hurt, laying on her broadside in six fathoms of water.

The *Blossom* spent some time among the Pacific Islands, visiting, charting and surveying.

A selection of the incidents in Bechervaise's voyage underlines both the similarities with the Old Navy and also the development of a more informal relationship between officers and men which was to become increasingly common in the Navy in the future.

The first shows the continued attitude of the sailors to women, though in this case it was not so much Royal Naval vessels, as whalers, which frequented the port of Woahoo (or Whahoo as Bechervaise calls it) in the Sandwich Islands.

One of the worst effects of civilisation is that females in great numbers flock to the ships. It was by no means uncommon of an evening to count two women to one man about our deck; they usually came off in one of our boats or their canoes, but in the morning they all jumped overboard and swam without betraying the least alarm at the numerous sharks swimming about the ship; many of them were children.

Not so very different from the scene on board a 74 during the Napoleonic Wars.

Inevitably drunkenness remained one of the major problems, as in the following incident at Woahoo.

Application was made to the Captain, by the young king for the aid of our sergeant to drill his troops, which was granted, and for the first four days the man gave such satisfaction that the young king told him if he would go home and procure his discharge and return to Whahoo, his passage out should be paid, and the king would give him one thousand acres of land and make him a Major over his troops with a regular salary. To a man like that, risen from a plough boy, what an offer! But, drink, that curse of human hopes blasted his prospects and for several days he came off so excessively drunk that the king had to beg that he might not again be permitted; thus he forfeited his hopes and lost the Captain's good opinion.

The relationship of officers and men was noticeably different.

At Kamtshatken they persuaded one of the inhabitants to provide them with a meal of fish for a Spanish dollar.

Just as we were sitting down to a comfortable meal of fried salmon, rusk and some wild birds' eggs, the master, Mr. Elson, a man universally respected by all hands, came up, and looking round him 'Hello,' said he, 'what do you call this?' he was offered to partake of our fare and willingly accepted, and for my part I scarce can tell when I made a more comfortable meal. It must be observed that provisions were not then abundant, nor is that strict line of distance to be preserved in these ships which is kept in regular commissioned ships.

The last statement was certainly true at the time. No officer would normally have cadged a meal off a party of sailors but in the circumstances the mate was most welcome and it seems certain that incidents such as this had a permanent effect in improving the relation between officers and men. The shared hardships brought them close together in a way that rarely seems to have occurred on board the old ships of the line. Undoubtedly Beechey was a kind and considerate commanding officer, as the following incident shows.

One afternoon as I stood in the gangway, it being my watch, the Captain came up and taking a turn or two on deck came towards me, and having pulled a paper out of his pocket presented it to me, saying, 'Here, read this and follow the instructions it contains; your exertions and good conduct merit my esteem.' To a man who has a family however trifling the addition of pay may be, it is welcome; but the addition was given me in a manner so kind, so gentlemanly, that it was doubly pleasing.

Officers had behaved in this manner before, indeed one can imagine one of Nelson's 'Band of brothers' telling one of their ratings of his promotion in just such a way; yet it would have been very surprising in 1800. It was less surprising in 1826.

Bechervaise, in return, always did what he could to help the officers, and frequently such actions were right out of the line of duty.

Even so, there were certain things that were better not said.

While surveying, I was ordered to walk round the beach and stick a pole up at the point with a flag at the top. I went away taking with me only a very small hatchet, very sharp, and which was kept in the boat for that purpose. The beach I observed as I walked along was composed of large blue stones, and about 10 or 15 yards from the water's edge was bounded with large birch trees and small brushwood. I had completed my work and was returning back towards the boat pensive and swinging the hatchet about, when happening to look upward my eye caught sight of a large she bear and cubs, very little would then have knocked me down; I certainly thought myself gone that time. Father of mercy, thought I—come all this way from home to be eaten by a Kamschatdale bear; to run was hopeless; the bear's legs were far better than mine—in water or up a tree were equally bad; but while thus deliberating upon a subject equally dangerous and delicate, the animal quietly walked into the wood leaving me a clear road to follow; and oh! did I not run—I never stopped till I got to the boat and there with my hair about upright and the big drops of perspiration chasing each other down my face, I fancied myself safe. The officer who had been spying at me nearly all the time made a laugh of it, asking me what the bear had said to me; it struck me to say that the bear had told me never to obey foolish orders again; I, however, kept in, sensible I was addressing my superiors.

During their three and a half year cruise they ranged widely round both sides of the Pacific coast. On their first expedition through the Bering Strait they spent some time surveying the area. They were there primarily to aid Franklin if he arrived. One of the *rendezvous* points was in Kotzebue Sound where they anchored for some time off the Uric Rocks in the large natural harbour.

As the time of Captain Franklin's visit was uncertain, if ever it took place, the Captain ordered a cask of flour to be buried as deep as possible on the top of the Uric Rocks, and something else was buried at the east end of Chamisso (an island in Kotzebue Sound) with a bottle containing directions; I was sent to the top of the Uric Rock to paint in large black letters upon the stone the bearing and distance of the articles buried. The spot on which I stood was a perpendicular cliff of such a height that I was really afraid to look down, and the rock being so rotten made it doubly dangerous; I however accomplished my task and left sufficient marks to attract attention.

While they were surveying in this area the ship went aground. The ship's barge separated from the *Blossom* for more detailed surveying and reached what they accurately claimed to be 'the most northerly point yet discovered on the continent of America'. This they named Cape Barrow after the secretary to the Admiralty. Bechervaise was not on this expedition, which was one of considerable hardships (*see illustration facing p. 32*). They found no trace of Franklin and erected two posts to indicate a message to the explorer, but the barge was set in the ice for some time and it seemed likely at one point that they would not get clear. Some indication of the hardship of this expedition is recorded in the official record of William Smyth the mate of the *Blossom*, who commanded the barge.

> We now began tracking the boat along (i.e. pulling it along by a rope from the shore) and proceeded for a short time without much difficulty; but the ice increasing fast and the pieces getting larger, she received some violent blows. . . . Nothing now but the greatest exertion could extricate the boat; and the crew, willing to make the most of every trifling advantage, gave a hearty cheer, and forced her through thick and heavy ice until we rounded a projecting point that had hitherto obstructed our view. This, however, could only be accomplished with considerable labour and risk; for here, as in many other places, we had to take the track-line up cliffs, frequently covered with hard snow and ice, which, hanging a considerable distance over the water, prevented the possibility of pulling round beneath. The rope was then obliged to be thrown down, and the upper end held fast, until the crew hauled themselves up one by one; and in this manner we continued along the cliff until the beach again made its appearance. But here even we found it no easy task to walk, on account of small loose shingle, in which we often sank to the knees; and having the weight of the boat at the same time, it became excessively fatiguing. (*See illustration facing p. 33.*)

While the barge was away the *Blossom* itself continued surveying. At one point Bechervaise went on shore with a party to try to shoot some deer that had been seen grazing inland. The weather had been beautifully clear but it suddenly became thick and snow fell fast. The pocket compass which Bechervaise had with him proved useless because of the closeness of the magnetic pole and the wind shifted making it dangerous either to go on or to turn back.

> I never during my life suffered so much as I did that night and the next day; my mental anxiety was almost beyond bearing; my companion who thought but little, suffered less, but for me I saw a potential death in all its horror among the snow, which must have been the case had the thick weather lasted. Sometime during the

ensuing day I almost fancied myself at home with all that was dear to me, but the fairy web was soon broken, and I as it were awoke to consciousness, with an aching despairing heart. During the night we felt a powerful desire to sleep, but all succeeded in combatting it, for we knew well that to go to sleep was a certainty of waking no more; for it is invariably the case that if a person oppressed with cold, ever give way to sleep they lose their lives. However, as in many other instances a blessed and merciful providence rescued us from our truly perilous situation. During the day it cleared up and gave us a sight of the dear old *Blossom* in the offing. Oh, the hopes, the joys of this moment; we very soon walked down to the beach and having a boat sent for us, soon got to the ship with my mind fully made up never to volunteer for any land expedition.

Shortly after the return of the barge, as winter was approaching, the *Blossom* sailed back south and visited San Francisco. During their stay, they surveyed the port. Bechervaise wrote that 'good living soon made a great difference in our size and looks' though Captain Beechey's remarks were more percipient.

This magnificent port which possesses almost all the requisites for a great naval establishment, and is so advantageously situated ... that it will, no doubt, at some future time, be of great importance.

After Christmas 1826 they sailed right across the Pacific to China and anchored in the Typer off Macao. From here Bechervaise was fortunate enough to go with the Captain to Canton, though he went with mixed feelings.

The East India Company's yacht was granted to take him (the Captain). For some reason, I am not aware of, I was selected to go with him; though gratified at the idea of seeing the great city, I felt less pleasure than I should have done had the coxswain gone, for I knew he was the person who had more right to the favour than myself; but as I hold it wrong to question the motives of my superiors I went without a word.

If the relations in the Navy have changed since then, relations with traders ashore have not.

In my little dealings I purchased some crockery ware, from the stand of a man who spoke broken English; sometime after I discovered that he had charged me just double the price I ought to have paid for it. I returned to him, much inclined to break a small portion of his ware, to make up for his roguery, but changed my plan, and only tackled him with having cheated me; the fellow with all the impudence in the world, put his finger up to his eye and laughing said 'he had been to London (Billingsgate)' and considered he had given me a very fair sample of it.

In April 1827 they sailed back to the North calling at Loo Choo and other islands on the way, and arrived back in Kotzebue Sound at the beginning of August. The barge was again fitted out to await the arrival of Franklin whilst the *Blossom* continued surveying south of the Bering Strait. They returned at the beginning of September but:

On the 6th. a few minutes after eight o'clock, while the ship was on stays, she struck on her keel first, and paying off rested on her broadside against a bank of some kind; when a few minutes afterward it cleared away, (for it had been thick all night), and we found that she was fast ashore on a bank from which she had but narrowly escaped the year before, and to which among ourselves we had given the name of Beechey's Bank. At this time it required no whistle to send the men on deck, all were ready to hand, the tide was ebbing; one of the ship's lower anchors and two kedges were immediately got out, and every man in her exerted himself to his utmost; much of the water was started and pumped out; our anchors were of no service in getting her off. Several bidairs (bidars) of natives came off, who appeared sensible that something was amiss, but they were not aware of the extent of our calamity. Towards noon the wind rose high, and the swell increasing the ship heeled over a great deal; in this critical moment every eye was fixed upon the Captain and Master, all depending (I mean the men) on their superior courage and judgement; both were alike firm; not the slightest alteration could be observed in the countenance of either, aware of danger, they seemed fully prepared to meet it, and provided resources for every necessity; and to the firmness of the superiors alone may in most cases of danger be attributed that prompt execution of orders, that ready and willing attendance which make the well regulated ship and respected Commander. At that moment we were deprived of two very valuable officers, one away in the barge and the other nearly blind. About three in the afternoon the wind still increasing and sea rising fast, as a last effort, sail was made in the ship, and in a short time during which she bent heavily, she gave one sudden spring, nearly ran over all the boats, natives and all, and in a few moments was in 8 fathoms, and increased it till she got to 22; our people cheered, the Esquimaux clapped their hands, and for a moment all was confusion; order was soon restored, the ship was again afloat.

However, the barge was not so fortunate. Bechervaise was given this account by the coxswain of the barge:

Having got as far as we could for ice, we returned to Kotzebue Sound in hope of finding the ship there, but not seeing her we supposed some accident had befallen her; our officer traded with the natives for provisions, in order to secure as much food for winter as it was possible to get; a party was also employed to collect wood, both for fuel and for building a home (in fact, an observatory). The barge was then anchored in the offing of a sandy bay, on the outer edge of a shoal, a cable's length from the shore, wind off the land. On the 7th. in the morning, the officer landed with all hands but one man and a boy, leaving orders that when dinner was ready they should make a signal. During the forenoon the wind shifted on shore, but as it was light, no apprehensions of her striking were entertained. About 2 p.m. we saw the man standing in the fore cuddy, making signals, which our officers supposing to be for dinner, ordered me to take the men to dinner and return as soon as it was over, but on getting on board we found that she was tailing in shore, and had already struck very heavily, for the water was level with her cabin. The dinghy and two men were sent to appraise the officer of our situation, but by the time she got on shore all hope of her coming back was over; (Beechey says that the oars were broken). The wind had risen to a gale; our anchor had come home; the barge had drifted broadside on the shoal, and the sea making a fair breech over her. There were then on board four men and a boy; the natives seeing our distress, launched their bidairs and three times had them turned bottom up, at last they gave it up in despair (Beechey records that Mr. Belcher compelled the Esquimaux to assist him in reaching the vessel; but the sea ran too high, and the natives not being willing to exert themselves, the attempt again failed); the men on board had nothing but death before them, either from cold or drowning. About 4, her casks and barrels came floating on shore; Thomas U—— not being able to swim, got her main boom and one of her sweeps, lashed them together and allowed the next sea to wash him off her decks, but a rope caught his foot, the spars slipped from under him and he perished; his body was picked up ten days afterwards and buried directly. S—— another man was a good swimmer gave himself up to a heavy swell and swam with all his might and had a good footing when a drawback took him away into deep water and he sank to rise no more.

Only two men and one boy remained; these having lashed the boy in the main rigging sat one on each side of the cross-trees and remained there, the sea often beating over them. The poor boy soon became senseless with cold and fatigue, slipped through his lashings into the cabin, from which the next sea took him and he never was seen again. About 2 a.m. it moderated and two of the men got off in the little boat; supposing the men at her mast head dead, they cut the lashing which held them, and they both dropped into the bottom of the boat senseless; they were taken on shore, where a keg of rum had just drifted, and were then rubbed all over with spirits, and a little poured down their throats, which recovered them; the officers also kindly purchased skin clothing from the natives, which under Providence greatly tended to their recovery; two men and one boy perished by this unfortunate disaster.

Altogether the second visit north of the Bering Strait was not a success. Previous to the wreck of the barge a man had been lost overboard from the *Blossom* and shortly after a second man also nearly lost his life in the same way. Even relations with the Esquimaux which previously had been quite friendly, deteriorated into open conflict.
Bechervaise adds:

The weather was now becoming severe and almost constant falls of snow made it quite necessary that we should leave; none left with regret, or if such a sensation did arise it was at our not having gone quite through the straits.

They left Kotzebue Sound and after a dangerous passage through the Bering Strait when they almost went aground, six weeks later they made land at Montery Bay (Bechervaise calls it Monte Re) where they had news from England.

A newspaper sent off shore gave us news that Captain Franklin after experiencing great suffering had returned to England; by this all hands were relieved from an oppressive weight, the dread of another visit to Bering's Straits. The news communicated to all hands caused such an uproar in the ship, that it was long before anything like order was returned, and though at a vast distance, home rose before our eyes with redoubled charms: every heart beat high with anticipated happiness, and we could in almost fancy behold the roof where dwelt some friend or partner dear, in fact we were 'homeward bound'.

It was not until September 1828 that they finally reached England.
In one sense the expedition was a failure; their major purpose—meeting Franklin or possibly even Parry—came to nothing. Yet at one point the barge was within fifty leagues of Franklin; they had reached the most northern point of the American continent, as Beechey supposed, and they had shown that an approach to the north-west passage from the west was indeed a practicable proposition. In addition

considerable scientific information had been collected both geographical and biological but probably for most on board the thoughts uppermost in their minds, when the chain again rattled through the hawse at Spithead, were those expressed by Bechervaise:

> I never in my life recollect having experienced such anxious feelings as I felt that day; I was then in sight of home, without knowing what might be the news I should get; however my anxiety was soon relieved for about an hour after the anchor was down, a respectable waterman came alongside with a letter to the Captain, which having delivered he came to me and said 'pray is not your name Bechervaise?' 'Yes', said I, 'well then, two hours since I saw your family in good health.'

Bechervaise gladly filled the man up with rum and was able to see his family for an hour. A fortnight later the *Blossom* was paid off.

Before turning to another account of Arctic exploration something further can well be said about Bechervaise himself and his views on the service in general. Unlike many of his predecessors on the lower deck, he came from a most respectable background. He was born in St. Aubin in about 1790, and his father was a successful and well-liked master mariner. John himself received a very fair education first at a small boarding school in the Isle of Wight and then at a larger one in Southampton. After various temporary jobs he determined to become a seaman and was apprenticed to a distant relation of his father.

> To this man I was apprenticed for those years to learn the art, trade, and mystery of a seaman; it was also agreed that during the winter months, while the brig was gone to market with her second cargo of fish, I should remain in Newfoundland, and keep the books and attend the stores, but by no means to have anything to do with the fishing, and to be supplied with good clothing, boots, etc.; and which I now decide a most improper indulgence was given me, that of having my meals with the master of the vessel in summer, and at the agent's table in winter.
>
> My being allowed to sit at the same table with the master, and the many indulgences he gave me, while it prevented me from feeling so awkward as I should have done had I been placed with the crew, still it in no wise tended to my comfort, for the other lads jealous of the preference shown me, exerted all their little powers to make me uncomfortable; besides the very great injury it did me in after years, for never having been a regular apprentice, and have neglected to obtain that practical experience necessary, I was unfit to take command of a vessel when placed in charge of one.

Indeed, Bechervaise was almost more content at home than on board and he worked so well for the agent during the winter months that when the brig returned the following May he remained in Newfoundland. Later he came into close touch with some of the Indians and acted as agent on his own. In time, however, he grew tired of this life and determined to return to England. He finally obtained a passage in the *Trust* which sailed for England in October 1808.

Captured by a French privateer, Bechervaise managed to recapture the vessel, but, unknowingly, he allowed a naval vessel to take off his prisoners and as a result the Navy claimed salvage. In consequence Bechervaise quarrelled with the owners of the *Trust* and although he was later awarded 80 guineas by a committee at Lloyds, he was now out of a job and after the winter signed on as second mate in a brig bound for Newfoundland. On the return voyage, although they sailed in convoy, they were scattered and the brig was captured by a French privateer off the Lizard. Fortunately they were soon recaptured by an English revenue cruiser, the *Active*. Back in Jersey he was very nearly pressed but fortunately for him, he had a 'protection' as a fisherman. His comments on the 'Old Navy' in comparison with the 'New' serve to underline the changes that he saw take place.

> The dread of a ship of war was next to a French prison, but it must be remembered that a ship of war of those days was very different to those of the present day, now that the service is better conducted, and the wonderful improvements which have taken place render the navy superior beyond compare to any merchant vessel. It is possible the pay may be a little less, that I allow, but taking into consideration the regularity of diet, routine of duty, and comfort of the whole system, it makes up for everything, and pensions for old age.

He made several more voyages in the brig but in 1812 his father died and left him a small bequest. On this he married and also got a berth as a chief mate. On his first voyage as chief mate the Master died but though he brought the brig safely back, he was not confirmed in the post of master. So he left the ship and bought the third part in a sloop of which he took command and sailed to Newfoundland. Unfortunately his partner went bankrupt and he himself had to spend a term in a debtors' prison. Following this he had great difficulty finding work. He acted for a time as a merchant's 'go between' plying between England and France and had a couple of unsatisfactory berths as a mate. Finally in 1820 he decided to cut his losses and volunteer for the Royal Navy. He joined H.M.S. *Rochfort* as a First Class Petty Officer. He soon settled down to life in the Royal Navy. Most of the commission was spent at Malta with an occasional cruise—mainly, as he

H.M.S. *Alert* in winter quarters. March 1876.

Men from H.M.S. *Alert* on the northern march. 8th April, 1876.

Dawn of 1876. End of the Arctic winter night.

Godhavn Harbour, Disco Island. 10th July, 1875.

says, 'In order to give Jack his sea legs, and prevent him from forgetting his sea duty'.

One very real advantage that he obtained was that his son was admitted to the Naval school at Greenwich.

We called at Greenwich to see our dear boy; it is really gratifying to the eye of a parent to see the cleanliness and comfort that pervades the place, they all looked cheerful and healthy; as for mine, who was but just ten years of age, a sweet chubby boy, had the glow of health and happiness on his cheek: how happy I felt while pressing him to my bosom and blessed the hand of those who had placed him in that happy institution. I begged permission to see the Captain now Admiral McKinley who then had command; on his appearing, I begged leave to return my sincere and humble thanks, not only for the admission of the child, but for the care that had been taken of him. I got permission for him to come out for the evening and also to spend most of the next day with me, which was a great favour as it was the fair week when none of the boys were allowed out.

This was after the *Rochfort* had returned to England in the spring of 1824 and she was then paid off. Bechervaise then had considerable difficulty in finding another berth. In January 1825 he joined the *Bulwark* under Captain Dunday. Unfortunately when the ship was almost ready for sea it was discovered that she had a faulty bowsprit and another ship had to be commissioned to take her place. It was not immediately clear whether or not the *Bulwark* would be paid off, and Bechervaise missed his chance of a berth in another ship. Now with a wife and family to support he was becoming desperate. He then ran across an old shipmate who had joined the *Blossom* and as a result joined her, as he himself said, not because he really wanted to set off on a voyage of Arctic discovery—but because she was the only ship in which he could be accepted as a Petty Officer.

After his service in the Arctic, he spent a period in H.M.S. *Excellent* and this was for him, as it was for many of his contemporaries, one of the highlights of his service career.

I had frequently heard of the *Excellent*, and that several of my late shipmates had joined her; I followed their example, and do now and ever shall, feel truly thankful that I did so. I was fearful that my eye might be an obstacle, but the moment the Captain heard the ship I came from, and saw my papers, I was immediately entered. Of all the places presented by Her Majesty's naval service for the good of seamen, I deem the *Excellent* the very best; those who wish to obtain a better education may have a good opportunity of doing so, and to

4

a man of low rank what is better than knowledge; is it not one of the greatest blessings it has pleased providence to allow us to cultivate? I know one Petty Officer who had joined the ship *Asia* but a few weeks before me, and on joining did not know his own name when placed before him; but before he left had gone through decimals. Here I passed 16 months in comfort, learned the art of naval gunnery in all its various branches, and on leaving her to join the *Melville* obtained a certificate class No. 1, well endorsed as to conduct etc.

Bechervaise gives an amusing description of the ceremony of crossing the line—a tradition that remained remarkably stable throughout the period:

There were a great number on board the ship of officers and seamen, who had never yet gone South of the Tropics, and consequently were to be initiated into the mysteries of crossing the Equinoctial line, and entering the dominions of Neptune; great preparations had been made since our leaving Woolwich, for an event which promised to serve part of the crew great amusement, to the other great fear; many a poor girl at Woolwich, and at Spithead had been deprived of some part of her wardrobe, to adorn Amphitrite; from one a night cap and gown had been stolen, from another some other part of the dress, and although I had no hand in it, I was as bad as the rest for I was consenting thereto. An immense grey horse hair wig, sufficiently long to reach well down the back of Neptune, had been purchased in England by subscriptions, accompanied by a venerable grey beard to sweep her aged breast; a tin crown and a trident completed the regalia. On a review of all those who previously had crossed the line, I was selected as Neptune; in vain I endeavoured to defend myself from being deified; it was useless, I must be Neptune, all remonstration was vain; I took it, resolved to use the trident with mildness. Now render fancy to yourself the writer of these lines with his legs and arms well blacked, his cheeks vermillion, short and very loose trousers, a double frilled shirt, from whose ample folds the salt water dripped plentifully, two swabs for epaulets, a long grey horse hair wig, and a venerable beard of the same colour, a tin crown, a trident, and to complete the whole, a hoarse church yard cough; fancy all this I say, and Neptune, your humble servant in his shape stands before you. The evening before we expected to cross the line, the lookout man reported at 8 p.m. a light ahead; presently a hoarse voice hailed 'ship ahoy' which being answered by the Captain, Neptune intimated his intention to visit the ship early next morning. Accordingly early in the morning the ship was made snug, the top sails were close reefed, courses hauled up, topgallant sails furled, a new sail was secured to the gunwhale of the barge on the booms, the other edge to the hammock netting, leaving a hollow of 8 feet, capable of containing an immense quantity of water; into the same the very men who were to be dipped into it, were employed in pumping and bailing water, little thinking, poor creatures they were making a rod for themselves. A gun had been dismounted on the forecastle, the carriage made into a car, on which were to sit Neptune and Amphitrite, and between them the Triton; in order to keep all secret, a sail was run across the forecastle to screen Neptune and his gang from observation. Just before the appointed time, all who were likely to undergo the dreadful operation of shaving were ordered below, the gratings put on, and a constable stationed to prevent the ascent of more than one at a time; a wise regulation for our number were nearly equal, and had they shown fight, might have 'conquered'; a rope was rove through a block on the main yard-arm, to one end of which was secured a handspike, astride of which sat a man with his hands fastened to the rope over his head.

At 10 a.m. the screen across the forecastle was withdrawn, and exposed to full view, Neptune and his followers. The Purser, who had never before covered the Equinoctial, and who beside was rather inclined to be miserly, applied to the Captain for his orders against shaving; 'hush! Mr. M——' said the Captain, 'Neptune commands today, and should I interfere might ask me some questions, I should find it difficult to answer.' A few minutes after 4 bells the crew was on the quarter-deck, the officers forming a half circle, in front of which stood the car, when the venerable old Neptune, apparently worn down with age and care rose from his seat, and addressed the officers, frequently turning to the Purser.

'A very appropriate address indeed Father Neptune' observed the Captain; 'will you take a glass of wine?' As it was offered so it was accepted; I drank a good health to the Tars of Great Britain. Another glass was handed to Amphitrite, who, mother like, offered some to the Triton by holding the glass to his lips, taking at the same time special care that not one drop should go inside his mouth; the Purser seeing that he was likely to meet with no support, and dreading the yard-arm and No. 1 razor, turned to me and said 'well Father Neptune what is it to be?' 'Oh just what you please sir, only remember that the rules of Neptune are like the laws of the Medes and Persians, they alter not.' 'Well then,' said the Purser, 'I will give you two bottles of rum and some porter for yourself.' But I could see it gave the poor Purser a terrible twitch to be forced to so much generosity; the business with the officers was very soon ended, as they were liberal; we gained nothing in the end by it. The first of the

ship's company that was shaved, who was brought up blindfolded by
the whole posse of constables, was the armourer, a weatherbeaten
honest old Hibernian, who had been a farrier in the Peninsular Army
for many years. At the reduction he had found his way as armourer of
some small craft, and then to our ship; on his entering for our
ship, so anxious was he to be within the given age, which was
30, that on being asked his age he gave it as eight and twenty
although 56 was written in legible characters on his old cribbage
face, which throughout the ship's company had gained him the
cognomen of old eight and twenty. On this man then the barber
had to perform his first function; a bucket was filled with all the
cleanings of the hen coops, pig-stys etc. and with it a due proportion
of tar had been mixed; with a large paint brush dipped in the
villainous compound, and his razor, close to him the barber stood
waiting the signal. My first question was 'What is your name, my
man?' 'John S—— your honour,' at the instant of opening his mouth
the brush went across it, when the face the poor creature made it is
impossible to describe, 'Phoo, what do you call that? What do you
call that?' I again asked the old man how old he was, 'eight and
twenty your honour, and so I am; oh I will speak no more, I will
speak no more.' As a last effort to make him open his mouth, I said
'If you mean to put him overboard, mind, have a good rope round
him for perhaps he cannot swim'. Terrified at the idea of being
thrown overboard the poor fellow said 'I cannot swim, oh, I cannot
swim,' but as the brush again crossed his mouth, he uttered with his
teeth closed, 'I will speak no more, by Jesus I will speak no more
if you drown me.' Amid a roar of laughter two men tripped the
handspike on which he sat and sent him backward into the sail
where the bear was waiting to receive him; it was soon over, he
escaped and stood by to see his shipmates share his fate. At the time
of his heavy shave he was not aware who Neptune was. When he
found out I could not get him to speak to me for some time; at
length Irish good humour conquered and we were friends again. The
shaving continued until after two o'clock, the decks were washed and
everything set to rights again; Neptune's gang cleaned themselves,
and in the evening attended at the several officers' berths to receive
the promised contributions. There was some demure as to quantity,
but what was given was even too much, for some carried on drinking
all night; for my part I was glad to get back to my hammock and
enjoy a privileged night's rest granted to Neptune's crew.

It is clear from Bechervaise's later remarks (and he served on into
the 1840s) that the situation of the men had already radically changed.

He himself connected this with the reduction in the rum issue. He has a number of cautionary tales about grog:

> The man who writes these lines would not drink one glass of ardent spirits though the empty glass were to be given him full of sovereigns. The many punishments I saw inflicted on my first joining the service, for crimes committed in drunkenness, induced me to say, that I never while I breathe would taste spirits, and thousands of circumstances have tended to confirm my resolution; years in great numbers have gone since the thread of reflection has been broken by drinking ardent spirits, and I think I may safely say it will please God to continue so.

And again:

> On Sunday evening, the drum had beat as usual, and the retreat was to follow in a few minutes, when I observed a man named Tooey, captain of the foretop, standing under the half-deck, ready to spring upwards at the first flourish of the boatswain's whistle. One glance convinced me that Peter Tooey had been cook that day; or in other words that he was by far too much intoxicated to go to the earing in safety. A few words with him confirmed my suspicions, I begged him not to go aloft; and promised that the second captain of the top should take his place. But, alas, my words were unheeded. Poor fellow! at the 'Pipe hands shorten sail,' he about flew up the fore rigging; it seemed to me that his feet scarcely touched the rat lines. Before the order 'Lower away topsails,' was given, he was ready to spring in the yard. Indeed he was standing on it before it was secured, and walking outward towards the yard-arm, but he walked too far; in his blind haste to be first he walked clear over the yard-arm, struck the fore chains, and passed aft a corpse. Nor was this all: a mate named Bett or Brett jumped overboard after him and very nearly lost his life before he could be got on board again. I heard his last piercing cry, and was the last person to whom he had spoken on earth. It operated powerfully on my mind, and it was a long time before I could overcome it.

Most significant was the approval he gave to the Admiralty's halving of the rum ration in 1824:

> Again, I say, I would not advocate the cause of total abstinence in the Navy, but this I feel assured of, that the less spirits are issued the better. The proof is easily obtained. If it were possible to examine the logs of two different ships of the same class, the one, at the time when half a pint of rum was issued to each man daily, and the

other (since 1824) when the allowance was reduced to one half that quantity, and then carefully compare the punishment at both periods, I feel convinced that it would be found that the number of lashes inflicted in the first period would by far more than double the latter period. Then examine the log of a ship of the present time, after having been three years in commission, and it will be found that one half the punishment inflicted has been for excessive drinking, or neglect or error caused by it. Seeing then, as every man may, who will consider for a moment, the dangers, the fatal accidents that occur from excessive drinking, would it not be possible to devise some plan for its decrease?

And the Admiralty attempted to do so for the rest of the century. In every respect Bechervaise noted a marked improvement in the Navy.

Acquainted as I am with the ship's lower deck, after a sojourn of twenty-two years, I can enter into all the feelings of my brother seamen, and see at a glance the vast improvement that has taken place, both in morals, and character.

He particularly stressed the improvement in education:

The establishment of libraries in the Royal Navy has more powerfully tended to improve the minds of seamen than can be supposed. For many years that I served as a petty officer before libraries were given, a book of any kind on a ship's lower deck was a great rarity; and in any of the messes that had one, it was read and re-read and lent from man to man, until it became difficult to tell the original colour; and even these were of a kind that frequently injured rather than improved the morals of the men.

One of the greatest comforts I enjoyed while serving as quarter-master in the *Asia* was a privilege granted to me by Lieutenant now Captain Henry, of taking any book I chose out of his cabin to read, keep clean and return; and this indulgence gave me a pleasure I can scarcely describe. Nor was it lost to others, for in many instances my mess mates and ship mates shared the benefit. In one, sometimes in both dog watches, I sat at a mess table and read to those around me. How different it is now; every one can get a book, and read for himself. He can go to the library, take out a volume from a well-selected stock of books, and one day with another at sea, can have three hours to read and improve his mind.

We have men now in the service, and I could name more than twenty from one ship, who, on their entering into her did not know one letter in the book; and now, within five years, have learnt to read, write and cypher merely at their spare time.

Of course not everyone supported these advances:

> I recollect once hearing an officer of the Old School observe, that 'the less of education seamen possessed the better they were fitted for the service; for,' continued he, 'when they have much learning they are generally great sea-lawyers, and upon the whole troublesome characters.' That such is the case in some instances, is beyond a doubt, but these, happily, are exceptions. Nor does it follow, because some few persons prove troublesome that the rest are to be kept in ignorance and denied one of the greatest blessings it has pleased Providence to bestow on men: and if proof were necessary, I could show that seamen with a liberal education do not prove more troublesome than others.

Then, on clothing:

> During the first six years of my naval career provisions and very rough clothing were all that was issued in a ship of war; blue jackets of the coarsest kind, with black horn buttons, on which were stamped a foul anchor, and 'sailor bold' for a motto; duck frocks and trousers, the trousers cut by a machine and double the size for a moderate man; and the frocks scarcely half long enough with a coarse felt hat, that you might bend into any shape, and as easily restore; check shirts with a collar one-and-a-half inches deep, and these very dear, completed the catalogue of clothes which the seamen possessed.
>
> Now see the difference; cloth, flannel and duck, all of good quality, silk handkerchiefs, drawers, in fact every article of dress necessary for a man at his entry; if he is not, he can be, in twenty minutes, new from head to foot; and in all this, no overcharge. The prices are so moderate, that it would be quite impossible for anyone ashore to get them at the same price. Now, if a seaman is careful, he need never be without money; it is paid at least quarterly in all ships, in proportion to the pay and rate of each man.

Over his ship:

> A seaman on entering the Navy has every opportunity of choosing his ship, so that he can have no excuse for returning from it. If he finds his ship different to his expectation, the time is limited; he knows that the end is fast approaching, when he will again be free to seek another. It is not now as it was in days gone by when perhaps, just returned from a long and arduous voyage, he is seated at the fireside with his prattling child on his knees, or worse by far, torn from the very bed of his wife, to share the perils of the ocean, and brave the battle. All these horrors are done away with; the system of

manning ships has improved with the march of intellect; and men who join the Navy, in nine cases out of ten gladly remain until they are promoted, or get pensions, perhaps medals for long service and good conduct.

Above all, he adds:

Among the various changes introduced since the Peace, for the benefit of the seamen of the Royal Navy, there is not one that has been so useful, or tended to so much good, as the medal and gratuity money, given for long service and good conduct.

Not that everything is better:

More real friendship existed among tars of the Old School, than among those of the present day. Men were then endeared to each other by mutual danger, mutual sufferings, and mutual privation as well as by length of service in one ship. Now all know the probable expiration of their period of service; and if the ship does not please them, at the end of the station they seek another—see fresh faces, have fresh shipmates, and little remains to recall those who are gone.

But he adds:

The rising generation of seamen are men far different from those of former years. It has been said by old officers that they have lost a good deal of that reckless daring that distinguished their predecessors. Admitting this to be the case, what is wanting in the one particular, is certainly well made up in judgement; it is seldom that a seaman's presence of mind forsakes him, even in the most imminent danger.

And finally:

I only wish to point out to those with whom I have spent so many comfortable days, the benefits offered in the Navy; as well as to assure them that I look back with sincere pleasure, after a long period of service, to the day in which I entered it; What real seaman is there in the Royal Navy who ever looked at his well disciplined ship without pleasure, and felt the conscious pride of a Briton, that of all ships in the world, those of our beloved country were pre-eminent, and their men the most daring.

4

Arctic Exploration—William Simpson

5th. February 1848

Strong breezes this day from S.S.W. with a heavy swell, which makes it rather uncomfortable for us, being so much crowded with provisions and stores we have scarcely room to move, but we must make the best of it. God grant that we may obtain the object of the expedition, then those little annoyances will be nothing as compared to the gratification we shall have of probably rescuing our missing countrymen from suffering and famine. The weather continued more or less boisterous till the 10th. when we battened down the hatches and placed the ship under storm sails and obliged to issue 'Preserved meals' to the ship's company, as we could not keep anything in the ship's coppers, ship rolling and pitching heavily. Our Captain (and indeed all the officers) are very kind, the weather being so bad since leaving England, induced our Commander to issue an extra allowance of Grog every night to the watch as they went on deck at eight and twelve o'clock and the poor fellows stood much in need of it being constantly wet while on deck.

So wrote William Simpson, Sergeant Royal Marines Master-at-arms, during the voyage of the *Plover* on their way to their search beyond the Bering Strait. The object of the expedition was to try to discover what had happened to a previous expedition led by Sir John Franklin. Not that their hopes were very high. At a dinner on Christmas Day that year they drank a toast to

Sir John Franklin, the officers and men comprising his expedition; may we find them, and in health and safety, and not in the lamentable condition to which it is feared they have been reduced.

Franklin's expedition had set out in the *Erebus* and the *Terror* with high hopes of finding the famed North West Passage. It had been equipped on a quite unprecedented scale and had sailed in May 1845

full of optimism for the success of its hazardous enterprise; no Royal
Naval expedition to the Arctic had previously met with disaster. The
two ships crossed the Arctic circle at the end of June and sailed up the
west coast of Greenland in fine weather. A month later they were
seen by Captain Martin of the whaler *Enterprise* and Martin spoke to
Sir John Franklin and several of his men. He was the last man to do so.
From that date Sir John Franklin and his total expedition were never
again seen alive. There is a story that six years later the mate of an
English brig saw the two ships stranded on an ice floe off the coast of
Newfoundland but the fate of the two ships is uncertain. We do know
now, though, the fate of the expedition itself. They sailed through
Lancaster Sound and Barrow Strait and the following year they
turned south and nearly reached the shores of King William Island but
were then beset in heavy ice (1846). An expedition from the ship
reached the island and the final gap in the North West Passage had
been bridged. It had not yet been navigated—this was not achieved
until Amundsen succeeded in 1905—but it had been discovered and
explored. From this point on disaster began to overtake the expedition.
On 11th June, 1847 Sir John Franklin died. Captain Francis Crozier
succeeded him in command of the expedition and yet another winter
(1847–8) was spent caught in the ice (at a time when the *Plover* among
others was on its way to search for the survivors); by April their stores
were almost exhausted and many years later a record was found left by
Captain Crozier in the north of King William Island. 'H.M. Ships
Terror and *Erebus* were deserted on the 22 April, 5 leagues N.N.W.
of this having been beset since 12 September, 1846.' Crozier's plan
was probably to travel along the west and south coasts of King
William Island in order to reach the nearest outpost of the Hudson Bay
company at Fort Resolution across the Great Fish River. But the men
were weakened with hunger and with scurvy. One hundred and five
officers and men out of the original complement of one hundred and
twenty nine started the journey; some may have turned back to the
shelter of the ship but the majority followed Crozier on his last tragic
march. Skeletons, graves and other remains were later found along
the route but from the journey not one man survived.

William Simpson and the officers and men of the *Plover* knew none of
this as they sailed across the Atlantic on their way to the Bering
Strait. Their destination was Kotzebue Sound, where Beechey and
Bechervaise had anchored twenty years before, though the *Plover* did
not reach this until the summer of 1849. They formed part of three
expeditions launched by the Admiralty to search for Franklin; of the
other two, one approached from the east by sea and the other overland.
The *Plover* under Commander Thomas Moore had sailed from England

on 31st January, 1848 and after the somewhat stormy passage already described reached the Falkland Islands on 7th May. The free relations that existed on these expeditions as already noted by Bechervaise, gave rise to certain problems. Simpson records:

> The commander called the whole of the petty officers on deck this day and reprimanded them, not only for the manner in which they did their duty, but also for the example shown by them to the men who performed their duties in a very careless manner. Indeed it was about time something was done as some of them appeared to think they could do as they liked not being in what is termed a regular Man of War.

Picked men though they were, they were not entirely honest:

> 24th. February
> Having a great number of Seal Skins on board, supplied by the Hudson's Bay Company to us for the purpose of lining our blankets, making coats etc. on our arrival in our winter quarters, they were got on deck this day, the weather being fine for the purpose of airing them, some evil disposed person concealed two of them under the bows of the Pinace stowed on deck, evidently with a view of stealing them, as they were covered with a coil of rope. This very much annoyed our commander who ordered me to use all possible means to discover the delinquents. I did so, but to no purpose. Whatever was the motive of the person who took them is hard to say as every man was given to understand they would have a sufficiency for his wants previous to our arrival in the arctic regions.

Still, the 'normal' customs were preserved as they 'crossed the line':

> 20th. March
> This day we crossed the equator. Received a visit from Old Father Neptune and his tribe and proceeded with the usual ceremony of shaving etc. and spliced the main brace.

And the 'normal' behaviour when they went ashore in the Falkland Islands.

> 11th. May
> There being an abundance of Wild Fowl here the Ship's Company had permission to go on shore to shoot but there were few who troubled themselves sporting, there being a grog store, they (most of them) just popped in to have one glass which brought another and another until they became careless as to any other amusement.

They left the ship about one p.m. and it was past twelve before we got them on board.

One wonders though what they really thought of the sermon given by the local clergyman.

14th. May

Reverend Mr. Moody (chaplain to the settlement) came on board and performed divine service. He delivered a most touching address touching on the object of the expedition which he drew our attention to by pointing out the necessity of preserving harmony and good feeling with each other, and as the eyes of the world were fixed on us, he trusted none of us would disgrace the Flag under which we served and concluded with a prayer to the great architect of the universe for the welfare and prosperity of the expedition.

On their voyage north they were kept at it:

June 1848

The carpenters are very busy doubling over the Pinace and otherwise preparing the Boats to encounter ice—Ship's company making Fearnought Sleeping Bags—stockings, gloves, caps etc. from seal skins each man being provided with skin for that purpose, also large sealskin cloaks for travelling parties—so that there was plenty of employment.

And Simpson himself had another unusual job to do.

I have to skin all birds caught and preserve their skins for the government collection. Rather a novel employment for a Sergeant of Marines taking into consideration he had so little to do before but as the Captain says this is no place for idle people, well he does his part, therefore we must not grumble.

Simpson was probably 'swinging the lead' a bit but while they were at Callao:

July 7th.

In the midst of Victualling, Watering Coaling etc. the hands were turned up to muster. I was then in the hold. On my going on deck to report it clear, I was much surprised to see the Admiral with his staff on board, here was a pretty mess, no one clean nor any to receive him. However there was no help for it, every one was too busy to think much about it as we had a deal to do and going to sea at daylight.

In spite of the urgency they arrived too late to get through the Bering Strait before the ice moved south and they were forced to winter off the Siberian coast in Emma's Bay Port Providence near Tschutske. Simpson found the situation bearable:

> Since our arrival here we have been very comfortable, at least as far as circumstances will admit, the weather is extremely cold, the temperature being 21 degrees below zero, but we must expect to have it colder yet, we have had some men frost bitten, but none severely. We amuse ourselves occasionally with Masquerades or Plays in which the Captain and officers take their part.

And there were other amusements, too:

> After dinner the football was got out and at it we went, dividing the ship's company impartially. The First Lieutenant (Lee) took one side and the Doctor (Simpson) the other till we completely tired ourselves, and although the weather was cold we soon came to a heat.

Some contacts were rare with the local population.

> November 20th.
> Performed this evening 'How to settle accounts with your laundress' which was performed with great spirit and elicited great applause from the audience who were chiefly natives there being 40 or 50 present. The natives are very friendly and some of them have a great desire to learn our language in which they have made great proficiency. We have found cases of theft amongst them which on being made known to the chiefs are restored. A few days since we had a thermometer stolen from the booby hatch, where it was kept but on being made known to old 'Accool' the principle chief it was soon brought back. We find the cold very severe, although we have a fire (stove) in the main hold and pipes leading from it round the lower deck, yet in the morning when we turn out of our hammocks there are icicles 4 and 5 inches long hanging from the deck and beams overhead. I have two men constantly scraping and wiping overhead by day, also two men to bring snow on board to make water for the people. On our arrival here we filled our tanks with ice thinking the heat from Sylvesters stove in the main hold would thaw it, but in this we were deceived, as there was not heat sufficient. The natives soon became much attached to me, in consequence of my having charge of the water (as soon as they arrived on board their cry was 'Memilk, memilk, Tagart' meaning water, water sergeant, the word they could never pronounce). I have frequently seen three of them drink two gallons taking only one drink each.

The high spot of the winter was undoubtedly Christmas Day.

December 25th.

Christmas Day. I cannot pass over this day without mentioning the very kind and handsome manner in which the ship's company were treated by their officers. I do not think it possible for any body of men to be more cheerful and happy considering the situation we were in. On the opening of the morn the usual routine was gone through as on Sunday. At 9.30 a.m. divine service was performed by the commander, after which all was bustle and activity preparing for dinner which was cooked the day previous. A table having been rigged on deck at 12 o'clock the band (two fiddlers, two fifes, tambourine and ship's drum) struck up 'Roast Beef' when at it we went to a most excellent repast consisting of—

1st. course—Fish, boiled.

2nd. course—A Deer roasted whole with preserved potatoes and parsnips.

3rd. course—4 Plum Puddings and 2 Cranberry Tarts.

This with a cask of ale the gift of the Gun Room officers, was excellent. The dish in which the deer was brought to the table was made by Old 'Riggs' the armourer from preserved potato cannisters and was 5 ft. 6 in. in length, 20 in. in width and 5 in. in depth. On the first course being cleared away and the second coming up the main hatchway the band struck up 'Sick a' getting up stairs'— we had several Tschatskian chiefs on board who were much surprised not having seen anything like it before, indeed, they eat their meat raw, never cooking anything. Doctor Simpson and Mr. Lindsay the Purser acted as waiters and I must do them justice, they did their duty nobly. On the table being cleared Grog was placed on the table of which we had double allowance of concentrated rum, and the crew assembled round it, conviviality being the order of the day, everyone was determined it should be obeyed to the letter. It is true we had no glasses amongst us but then we had a good substantial Panikin, which answered our purpose very well, and which were nicely polished with water for mixing in bright copper measures —our worthy chairman, old Riggs the armourer (on all being seated) rose, and addressed the company in as good terms as can be expected from a rough old man-of-war man, and proposed 'The Queen and all the Royal Family' with three times three, Band playing 'God save the Queen', the next toast from the chair— 'Sir John Franklin, the officers and men composing his expedition; may we find them, and in health and safety, and not in the lamentable condition to which it is feared they have been reduced', drunk with cheer, band playing 'Rule Britannia'—the rest from the vice chair, a quartermaster 'Captain Moore, may he be prosperous in the objects of the expedition.' Band: 'See the Conquering Hero Comes'. The next from Dear (Gunner's Mate) 'Lieutenant Lee and the officers of the ship.' Band: 'They are jolly good fellows.' Again the glass went round; all was good order and good feeling. The next toast given by myself on taking the chair which was vacated, Riggs having taken it 'pro tempore' while I was officiating about the Grog, beer, etc.—'Shipmates, I rise to propose a toast which I think you will all join in with pleasure, we are now, far, far away from our native land, that great and glorious architect of the universe only knows if we shall ever return to it, we have many difficulties to surmount—I beg to propose the very good health of our Parents, our wives, our children, not forgetting our sweethearts and all those dear friends we left behind us, may they have many returns of the day, and may we return to them with credit to our Country, ourselves and them,' drank with three times three, Band playing 'The Girls we left behind us.' Everything went on very comfortable, at 7 p.m.—cleared table and placed supper, after which we again sat down. The ship's company having asked me to request the Captain to come on deck I did so, and on his coming up the afterhatchway, he was greeted by 4 petty officers and placed on a chair and carried to the head of the table amid the cheers of the crew and placed at the head of the table, it being vacated for that purpose, and having made an appropriate speech and drunk their healths, carried back, Lieutenant Lee and the remainder of the officers were brought up in rotation.

In a short time the officers came up and did us the honour of joining the social board. Nothing was to be seen but cheerful and contented faces, there we sat enjoying our Pipes and our grog. In honour of Mr. Lee our worthy First Lieutenant the chair was vacated and he took it. I sat on his left. After a few minutes he gave me a kick and then rising said as near as I can remember, 'I beg to propose to you a toast and one which I flatter myself will be drunk by you all with pleasure; it is the health of one of yourselves, one who in my opinion has done his duty, and that straight forward. There is but one fault I have to find with him viz. (laughing) he does not report you fellows as often as he ought to do, you all know to whom I allude I therefore propose the health of Sergeant Simpson' (Drank with cheers). On order being restored, he resumed: 'I have a duty now to perform which ought to have been done before, but by some chance has been neglected. I am sorry for it but I trust it is not now too late. I allude to the charge which was brought against Sergeant

Simpson in July last, relative to the "Lemon Juice". I am happy to say it has been satisfactorily proved that he was entirely innocent and not only myself but every officer in the ship is sorry it should ever have happened.' He then turned to me and holding out his hand said 'Sergeant Simpson I feel much pleasure in having it in my power to speak thus of you. May you go on as you are now and prosper.' He then sat down amid the cheers of the men and officers. I shall never forget our Doctor, Mr. Simpson—he to strengthen it got on the table and gave his testimony. Indeed they were all alike for that. Upon order being restored I rose and made some sort of speech but as may be supposed being a little surprised and rather confused I do not well know what I did say. For several days after this there was but little done in the shape of work. Indeed we could not do a great deal as the days are at this time of year very short; the daylight we have in this month being little more than twilight.

Clearly a good time was had by all, officers and men included. One wonders what the hangovers were like.

The incident which the First Lieutenant, W. A. R. Lee, referred to, took place in the Falkland Islands. The purser had obtained a quantity of lime juice and about 30 lbs. of it disappeared. Simpson was accused of making away with it.

The whole ship's company called on deck and requested to state if they had ever seen me sending any Lime Juice out of the ship or in any other manner doing anything wrong but did not receive any answer. My belongings were searched but nothing found. Commander said 'Darn me, I thought we had got rid of the only "Thief" I had in the ship.' I replied, 'Captain Moore, you have accused me of theft. I trust you will investigate this charge, and should I be deemed guilty of course must abide the consequences but if on the contrary such is not the case I have to request on our arrival at Baha you will send me out of the ship.' He ordered me to keep silence and threatened to seize me up at once and give me four dozen. I told him it was very hard because one sergeant had disgraced himself by theft that not only myself but that the whole corps should be disgraced and stigmatised without first having obtained a fair trial.

The case was postponed during dinner when the Captain of the Hold accused Simpson of taking the lime juice and that two marines would prove it. Immediately Simpson took them on deck but they would not be pinned down and one positively denied it. Later a Board was assembled to look into the matter and Simpson was asked to confess but he refused. Application was therefore made to the Admiralty saying that suspicion had fallen on Simpson and asking what was to be done about it. Simpson himself was urged by the First Lieutenant to pay for the missing lime juice which he refused to do and retaliated by demanding a Court Martial and saying that he assumed he was under arrest. However, Commander Moore sent him 'to his duty, where everyone looked on me with an eye of suspicion'.

Here the position rested for a month. A very awkward situation for anyone, but especially so for Simpson, who as Master-at-arms was in charge of the general discipline of the lower deck. It was more by chance than anything else that the situation was resolved.

August 7th.

When some misunderstanding having arose, relative to the quantity of chocolate on board the ship, the holds were ordered to be cleared to search for it when a case of lemon juice was discovered in the spirit room which made the four full cases on charge at the time I was accused of making away with the 30 pounds. I immediately drew the attention of the First Lieutenant to it who said 'Thank God, Simpson, this will clear you beyond doubt.' He went to the Captain who sent for the Purser and myself, when it was discovered that the case of Lime Juice which had been the cause of dispute had been sent on board from the Falkland Islands the day I was on shore buying meat and directly stowed away so that I had never seen it. The Commander then said Mr. Lindsay was to blame for not acquainting me with its having been sent on board and therefore exonerated me from blame. I replied, 'It is lucky, Sir, this did not take place before we got to Callao. If it had, in all likelihood I would have been reduced and probably my innocence never made known as I feel convinced you would not have been made acquainted with the discovery had I not been on the spot myself.' He said, 'I am happy it has taken the course it has; it certainly looked suspicious but continue to go on with your duty as you have and you shall not be forgotten.'

The speech by the First Lieutenant on Christmas Day removed most of the hard feelings which Simpson somewhat naturally harboured.

Among other incidents noted by Simpson that winter was the Aurora Borealis.

January 2nd.

Observed the Aurora Borealis beautifully variegated this night. I think the prettiest thing I ever saw without exception and 15th. again itself about over the whole horizon. I could stand for hours

5

watching this beautiful luminary, no painter, no tongue can speak or describe the beauties you behold.

And the winter passed away quickly.

To enliven us and make the winter pass comfortably as well as to exercise the people, our commander very judiciously encouraged of an evening, once or twice a week, masquerades or Plays at which I can assure you some of our characters would not have disgraced the boards in some of our minor theatres at home. This with the ordinary duties of the ship and school occasionally (at which I have to officiate as master) we passed the time until April when we got the housing off the ship rigged ready for the breaking up of the winter. However, finding that in May there was no appearance of the ice breaking up in the harbour although broken up outside, we commenced on the 21st. May to cut a passage for the ship and after having cut a canal about 1¼ miles in length, the ice averaging from five to eight foot thick, we warped out on 13th. June but owning to the sea outside being covered with floes, we did not get fairly out till the 1st. July.

Finally, on 14th July they anchored in Kotzebue Sound.

Our boats, the Pinace and gig had been already prepared to proceed manned, armed and victualled for seventy days to the Mackenzie River, to gain, if possible, information of the probable fate of Sir John Franklin's expedition and under the command of Lieutenant W. A. R. Lee.

Simpson remained in the *Plover* and the party returned some time later having, not surprisingly, found no trace of Franklin's expedition. They spent the next winter in Kotzebue Sound and it passed much like the previous one. Simpson held 'school', occasionally kicking a football, and a little shooting, but he found life much less pleasant primarily because he began to suffer severe pain in his limbs which he put down to rheumatism. He was not even able to enjoy much the festivities on Christmas Day and such tasks as scrubbing hammocks, bedding and clothes were quite beyond him.

By this time the other two searches had returned home, and the Admiralty now launched a larger and more comprehensive search. Two further naval ships, the *Enterprise* and the *Investigator*, were sent out to probe further east from the Bering Strait. In addition, seven British vessels and two American brigs led the search from the west.

On 29th July H.M.S. *Investigator* arrived from England and it was announced to the ship's company of the *Plover* that anyone who wished might go home. Simpson records.

I, for one, much as I wish to see my friends would be sorry to leave
the expedition till it is finished but I am much afraid I shall not be
allowed to remain as I have been suffering from rheumatism since
Christmas and am much afraid it is getting worse.

And this was indeed the case. He was transferred to the *Herald* for
passage to England on the grounds of ill health, and finally sailed
from Kotzebue Bay on 23rd September, reaching England at last in the
spring of 1851.

Unfortunately we know little else of William Simpson. He undoubtedly was a lower deck lawyer, and whatever the First Lieutenant
may have said on Christmas Day he was certainly not easy to befriend.
For a time he was made to do the job of Purser's steward (which was
why he had charge of the lime juice). He tried several times to change,
and only succeeded after the lime juice had disappeared. No doubt a
little of the Captain's displeasure was caused by Simpson's prior
attempts to give up the job.

In general, though, the officers seem to have found his conduct
satisfactory. At least Simpson himself thought so:

Commander Moore expressed himself perfectly satisfied with the
manner in which I had conducted myself during the time I was on the
ship as did Lieutenant Cooper and others. Commander Moore
said he had written to the Admiralty for promotion for me.

The search for Franklin went on led by a somewhat reluctant
Admiralty, and it was not until October 1854 that any definite news
came. Dr. Rae who had taken part in the overland search in 1848 heard
from some Eskimoes that they had seen a party of white men hauling
their boat towards the Great Fish River and then he found the remains
of thirty men from Captain Crozier's party together with personal
possessions which established their identity beyond doubt. In the
following year further remains were found including part of a back-
gammon board presented to the *Erebus* by Lady Franklin, and there the
search ended from the Admiralty's point of view. But Lady Franklin
herself would not give up; bit by bit over the next twenty years the
whole tragic story was pieced together.

The end of the Admiralty's interest in the search for Franklin did
not finish naval exploration in the Arctic, and at least equipment was
improved (*see illustration facing p.* 48). When the body of Harry
Pelegar, Captain of the Foretop of H.M.S. *Terror* was found he was
wearing trousers and jacket of fine blue cloth over which he wore a
blue greatcoat and a black silk neckerchief. This was the Arctic
clothing of a Petty Officer on Franklin's expedition.

One final footnote. If one is sympathetic with the hardships which the seamen suffered in the Arctic a bored remark made by Simpson while they were in Hong Kong on their way home will put things in perspective.

59th. Regiment here. Not uncommon to find eight to ten men dead in their beds of a morning.

5

Arctic Exploration—Daniel Harley

We were very thankful of the chance of getting out of the pack. Sent the watch out on the ice to bear out the broken pieces as the ship steamed ahead and cut it, which is not a very nice job as one stands the chance of a ducking and the water is rather cold. Anchored to a floe inside the bay about 2.30 p.m. where the ship perhaps will have to remain for her winter quarters but there is not a man in the ship but lives in hope of rounding Cape Union and getting further to the North in the ship than anybody has been yet but we don't despair and we hope there will be better luck before the winter.

The Captain thinking that he would like to get the ship closer to the shore as the bay lays rather open and it would be a better shelter. Got No. 1 saw to work under the superintendance of the Captain and commander. Began cutting the ice to make a passage for the ship, during which performance I managed to go through some rotten ice and of course got a ducking which was not very pleasant. After sawing away for some time the commander sent the steward to serve out our ale $\frac{1}{2}$ pint per man which came rather acceptable although a very cold drink.

This comes from the diary of Daniel Harley, a Petty Officer on board H.M.S. *Alert* on her Arctic expedition in 1875. The next day a gale sprung up, the ice opened and:

September 1. Hauled in hawsers and anchors. Made sail and ran before the wind. Noon: Passed Cape Union. Went through the ceremony of claiming the remainder as we are now farther north than anybody has been yet. Hoisted the English Ensign to the peak.

That evening they met a solid barrier of ice across their path and had to turn back again.

September 2. During the afternoon there was a very heavy fall of snow; the snow here does not fall in flakes like in England but nearly as fine as flour.

They then made themselves secure for the winter:

September 4. Freezing hard the thermometer shows 15 degrees of Frost. Preparing for winter quarters as it is quite likely we will not get any further with the ship.

Indeed the Arctic winter had begun.

September 5. The weather is getting very cold as anybody might guess when one's whiskers and moustache freezes—one's moustache sticking out like porcupines' quills owing to the breath freezing as it leaves the body and only fifteen degrees of frost yet.

And a sad little touch.

During the night one of our pet dogs died—poor Fanny.

They had indeed sailed further North than the American expedition which had preceded them and their first objective had been reached; their next was to plant the Union Jack beyond the point reached by the Americans and so counter the drive of the American whalers who had followed in the wake of their American predecessors Elisha Kane and Charles Francis Hall. The expedition consisted of two ships the *Alert* and the *Discovery*, and was commanded by Captain George S. Nares.

They had sailed from Portsmouth on 29th May, 1875 and had a rough passage across the Atlantic, losing one of their boats. A month later they were among the ice:

June 29. Ice all around us. Some very large floes. We have to make two or three attacks at some pieces before we can get through. Seen some large seals for the first time. Weather fine and mild but very foggy.

And two days later:

July 1. Preparing for dredging for specimens of anything from the bottom. Sighted the *Discovery* steaming close to the land, the first time we have seen her since the 11th of June. We were very glad to see her as we did not know what to think about her. She also had a knocking about and lost one of her boats.

Unlike their predecessors the *Blossom* and the *Plover* the two ships were powered with steam engines as well as sail, though these were expensive on fuel. As coal was a problem, the engines were only used when absolutely necessary, and so the expedition remained to a considerable extent dependent on the wind. Healey writes at a later point 'having to study economy with our coals now as there is no more chance of getting more now'. Whenever they were caught in the ice, screw and rudder were lifted.

On 4th July:

6 o'clock: served out ale, some that was made a present to us before leaving England. I note this as it is the first I have tasted since leaving England; and also entered the Arctic circle at 6 o'clock.

The same day at church

Parson preached on the upper deck with his cap on. The description of the pulpit were a salt meat cask and a box of sundry broken crockery belonging to the Wardroom with the letter Y flag thrown over them. The text from the fourth chapter and the eighteenth verse of Proverbs. (But the path of the just is as the light, that shineth more and more unto the perfect day.)

Harley does not record how much he enjoyed the service, but he probably found the following week's sermon more fun as during it one of the ship's kittens,

Thinking he had something to do with the service, perched himself on top of the pulpit but he was very soon dethroned by our chaplain.

Two days later they arrived at Disco, 'the long looked for place of destination after a very long passage of thirty-eight days'. There they were able to get ashore before 'preparing for sea, ready to battle with the ice'.

July 8. Gave leave to them that wished to go on shore, just to stretch their legs on Terra Firma. The men mostly went on shore for the novelty of the thing as there is not much to see. There is only a few Esquimaux and a few Danish people here as there is a Danish settlement. There is a most excellent band, therefore we amuse ourselves on shore by dancing with the Esquimaux girls. They are very nice dancers and their dress is quite amusing. The band is composed of two fiddlers so there is quite a nice assortment of instruments.

But before sailing, on the Sunday:

forced to give up for our own safety, for a lump of an iceberg is a rather nasty customer to come in contact with, especially if it is a rotten one so that it will land a nice lump inboard which they will do. When some of the large bergs break the falling of a piece makes a tremendous noise. During the time we were trying to bear up on the *Valourous*, we shaved a very large iceberg which touched our port bows but did not do much harm. If we had of been another foot nearer we should of lost the whole of the port boats, and given us perhaps a nasty shaking. The hands were turned up to put the ship about with a view to clearing it, but we were too close upon it so that it was no use. The weather still very foggy.

Sighted a large berg, just what we were looking for as we wanted to make the ship fast to it. We steamed slowly up to it and lowered two boats. An Ice Quarter Master by the name of David Douques was sent in the whaler to examine the berg and to dig holes to hook on our ice anchors. Himself and a man by the name of Terancombe had got out of the boat onto the berg the Quarter Master giving it the first tap with the ice chisel, the berg parted throwing Terancombe into the water and wetting Douques up to the middle. Douques managed to stick to the piece of ice as it turned over. (It was rather a lucky job that the broken piece capsized from the boat or else it must of crushed her.) We did not hook an ice anchor but passed the bright of the hawser around a part of the berg.

For the next month they forced their way North. Baffin Bay was fairly clear of ice and they stopped in Proven for a couple of days, which provided some amusement—both ashore:

There was plenty of dancing on shore some of our officers joining in the sport. The Esquimaux seem all to be pretty good dancers. It seems to be part of their existence.

—and on board:

About half past (two) the whole of the female inhabitants came on board the ship which caused a good deal of fun—and a great many spectators as they are rather a peculiar lot of people to look at owing to the seal skin suit. They had a look around the upper deck then making their way down the fore hatchway made a halt on the lower deck sitting down in our messes. They were given some victuals that was left from our dinners and some biscuit which they seemed to devour as if they liked what they had given them. The party left about half-past three or four o'clock and seemed to be highly amused at what they had seen.

For a time they had to tow the *Discovery* and at one point disaster nearly struck:

We ran ashore on some rocks, but the rock being a smooth ledge did not place us in a dangerous position, but the *Discovery* having weigh (way) on her ran into our stern pushing us further up. After trying to get her off by backing our propellers and rolling her, gave it up for a bad job and left her until the tide rose. Captain Nares going on shore discovered there was fresh water to be had. So thinking it would be a good chance for the men to wash their clothes, and also a very good way of occupying the time while the ships were on shore he gave the men liberty to go on shore to wash their clothes. half-past eleven gave her another trial with the engines which brought her off a little. Fired a signal mortar as a signal for the men to come off shore as there were hopes of the ship sailing off which she did after two or three good tugs astern. About half-past eleven the men being all on board we started on our journey again with the *Discovery* still in tow.

Life was by no means dull. There was also the shooting:

Saw an immense Great Bear which we eagerly took the advantage of thinking about having some sport. We procured our rifles and a party of men and officers manned our whalers, and a couple of officers manned the dingy pulling to the shore in the direction of the bear but Bruin was just as cute as we were, a few shots fired at him, one landing on the ice, but he was a good distance off then. We steamed round the floe in the direction of where Mr. Bruin was running and came as close as we could to him which gave us a chance of having a shot at him from the ship but we did not succeed in securing him so returned to the ship rather sorry at not being able to capture him. This is the first bear we have seen. We took three of our dogs with us in the whaler and landed them on the floe with us for to assist in our sport thinking that the bear would scent them, but in coming back we had to leave one of them on the floe as it was rather dangerous to attempt to entice him to come back. One of the men did catch hold of him but he flew at him twice but I rather think he feared worse for I expect he made a good supper for Mr. Bruin.

They may have been unsuccessful with 'Bruin' but

Seeing three fine large walrus asleep some distance from the ship and on the ice, we determined to try and secure one or two. Lowered the whale boat and went away wending their way through the small ice; got pretty close to them. Captain Fielding (the Naturalist with the expedition) went on the floe also with his rifle and fired at them. The harpoon being fired at the same time succeeded in securing one fine fellow, Captain Fielding wounding him in the jaw, and the harpoon entered his back which held him after it was dead. It was brought alongside the ship hauled up on the ice and flinched, headed up in casks for the dogs, but the flesh is very good for human food also. I made a very good dinner off its liver which tasted very good. It is far better than the salt provisions in the ship.

Presumably it tasted better than the musk-ox. There was also football:

Being a fine evening and nothing on, we thought we would like a little recreation on the ice it being a fine large floe nice and flat and being about fifteen miles in circumference. The *Discovery* being alongside of us made up two parties and had a fine game of football which amused us greatly. The officers joining in with us.

Presumably *Alert* lost this time, as the next time they played, Harley records that 'We were fortunate enough to beat them'! Tiring of football, the *Discovery* got all their dogs on the ice and had a little sledging.

Some days later they rounded Cape Alexander, and sailing north, managed to break through into Franklin Pearce Bay. Progress continued to be slow and laborious. At times the ice would open up and they would succeed in travelling some distance, and then it would close in about them again, trapping them and putting them in danger of being 'nipped'. The Captain would go on shore to a high point of land to see where the 'leads' were and attempt to break through to one. Then as Harley wrote, 'In this country open water might be seen for miles and in half an hour after or less one will see it a solid mass of ice. It is really surprising how quickly the ice closes together.'

By forcing a way through the middle of the Channel instead of keeping close in shore, they managed to force a way through Kennedy channel, the narrowest section which they had to traverse. This took them further north than their American predecessors. After this the *Discovery* anchored for the winter whilst the *Alert* sailed on, though at first at no great pace:

Weighed anchor and steamed close to the *Discovery* they giving us a good round of hearty cheers and wishing us success on our journey towards the Pole but we did not get far, the tide setting in brought the ice in with it, blocking our passage. The Captain turned the ship's head towards the land as he wanted to make fast to a hummock, but in doing so we ran ashore there being only 2 fathoms of water forward. Turned the hands up, lowered all boats. Steaming the ship astern soon brought her off into deeper water. Made her fast to a couple of hummocks; hoisted the boats up and waited for the tide to turn hoping it will not take the ice out again.

They did not lose sight of the *Discovery* for another two days. Finally they did manage to pass Cape Union, and settled in their winter quarters shortly afterwards. Not that this was the end of their work. The aim was now to press on with sledges as far north as possible and they even hoped to reach the North Pole.

On 8th September the *Discovery*'s sledge party which had been brought on board the *Alert* set off and the following day a party consisting of three dog sledges, four officers, four men and twenty-four dogs left the ship for a sledge journey in order to survey and build snow houses for the autumn sledge parties. Three days later Harley himself went on one of these sledge trips and he describes it:

Organised three sledging parties. Told the crews off to lash their sledges, get the tents, cooking apparatus, sleeping bags, duffle suits etc. as the Captain wanted to get off as soon as possible as there was a splendid lead of open water reaching pretty close to Cape Joseph Mary, our object being to go as far as possible by boat and taking the sledges and equipment in the boat with us, viz. 2 8-man sledges, leaving the 5-man sledge to travel and meet us. As she had the quarter part of the provisions and she being rather heavy laden, gave her four extra hands from some of the 8-man sledges. Started about 11 a.m.; made sail in the boats with the wind aft; with the usual good-bye made a pretty good run for about 7 miles, passing through a good deal of pancake ice. As we could not get any further by boat we ran close to the edge of the hummockey ice that were fast to the land and unloaded the boats, loading the sledges again after the sledges were landed. Hauled the boats up on the ice. Leaving the boats there, we made a start with the sledges to get as close to the land as possible, but we had very hard work before us as the ice was very hummockey. About 9.30. p.m. as we were rather tired and it would of been no good of trying to bring the boats up that night, we pitched our tent on a nice piece of floe under the lea of some large hummocks. As we were pitching them Lieutenant Parr arrived with his sledge and hitched their tents alongside of us. The cooks then set to work getting the supper ready which is a very unthankful billet as it takes a long time to thaw the snow and condense enough of water for the tea and rum, as we have our rum at night. And the cook being cold and hungry himself into the bargain makes it not a very pleasant job especially as he has to serve everybody else before he serves himself, but he has to rub over it as cheerfully as he can as it only comes to his turn once in six days. While the cook prepares the supper the remainder of the men brush the snow off their boots and clothes before getting into the tent. After getting inside they take off their snow suits and boots and boot hose and blanket wrappers which are wet and frozen and putting on a dry pair of blanket wrappers and a dry pair of stockings and a pair of moccasins for sleeping in, these things being carried in the canvas knapsack. After that they get into their sleeping bags and settle down in their allotted sleeping place for the night. The snow suits and bags have to be put under one while asleep to keep them from freezing or else you would not be able to put them on next morning. For some to have the weather below zero, they would be pretty stiff. Stockings and wrappers are taken in the bag with you to insure their being thawed by the morning because they have to go on again wet or not and the dry ones that are taken off are placed in the knapsack again. After settling down in your bags the topics of the day goes around or a talk about home or something else until the poor cook cries out 'supper', when in comes the allowance of Pemmican through the small windows of the tent in his panicans. Every man carries his own spoon which is made of horn. After the Pemmican is disposed of the tins are passed out again; then the tea is passed in in the same tins just as they were passed out, as the cook cannot make hot water to wash them out so that the tea slips down pretty well as it is nice and greasey; but a tin of hot tea is prized too much to take notice of that. After the tea is passed in, the cook manages to get his supper while the water is condensing for the rum and to put in the water bottles. After that the cook clears up a little and gets the cooking apparatus ready for the morning, but his trouble is not over yet; brushing himself and taking off the necessary clothing he settles down in his bag, his billet being close to the door or porch which is not a comfortable place and is colder than the remainder. The cook being settled, the grog is served out and then around goes the songs and stories until getting sleepy the coverlet is spread and the bags buttoned up; it does not take us long to fall into the hands of murphy. Next morning the cook has to be up some two hours and a half before the remainder, to prepare the breakfast. After breakfast the bags are rolled up, and the snow suits and boots and everybody dresses. The tent is struck and rolled up and the sledge packed all ready for a start, but after billetting that night we did not strike our tents as we had to bring the boats up and we intended remaining there for another night. Thermometer at zero. September 12th. 9:30 a.m. Started to bring the boats up taking the eight-man sledges with us, namely the Marco Polo, the Commander's being called the Victoria, and Lieutenant Parr's, the small five-man, being called the Nil Desperandum. Arriving down to the edge of the ice where we left the boats, to our surprise the whole of the open water that we had passed through the day before was one solid sheet of young ice. So much for an autumn night in the Arctic! Lashing the boats on the sledges we made a start which took us until late in the afternoon when we stopped at our encampment for lunch. After lunch made another start with the boats taking them about another 7 or 8 miles further on to another very low point of land, leaving them there. Brought the sledges back to the encampment where we arrived late in the evening pretty tired after a rather hard day's work. Put the dog sledges on the road as they were coming back to the ship. Got into the tent after brushing ourselves and retired for the night.

September 13th. 8 a.m. breakfast rolled up tents bags etc. stowed sledges.

9:30 a.m. made another start marching our way to where we had left the boats. Arriving where the boats were left, unloaded the sledges and placed the boats upon the sledge and putting the sledge equipment tents, gear etc. inside the boats made another start. But coming on to blow very heavy and making it very hard for travelling, when we stopped for lunch all ready for encamping for the night as Commander Markham did not think about going farther unless the wind abated. But as we wanted to get the boats farther on, some three or four miles distant so we all agreed to take the boats. As the wind did not abate we made a start taking a small depot of provisions with us. Taking the boats as far as we could, hauled the sledges some distance upon the land, unloaded them taking the boats off the sledge, turned them bottom up, placing the depot of provisions under them. After finishing, returned to our encampment again for the night, the boats being left now upwards of twenty miles from the ship but in travelling that twenty miles the sledges had to make a much longer march of it, owing to having so much hummock and having to travel by the land and autumn travelling is very heavy.

September 14th. 9:30 a.m. Struck tents and loaded the sledges. Formed the order march and made tracks for the ship but we had a very long march before us. Continued to blow very hard, freshening to a gale from the southard and westward; kept on the march until about two o'clock in the afternoon when we pitched tents for lunch under the lee, out of the wind, of some large hummocks, but in the middle of our lunch as we were drinking our panicans of hot tea, the ice broke away from the land and we should of soon been out to sea if we had not of struck tents at once and loaded the sledges and got on the march at once. Marched on again blowing a gale and the snow blowing off the hills nearly blinding us as we were marching head to wind. Towards the evening as we were getting very tired, the commander asked whether we would pitch tents, but the place being very open we should of had rather a job to pitch, so we agreed to try and reach the ship although we were all very tired as we had been marching up to our middle in wet snow a great many times which is very hard travelling. About 6 p.m. as we intended to try and reach the ship the Commander gave orders to halt for a short time and served out our stipulated allowance of rum. A traveller might travel some hundreds of miles in this country before he meets with a half-way house. After drinking our rum we made another start but did not get far before one of the men belonging to the sledge was forced to give in through exhaustion. As he was rather bad the commander gave orders to pitch the tent but as we had a deal of trouble to pitch owing to the strength of the wind and the place being very open; as the man was getting worse and we were frightened of him getting frozen, we resolved to try and reach the ship although we were that tired that we did not know how to move one leg before the other. But there was a man's life depending on us, so placing the man in a sleeping bag and covering him with his coverlet and tent gear we lashed him on the sledge making the best of our way to the ship. But it was very hard work for us to push on as it was dark and the snow nearly blinding. We left the other sledge crews encamped for the night. We marched on with our load as cheerfully as possible until we got within about a mile and a half from the ship when we got to the bluff of a hill as we had to take to the land which made it harder. We had to make standing pulls with the sledge dragging her up a few inches at a time. We were nearly fagged out, our strength gone. The commander cheered us up as much as he could.

Unfortunately the next few pages of Harley's diary have been erased but we do know that the party reached the ship safely.

This trip and the others were simply preparation for the major assault towards the Pole. The most successful of these was that led by Lieutenant Albert Markham the First Lieutenant of the *Alert* the following summer and they reached a point 83° 20′ N—only four hundred miles short of the pole but there they were forced to turn back greatly weakened through scurvy which dogged nearly all the various sledging expeditions. On an early expedition one of the boats had to be abandoned, five men had to be carried on sledges and only two officers and six men were left to haul. Among the hundred and twenty-one men on the expedition, there were fifty-six cases of scurvy.

Harley himself remained with the ship which itself did not have too easy a time, twice being nipped and forced on shore, though without any serious damage. Indeed when one of the *Discovery*'s sledging parties reached the *Alert* after a report that they had had to encamp further north through sickness (scurvy) having been helped in by a party from the latter ship Harley records that 'They all look pretty well considering. The fresh provision they have had has brought them around greatly.'

The *Alert* remained in its wintering place until 10th August and then sailed south to rejoin the *Discovery*, 'nearly twelve months since we left her'. It was not until 20th August that they really began to move. Then they found a 'splendid lead and Thank God, we are now on a fair road again southward'; but the very next day they had to seek shelter in a snow storm, and were then nipped in the ice and driven ashore, their boat heeling over at an angle of 25°. They got off the shore but remained caught in the ice, and on 30th August

> Captain gave orders to get up steam; being up steamed ahead a little but the young ice that had formed was very hard to push through; but after cutting and boreing our way until nearly 6:00 p.m. the Captain had to give in and both ships made fast to the floe and wait patiently for another chance. If we do not get wind it seems quite probable that we are doomed for the second winter.

Eventually a gale did spring up and helped to clear a passage through the ice, but it was not until 25th September that they got back to Godhavn, and over another month again before they finally reached England.

Undoubtedly the expedition was a considerable success. Though they failed to reach the North Pole itself they went further than any previous expedition, and their approach remained the nearest for ten years when it was beaten by only four miles. Also, though they suffered severely from disease the expedition returned to England almost intact. This was a real achievement, since the problem of scurvy was to remain a scourge for over a generation; Scott's expedition was severely weakened by it.

Nevertheless this was the last Naval expedition of its kind. Never again were heavily manned naval vessels working under service conditions to explore the Arctic. Aside from the dogs (which were not a great success), and some improvement in diet, their equipment differed only marginally from that of Franklin's ill-fated enterprise. Their success was achieved only by superb courage and morale. Harley's description of the ice as 'hummockey' is very much an understatement. The strength and endurance required to drag heavy sledges over this difficult terrain could be achieved only by men determined to 'do their duty'. This was indeed the Victorian Navy at its apogee.

Overall the Royal Navy's contribution to Polar exploration was outstanding. Even in the Antarctic, where to this date the Navy had contributed less than at the other pole, the ill-fated *Erebus* and *Terror* reached the shores of the continent. Two voyages in the early 1840s under Sir James Clark Ross reached the farthest south yet, and though it was not to be a British Sailor who was to be first at either of the two poles, this lay still in the future.

The future was more tragic for Petty Officer Daniel Harley. He was to lose his life only two years later in the tragedy of H.M.S. *Eurydice* to be described later in the book. He was then still five months short of his thirtieth birthday.

'Reefing Topsails.'

H.M.S. *Samarang* in a gale in the bay of Biscay.

The crew of H.M.S. *Dauntless* prepare for the Crimean War. 8th April,
1854.

The sick bay of the *Bellisle* (Hospital Ship), Faro Sound, 1855.

6

Surveying and Charting—Joseph Stratton

Dear Father,

I received your kind and welcome letters dated September and November upon our arrival here, after a very long and tedious cruise, and was heartily glad to learn that *Julia* had received my letters, I thought we should have had some orders respecting our ship. There is a report that she is ordered home, but I am of opinion that there is no chance of that for some time. Since my last we have been at Sarawak attended by the *Phlegethon*, East India Company's Steamer. We conveyed the Rajah and his suit to Borneo Proper and left him as Prime Minister he having resigned as Rajah of Sarawak and given that part of Borneo with a very beautiful island named Pulo Labuan lying off the mouth of Borneo river to the English Government. We have surveyed it and found a abundance of coal. There is a fine bay and harbour which we have named Victoria Bay. Our Government has sent out Captain Drinkwater Bethune R.N. to hoist the English flag upon the island which will eventually be the island for steamers to China. After being three months from Singapore we called at Manilla for provisions and was informed by the English consul that a Bark named 'The Premier' had been wrecked near Curran Bay off the coast of Borneo and the Captain and crew had been taken and sold for slaves by the Natives who are all Pirates. We sailed after staying here a few days to the relief of the sufferers and arrived the Day after Christmas. (I hope you were all more happy that day than I was.) We expected to meet with a strong opposition from the Natives. The town was situated sixty miles up a river, our boats were all armed and manned, (five in number) the two barges had each a six pounder, the two cutters had each a three pounder, and Captain's Gig had Congreve rockets besides small arms. When the Natives observed us making towards their tower they made signs to us to go back and pointed their guns and spears but we were not to be frightened quite so soon as they

6

fancied. The Captain landed and had an interview with the Sultan and soon came to terms. A Salute was fired from our boats which struck them with surprise; they returned it. We stayed three days and succeeded in getting the crew of the Bark. They were natives of Calcutta. The Captain and mate had been taken away by a Dutch sloop shortly before our arrival. I went to the wreck; she is lying on an extensive coral bank—she was set on fire before the crew left her, there is not much of her to be seen. The Natives are a most strange looking race, they are all provided with a knife or sword, spears and Blow pipes, the blow pipes are ten feet in length bore with a small hole not more than three eighths of an inch and very nicely made. The arrows they blow through are poisoned. I have a number of these weapons that I purchased off them and some taken from the boats we captured. You wished to know if we lost any of our crew. I am happy to inform you that not one had a scar beside the Captain and he has quite recovered. After this cruising we went to Manilla, from there to the Bashee island and then to Hong Kong where we are at present. I believe we are going to Formosa. Hong Kong is rising fast. There is a great improvement since we arrived the first time. Fine houses are rearing their heads as fast as the hands of Chinamen build them,—the hills which are very lofty supply them with abundance of fine granite. I have been on shore here very frequently and there are Chinese employed cutting into the granite within a few yards of the buildings in fact there is one continual chipping, others forming the blocks of stone into designs of various orders. There are a few English workmen but not many compared with the others. I don't think it will ever be a large place on account of the hills or rather mountains which slope down to the sea. However it will be in a short time a beautiful city; at present it looks very well from the shipping. I have a number of small things purchased here which will afford much pleasure to you on my return. I was sorry to learn that Isabella was still at home and no better as to behaviour. Tell George that if he pays attention to his work it will be far better than going to sea and when I return we may be able to do something together for I can assure you that I shall never think of going to sea any more. Give my love to mother and assure her that it is impossible for me to forget her. I shall write to you again before we leave here and then I may be able to inform you more about the ship. Give my respects to all who may feel interested to inquire and that I am in good health, thank God. I intend writing to uncle this leave and aunt Kate. I have not received any answer from Julia. Adieu, God bless you and may we meet shortly and believe me your dutiful son

J. J. Stratton.

So wrote Joseph Stratton from H.M.S. *Samarang* during a commission in the Pacific under Captain Edward Belcher (who had commanded the barge in the *Blossom*). The major object of the voyage was to survey and chart the coasts and islands of the Eastern Archipelago (i.e. from Korea to Singapore) which had been 'opened' as a result of the treaty between England and China following the Opium War in 1842.

Joseph Stratton also kept a diary of his time in the *Samarang* but aside from an occasional remark such as 'Here we saw the Great Comet' and 'Took seventeen Chinese out of a sinking junk, one severely hurt' it is simply a list of the various places that they visited. Although his first entry is

5th. December 1842. Joined Her Majesty's Ship of War *Samarang* 26 guns Captain Sir Edward Belcher C.B. on a voyage to survey various Islands in the North Pacific ocean and Chinese Seas.

he makes no further reference to the major objective of their voyage—surveying. He does not even mention it in his letters. This is hardly surprising; it was a tedious, monotonous task, especially for the ratings who would spend long hours in open boats, measuring and sounding the bearing of the ship and the depth of the water. They would have to make difficult landings on rocky shores to fix the positions of bays, inlets and other features. For the Captain who could see the growing pattern of the chart, it was an exciting and rewarding enterprise; for the sailor it was simply a boring, repetitive and even dangerous task. It was all very well for the Captain to use his sextant and the ship's compass on board to obtain a true bearing between one floating mark and another; it was less enjoyable for those who were the floating marks. Yet absolute accuracy was essential. One error of position by the officer in command of one boat would jeopardise the whole day's complicated plan. Belcher himself did not help matters. He was a brilliant and utterly dedicated surveyor. On one occasion after being fired on by a group of natives off the coast of Gillolo, though temporarily retiring to the barge, he insisted on completing his observations and readings. Having done this he proceeded to attack the natives whom he called pirates and though shot in the thigh continued in command and succeeded in routing them. Although they were flying a Dutch flag he managed to have them classified as pirates and received £10,000 bounty for the officers and men of the *Samarang*. On the other hand when the boats went away, the Captain's would be filled with delicacies. The others would have to put up with naval issue of salt beef and biscuit.

The officers might complain about the time spent in open boats and more justifiably at Belcher's arbitrary decisions. One Christmas, for example, after everyone had made arrangements to spend the festival at Manila, Belcher suddenly decided to take the ship off without warning and spent the festival surveying a remote and cheerless bay.

The Hydrographer of the Navy, Admiral Sir Francis Beaufort (remembered among other things for the Beaufort Wind scale), did not have the same view of Belcher's activities. 'The harvest I look for at your hands,' he wrote to Belcher 'does not stretch beyond the reach of a deep-sea line and all the credit I crave for you, and through you for myself, must be won in the kingdom of science and reaped in hydrographic fields.' Probably more than any single person Beaufort was responsible for the adoption by the Admiralty of a system of scientific surveying and charting so that at his retirement in 1855 he left a series of 2,000 charts covering every area of the world and during his last year of office alone, 140,000 copies were printed for sale or for issue to the Royal Navy. The foreknowledge of this would have been of little consolation to Stratton and the officers and men of the *Samarang*.

Belcher was a flamboyant and boisterous character, and not well liked by his officers and men. At one point a Court Martial was held at the request of the First Lieutenant of the *Samarang* on the grounds that Belcher had slandered him by accusing him of conduct unbecoming an officer and a gentleman. Fortunately for all concerned the Court was dissolved before a verdict could be reached though the First Lieutenant was returned his sword without a stain on his character. Only a short while later the *Samarang* was delayed in Hong Kong because of a row between the Captain and the local Commander-in-Chief, Admiral Sir Thomas Cochrane, who accused Belcher of insubordination. The *Samarang* was at no point a happy ship and the end of the commission was greeted with frantic joy.

Even though the entire task of surveying had not been completed, a great deal had been achieved. Much of the Eastern Archipelago had been charted, together with the coast of Borneo, and parts of the coast of Korea and the Majico Sima Islands.

Nor was this the only achievement. Belcher had joined with his boat's attacks mounted against pirate lairs on the Borneo Rivers; he organised an expedition to rescue a European woman supposed to be living in captivity at Amboor on the north coast of Borneo (though she was never found); he signed treaties of friendship with the Sultans of Gunang, Tabor and Bulungang. All this was in addition to the incidents recalled by Stratton in his letter (though the amount of coal was far less than Stratton implied).

The voyage had its share of minor mishaps, as the following incident recalled by a young officer on board recalls.

September 8th. It being calm, the ship's company were permitted to bathe. In a minute all those who could swim were in the water, playing about in every direction round the ship, and enjoying the luxury. While this continued, the man at the mast-head reported a shark close at hand. The word to come in quickly was given by the first lieutenant and all the officers. It required no second call—every one knew why, and swam to the ropes, which were thrown in every direction. It was touch and go as the saying is—one of the marines who was last, was actually touched by the shark, who made at him; but before he could turn and bite, the fellow had jerked himself out of his reach. It was very fortunate that the man at the mast-head kept so good a look-out for generally they are more occupied with the gambols of the bathers than looking out for sharks. As it was, many of the swimmers were so unnerved that it was with difficulty they could get out of the danger. After the men were on board again, the great object was to have revenge upon the animal who had thus put an end to enjoyment. The shark hook was baited with a piece of bull's hide and the animal, who was still working up and down alongside the ship, took the bait greedily, and was hauled on board. The axe was immediately at work at his tail, which was dismembered, and a score of knives plunged into his body, ripping him up in all directions. His eyes were pushed out with fish-hooks and knives and every indignity offered him. He was then cut to pieces, and the quivering flesh thrown into the frying-pans and eaten with a savage pleasure which we can imagine only to be felt by cannibals when devouring the flesh of their enemies. Certainly, if the cannibal nations have the same feeling towards their enemies which sailors have against sharks, I do not wonder at their adhering to this custom, for there was a savage delight in the eyes of every seaman in the ship as they assisted to cut pieces and then devour the brute who would have devoured them. It was the madness of retaliation—an eye for an eye, and a tooth for a tooth.

The surveying work was all carried out at a time and place when the Navy was at its lowest ebb. On the same station another naval vessel, the *Royalist* (not to be confused with the Rajah of Sarawak's yacht), demonstrated its desperate inefficiency. In a period of twelve months she had lost three commanding officers through illness and death; no official communication had been received by the brig for eighteen months. In desperation the acting second master promoted himself and without orders sailed the vessel to Singapore to find out what they ought to be doing. It turned out that the new Captain had apparently been unable to locate the vessel and had waited at Hong Kong hoping

that she would turn up. All credit then to Francis Beaufort and the
hydrographers and surveyors who charted the world's oceans in such
difficult circumstances. Changes could only come after the old generation of officers had passed away.

Joseph James Stratton left the Navy when the *Samarang* paid off
and became a licenced victualler, keeping a number of public houses
including the Prince of Prussia at Camberwell and the Albion in
Hammersmith. His son Frederick also went to sea, but in the merchant
service. On his first voyage he contracted malaria and was buried in
Suez.

7

The Crimean War

We had five of our company very slightly wounded in the trenches.
I saw one of our men chasing four or five Russians with admirable
gusto. I had one or two very narrow escapes. It is very good sport
at present; but when it comes to storming the town, I fear it will
prove a very lamentable affair. I shall be heartily glad when it is
over . . .

I saw an awful sight yesterday;—a bomb shell dropped into the
battery near where I was lying and exploded, when I saw the
mangled remains of a sailor in the air: he was literally blown to
pieces. Here is a new addition to the features of a camp life. You will
hear mingled with the sound of the boatswain's pipe a hoarse voice
calling out 'All hands to muster'. The Jack Tars are curious animals
in camp.

So wrote a young rifleman of the Green Jackets living in siege before
Sebastopol. The sailors he mentions were members of the Naval
Brigade who were sent ashore bringing with them a number of the
ships' guns. Unfortunately no lower deck account of the Naval
Brigade's exploits in the Crimea appears to have survived and so it is
appropriate to include a description by a soldier who fought alongside
them, a rifleman who was decorated with a medal and two clasps from
the Admiralty in commendation of gallant and honourable service.

During this battle three seamen, Thomas Reeves, James Gorman,
and Mark Scholefield won the Victoria Cross. In the words of the
despatch sent by the commander of the Naval Brigade, Sir Stephen
Lushington:

At the battle of Inkerman, 5th November, 1854, when the right
Lancaster Battery was attacked, these three seamen mounted the
banquette (a low bank) and under heavy fire, made use of the disabled soldiers' muskets which were loaded for them by others under

the parapet. They are the survivors of five who performed the above action.

The riflemen had nothing but admiration for the bluejackets. Some months later one of them described an assault on the outskirts of Sebastopol:

We made an attempt on the 18th. of June to storm the Redan Batteries, but in consequence of the affair being misconducted, we met with no success. It seems as if they had expected a small party of our men to do the whole of the work. It was arranged as follows: Each regiment of the light division was to furnish a certain number of men to carry scaling ladders (ours furnished 160); they were to advance at a given signal towards the enemies' works, accompanied by a party of men carrying woodstacks to fill up the ditch; in rear of them was supposed to be the support, closely followed by a strong working party. The signal was given by fireworks from one of our batteries one hour before daylight, and the riflemen, with about two dozen *volunteer* Jack Tars, made a dash, and in spite of the sweeping volleys of grape and canister etc., some of them managed to reach the Russian works, but where was the support? (red soldiers under cover?) Not forthcoming, by some mismanagement. (According to the official version they got held up by a large number of non combatants directly engaged who also wished to take part!) These were detained in the advanced trenches, and out of 160 of my comrades (riflemen), 70 were killed and wounded, and I am sorry to state, a number of the sailors were killed. God bless them! They are England's bravest men. I saw one sailor, a very little man, struggling through a crowd of soldiers, which his chum, who was twice his size and mortally wounded, on his back. The soldiers expostulated with the impropriety of carrying him home, but Jack was determined to effect his object, or die in the attempt. A sailor will run a mile to give a wounded rifleman his grog.

Certainly the sailors might have been more comfortable on board a ship in a force eight gale.

Up to my neck in mud in all weather, and doing my natural sleep every night in a puddle of water . . . for my own part I have given up all hopes of ever getting dry again. We cannot live in tents; in fact the tent that I used to live in, has long since become non-effective. We awoke one morning and found that the wind had made a large back-door into it; so we were obliged to take our canvas and dig a large hole in the ground to live in; but before we could finish it, the wet weather commenced, so we are living in a well almost. We have the remains of our tent covered over, but that is anything but water proof; certainly we can luxuriate ourselves with a shower bath as often as we like. There is no moderation in the weather here at all. I expect the weather agent for this district has been defunct long since. I cannot explain to you properly the position I am sitting in now, but it is something after the style of nose and knee fashion, as father used to term it; with a little spring issuing from a rock on my right, my feet imbedded in mud—but now for the sublime part— a fireplace of my own construction on my left with plenty of wood on. The late shipwrecks will supply us in wood all the winter if the weather will admit of our getting at it. We have to descend one mile and a half before we can get it, from this to the beach. I went to the town of Balaklava yesterday to try and purchase a few articles to make something in the shape of a Xmas dinner. I could not get flour, even at ten shillings a pound; they even asked about two and a half for a small loaf about the size of Quick's penny tea cake.

The sailors were not responsible for one apparently typical incident:

I often think how happy you ought to feel and how grateful you ought to be to the Almighty for His protection in preserving your homes from invasion. I have often seen some of our men enter a comfortable cottage, and actually rob the inmates and turn them out of their own home, and before night the pretty cottage would be in ruins. I saw a daring fellow enter a poor woman's cottage, and after turning every rag over the poor old girl had left, he took her workbox from under her arm, despite the poor old lady's bewailing. She looked sorrowful indeed when she saw the ruffian depart with her only treasure; and, more than that, in passing through the garden, he took a hive of bees, which probably had been the old lady's only pride. Oh! how I wished I was her son that I could take revenge. I would have taken his heart out and burnt it! But such deeds are common. I tried to pacify her, and while doing so, I thought of mother, and that thought brought tears to my eyes; the old woman saw it, and blessed me. I could not assist her, and so she wandered forth to find a fresh home. I often pass the place where her cottage stood, but not a vestige remains.

The Army Commander-in-Chief himself wrote, after the final capture of Sebastopol:

The Naval Brigade, under the command of Captain the Hon. Henry Keppel, aided by Captain Moorson and many gallant officers and seamen who have served the guns from the commencement of the siege merit my warmest thanks.

And the Naval Commander-in-Chief at the same time wrote to the Secretary of the Admiralty.

With the exception of the Naval Brigade it has not fallen to the lot on this occasion to perform distinguished deeds of arms such as those of their gallant brethren in the army.

And one of the soldier's wives, a Mrs. Henry Dauberly wrote:

These seamen appear to work with the greatest energy and good-will. One meets a gang of them harnessed to a gun, and drawing with all their might and main; or digging at entrenchments singing, laughing, and working heartily and cheerily. But their experience of camp life is short indeed in comparison with that of our poor soldiers with whom they contrast so gaily.

The Naval Brigade, now that there is no longer need for the Sailor's Battery, are all ordered on board their respective ships. I think there are very few but are sorry to leave their comparatively free life on shore for the imprisonment and the strict discipline of a man-of-war. They would be (if we were to remain the winter) a very serious loss to us as there were no workmen, carpenters, joiners, builders, half so handy or so willing to assist as those in the Naval Brigade. There was certainly no camp in which more kind considera-tion for others, more real active help, has been afforded to all than in that of the sailors; and their cheerfulness and willingness to labour encouraged and comforted all through the difficulties and sufferings of last winter.

Indeed the stories of the exploits of the Naval Brigade are legion. One army officer describing their behaviour wrote:

There is a recklessness about the seaman's courage. For instance, whenever a particularly affective shot issued from one of their embrasures, the tars would leap *en masse* upon the parapet, wave the Union Jack, and cheer like devils. A defiance that had the effect of bringing upon the brave, but thoughtless, fellows, an augmented dose of iron.

And he goes on to tell the story of a bluejacket who

chivalrously anxious to obtain a genuine trophy from the person of a *living* 'Rooshian', chanced to catch sight of a big flat-capped, long-coated Calmuck, dodging among the bushes and stones near the naval battery. Like a shot, Jack leaps through the embrasure, and away, over the open, after Johnny Russ, who, finding himself pursued takes likewise to his heels. It is a short, and unfair race; it is a shorter and more unfair encounter. In a few seconds, the nimble footed seaman is aboard the lubberly marksman, has gripped him by the nape of the neck, has shaken him as the pedagogue shakes a stupid school-boy, has wrested the musket out of his hand, has applied a valedictory kick or two to the terrified creature's posteriors, and is back again in the battery, with the coveted prize so honestly won. When asked by his messmates, 'how it was he hadn't brought the enemy along with him,' our hero replied, 'Why, what'ud have been the good in him, poor chap. Don't you see any how I've got his firelock? Them sodgers be worse nor lumber when you've taken their *harms* from em.'

Of course the Royal Navy's involvement was not confined to the Naval Brigade nor even to the Black Sea. Engagements took place in the Arctic, the Far East and the Baltic. An attack was made in the White Sea, which was blockaded, and a minor engagement took place in the Far East, which was most notable for the action of the British Commander in the area, Admiral David Price. He was possibly too old for the job, but he had a distinguished record. Shortly before an attack on a well-defended position in Avaloka Bay by the combined British and French fleets, Price 'lost his head in a most unaccountable way'. He retired to his cabin and shot himself. The attack was suspended until the following day.

In the Baltic, the naval offensive took the form of an attack on the Russian Baltic ports by a combined British and French fleet. It achieved very little and the major argument has since been over apportioning the blame. The British admiral, Sir Charles Napier, has been severely criticised. At 68 he was too old for the task, and far too timid.

He had not helped relations at home by sending a signal to the fleet when he took command saying:

Lads, war is declared with a numerous and bold enemy. Should they meet us and offer battle, you must know how to dispose of them. Should they remain in port, we must try and get at them. Success depends on the quickness and precision of your firing. Also, lads, sharpen your cutlasses, and the day is your own.

Not surprisingly, rapid action was expected, particularly as fourteen years previously, following a dashing bombardment and attack from the sea, Napier had helped to capture Acre. The expectations for success in the Baltic were unreasonable as Napier's fleet had neither the trained men nor the material to reduce the Russian fortresses. Bomarsund was captured but this alone was not an adequate achievement either for the Admiralty or for the general public, and Napier was the inevitable scapegoat.

The main reason for failure was the system of officering and manning the Navy. The problem of the officers was primarily one of age. There was no proper system of retirement. Napier had been made a Captain in 1809 and at the time of the Crimean War was 68. Yet also considered for the post was Thomas Cochrane, Lord Dundonald, who was 79, and who was not even rejected on the score of age. The Commander-in-Chief at Plymouth was 81. The block in promotion in the smaller Navy after 1815 was not really eliminated until after 1864.

The problem of manning the lower deck was even more serious. Here a large trained reserve was needed but there was no machinery for this apart from the Press Gang, which public opinion would not stand, and no responsible naval officer even suggested restoring the press. Yet the problem of manning had to be solved. Even in peacetime it was intractable, but the rapid expansion required by the war simply could not be achieved. There were thus two separate problems: manning the Navy in peacetime and providing a trained reserve for rapid expansion in emergencies.

After the Crimean War the problems were tackled, but this was too late to help either Napier, or the British fleet in the Black Sea. A pay-rise granted in 1852 had helped a little, (the Able Seaman's pay went up from about 1/1 a day to 1/4), but an Act to establish Naval Coast Volunteers passed in August 1853 came too late. The seamen who were raised in 1854 were a motley and generally unskilled collection and this added to Napier's problems.

In the Black Sea the situation was a little better. The fleet was based on ships from the Mediterranean, and the majority of these were in good order, though the seamen there were barely literate, as a verbatim copy of a letter sent by a seaman in H.M.S. *Bellerephon* shows. The ship was in the Mediterranean at the beginning of the war and later returned to England.

Feb. 6th. 1855

My Dear Mother,

I take this opportunity of writing to you, hoping to find you in Good health as it leaves me at present thang God for it. we arrived here last Tuesday from Gibralter; dont no when we shall leave here but there his talk of us leaving here about next June or July. so you heard from Bob and he is goen to America; i daresay we can do without him. I wonder Bill dont go Coasting instead of Lumping i should think it would Pay him better but he knows best

I should have wrighting to you before bu we could get no regular mail i received your very kind letter but was very sorry to hear of Sarah's ill health you never mind sending me a newspaper if you cant afford it I dont wish you to put yourself out about me if Sarah

can is well enough to wright tell her too did Jim give you any
directions where to wright to when he wrote if he did let me hear i
dont know who this Sarah Bussell his tell me i dare say we shall go
up along before we come home they say we are going to bring
Admiral Harvey if so we shant be long i often have a talk about the
Blackheath lions to Bill Johnson his mother lives in Royal Place i
shant forget Bobs kindness in not getting a letter wrote to me i
dont kno what else to talk about my news his all spun excuse my
bad wrighting if Sarah has made that ring she may send it between
two cards with a page for to lay in sticthed to the card. tell Sarah i
Broke my flute send the price of the ring so no more at present
from your affectionate son.

John Franks
a chap wet my hair yesterday but I did not of what you as said in one
of your letters ill think next time. give my love to all Friends and
Old George.

John Franks served out his time in the Navy and later became a
merchant seaman.

When the Mediterranean fleet reached the Black Sea, its major
task was to support the army. For almost the first time in British
history, relations between the two services were very friendly. The
Navy's first task was to escort the transports to the Crimea. Then at
the Battle of Alma it rendered 'Invaluable assistance and never ceased
to provide for the sick and the wounded and to carry them down to the
beach; a labour in which some of the officers even volunteered to
participate.'

A base was then established at Balaklava (famous for the Charge of
the Light Brigade), and at Inkerman, which has already been mentioned.
Eventually Sebastopol itself was stormed by the army, assisted by the
Naval Brigade, and this brought the war to an end. But it was a
soldier's, not a sailor's war. The Black Sea was cleared of Russian
ships, but no major engagement took place. The Russians scuttled a
number of their ships in the entrance to the harbour at Sebastopol and
these together with the shore batteries made any attempt to attack from
the sea virtually impossible. A bombardment was attempted, with
the British and French fleet anchored across the mouth of the harbour,
and W. H. Hankin, the coxswain of the *Sans Pareil*, wrote:

Engaged in the bombardment of Sebastopol Tuesday 17th. October
1854. Having fired between 1400 and 1500 rounds from our guns,
the casualties were 11 killed (including one midshipman) 59 wounded.
The vessel was struck a great number of times by shot, shell and
other misiles; also a great deal of other damage to spars rigging etc.

The magazine had to be cleared for some time owing to the bends being on fire. I was Captain of the 10th. gun on the main deck.
P.S. The ship was anchored with a kedge anchor astern during the time we were engaged with the batteries.

Altogether this was not a successful enterprise, and no similar action was attempted. The French had insisted on anchoring rather than attacking the forts under way, which made the ships a relatively easy target. The forts themselves were very strong and the ships did little damage. In return the fleet suffered heavy casualties. Altogether 46 were killed and 271 wounded. Every ship was more or less damaged, and fire broke out in the *Britannia* when a red-hot shot buried itself under the hammocks on the poop. Two ships had to go to Constantinople for repairs, though the remainder were patched up on the spot. It was 'no more than a mere diversion in which an imminent and fatal disaster was risked for little or no adequate advantage'.

Minor bombardments by the steam frigates on forts along the shore from Balbeck to Sebastopol were more successful. The ships' guns outranged those of the forts and therefore were not themselves in danger but they were a considerable irritant to the Russians. The bombardments were later discontinued at Lord Raglan's request because they had the effect of 'disquieting the army'.

More successful still were the attacks in the Sea of Azov on the Russian lines of communication, Raglan wrote of them: 'The gallant exploits of the navy have spread joy in our camps and afforded vast satisfaction to every individual in the army.'

The Navy thus acted in a subsidiary role. What honours there were lay with the army and those sailors ashore who formed the Naval Brigade. No detailed account by a seaman of the actions seems to have survived, but a number of sailors did distinguish themselves, no fewer than ten winning Victoria Crosses (this award was created about this time as a decoration for the highest gallantry). Joseph Trewavers one of the seamen honoured, was particularly mentioned by Admiral Lyons the naval commander for having

Cut the hawsers of the floating bridge in the straits of Genitchi under a heavy fire of musketry on which occasion he was wounded. This service was performed by the crews of the Captain's gig and one of the paddle-box boats of the *Beagle*, under a heavy fire of musketry at a distance of eighty yards the beach being completely lined with troops and the adjacent homes filled with riflemen. Joseph Trewavers is especially mentioned in the dispatches as having been the person who cut the hawser.

Trewavers himself came from a fishing and seafaring family. He was born at Mousehole in Cornwall on 14th December, 1835. With the outbreak of war he went to Devonport to join the Navy, and there he was drafted on board H.M.S. *Agamemnon*, which shortly afterwards sailed for the Crimea. He took part in the bombardment of Sebastopol already mentioned and a week later was landed with the Naval Brigade. He was then lent to the *Beagle* and it was in this ship that he sailed into the Sea of Azov, the object of the mission being to disrupt Russian communications and destroy ships and stores. One important route to Sebastopol passed through the town of Genitchi across a floating bridge, operated by hawsers, and so along the spit of Arabat. Lieutenant William Hewett (later Admiral Hewett) in command of the *Beagle* decided that the hawsers securing the floating bridge must be cut. One attempt failed but under the cover of a small paddle-steamer with one gun, Trewavers started again in a four-oared boat. Unfortunately after firing one round, the gun in the paddle-steamer collapsed and remained useless for the rest of the time. Rowing up to the pontoon, Trewavers leapt on to it and cut the hawsers. The Russians realising what was going on opened up a terrific fire on the party, but in Trewavers' own words:

> By coolness and pulling for dear life, and by the Russians shocking aim, we get back to the ships. The boat completely riddled and up to the thwarts in water.

Trewavers received the award of Knight of the Legion of Honour, and also the Crimean medal and the Turkish Crimean medal. He was immediately promoted to Able Seaman and later became a Leading Seaman, but he was not wedded to the Navy. When the *Agamemnon* returned to England and was paid off on 22nd May, 1857 he retired from the service. A month later at a great parade in Hyde Park he received his V.C. from Queen Victoria. He returned to Cornwall and became a fisherman at Penzance continuing to go to sea for a number of years. He married in 1866 and had three children, a boy and two girls. Eventually he retired from the sea returning to Mousehole where he had been born and died there on 20th July, 1905.

John Sullivan also won his V.C. in the Crimea. During the attack on Sebastopol he volunteered to take out a flagstaff and place it on a mound so that the direction of a hidden battery could be bombarded. On reaching the mound, he looked both ways to see if he was in a direct line between the British and Russian lines. Satisfied that he was in the right place he scraped a hole for the flagstaff and gathered stones to bank it up. All the time he was under continuous fire from Russian sharp-shooters, but although one fired three shots at him in quick succession, Sullivan reckoned that the man's movements were too rapid and excited for accuracy, and he completed the task. He was later promoted to a warrant-officer and was for many years a boatswain in Portsmouth dockyard.

The last words on the Crimean War come from the young rifleman whose letters home opened this account. He began his last letter:

August 24th. I must tell you how the Russians were treated on the 16th. instant. There was a large force making its way into Sebastopol, but previous to reaching their destination they thought they would try for a soft place in the French and Sardinian lines; consequently they diverged from their road and made for Balaklava. Our allies waited very patiently until they got well into the net, and then walked into them like butchers, I guess, but the Sardinians were too eager for a touch of them, as usual. However, they worked very well, and before 12 a.m. they managed to cover the plain with dead and dying Muscovites. We took no part in the fighting, but our fellows were on the making system. You could see them going from one dead man to another, trying for a pair of boots, and cutting their trousers up to look for money etc. You could see every man return with a Russian gun or two. The ones were off duty that day. We were very unfortunate on the 18th. of this month. Some of our batteries opened fire on the enemies' works, and to prevent them from repairing their works at night we were ordered to keep up a continuous rifle fire, which brought a heavy fire from the Russian shipping on us; the shells in the air were as thick as stars, and we were hopping about like cats on hot bricks. That night, in killed and wounded we lost 23, a considerable number considering we were behind trenches. The next day I had a good bit of sport with a Russian. We were firing at 100 yards: each of us had a loophole about 6 inches square, and we were firing shot from morning 'till night. We could only see the half of each other's faces . . .

This letter was unfinished. He was mortally wounded at the storming of the Redan and was found in Sebastopol, naked and covered with bayonet wounds.

The Main Battery, H.M.S. *Alexandra*.

'Blue Jackets to the front.'

The war in Egypt: a Naval Brigade clearing the streets of Alexandria
with the Gatling gun.

8

Mid-Century

It is not the object of this book to give a description of all the engagements in which the Navy was involved during this period. In the first
place it was engaged in every part of the British Empire, and that
Empire by the end of the century covered a quarter of the earth's
surface and included a quarter of the world's population; even an
attempt simply to list the engagements is meaningless except to the
specialist. Second, in spite of their number these engagements bore a
considerable resemblance to each other—the bombardment of a hostile
shore or a landing in support of the military or civil power.

The only major campaign—the Russian or Crimean War—has already
been examined in detail. The suppression of the Slave Trade, which did
involve action of a different kind, will be treated separately. There
remain the other engagements which occurred in almost every year in
one or other part of the growing Empire. Even a list of these would
be tedious. Wherever trouble occurred the Navy was first there to
help clear the matter up; often the sailors alone were sufficient. The
rising or rebellion that had occurred which threatened the life and
property of British citizens was put down simply with the landing of
a detachment of naval ratings. The mere appearance of part of the
British fleet was sometimes sufficient by itself to reinstate a ruler who
was fortunate enough to enjoy British support. Even when the army
was called in, a Naval Brigade generally lent assistance—and these
actions by Naval Brigades ashore were the Navy's main active part.

One famous occasion when the appearance of the British fleet
was sufficient was the case of Don Pacifico. He was a Portuguese Jew
living in Greece but, having been born in Gibraltar, was a British
subject. Like many money lenders he was not popular with his clients,
and his house and records were burnt by the local populace. The
Greek government were not sympathetic. Don Pacifico appealed to
Palmerston, who sent the British Mediterranean Fleet into the Piraeus,

until the Greeks paid compensation. In the face of such a threat, the
Greeks speedily capitulated. Palmerston was attacked for his high-
handed behaviour but he defended himself in a brilliant speech in the
House of Commons:

> As the Roman in the days of old held himself free from indignity
> when he could say *Civis Romanus sum*; so also a British subject, in
> whatever land he may be, shall feel confident that the watchful eye
> and the strong arm of England, will protect him against injustice and
> wrong.

What was unique about this incident was not so much the action
taken (the occasion was very similar to that described by Joseph
Stratton off Borneo) but the fact that the government upon which
pressure was placed was European. In a small way, incidents similar to
the Don Pacifico affair occurred frequently round the coasts of every
continent in the world. These activities do not feature significantly in
the journals and letters of the seamen themselves. Black, yellow, brown,
or white was generally a matter of indifference to the British sailor. He
was confident of his own ability and even superiority—the British
were the best, and British Sailors best of all. Who ruled whom was not
a matter of very great concern—local politics was a matter for the
locals. The ship itself provided the interests and the sense of community.

> If we were at a place where we could land, walking, running, fishing,
> cricket or even football was engaged in. If in a place where landing
> was impracticable, then boat racing, bathing or swinging the monkey
> while it was daylight; and after dark an entertainment by one of our
> many entertaining groups.

This was in the 1880s. But throughout our period the sailors fought
the natives ashore if they were ordered to do so, yet they remained
totally uninterested in their governments and habits.

At times the appearance of a warship was not in itself sufficient.
During the twenty-five years after the Crimean War, seven Royal
Naval ratings were awarded the Victoria Cross. The areas in which
these awards were gained give some indication of the range of naval
activities. Three were in India during the Mutiny; two were won in the
Maori wars in New Zealand; two in Japan and one in China.
Significantly, all these awards were given for service ashore, the first
three during the siege of Lucknow. In the Indian Mutiny, large numbers
of native troops had revolted against their British officers and attempted
to destroy British power in India. One of the key strongholds was in
Lucknow which held out against the mutineers. A relief force was sent
to the town, including a Naval Brigade of over 500, which fought its

way into the residency to free the defenders. A strategic point was the Shah Neyiff, a large domed mosque with a walled garden, and the Naval Brigade under Captain Peel bombarded it for three hours. Captain Peel (who had previously won a V.C. in the Crimea) behaved 'as if he had been laying the *Shannon* alongside an enemy frigate'. Eventually the guns were moved up to within twenty yards of the wall and the Captain of one of the guns, William Hall, a petty officer from the *Shannon*, was awarded a Victoria Cross for this action. Describing it he said:

> I remember that after firing each round we ran our gun forward until at last my gun's crew were actually in danger of being hit by splinters of brick and stone torn by the round shot from the walls we were bombarding. Our Lieutenant, Mr. Thomas Young (who was also awarded the V.C.) moved from gun to gun with a quiet smile and a word of encouragement; and when at last the gunner next to me fell dead, Mr. Young at once took his place.

During this action one of the Indian mutineers perched himself on top of the wall and picked off a number of the sailors at the guns. Peel called out for a volunteer to climb a tree and shoot this marksman, but the first sailor to attempt it was shot dead as he reached the top of the tree. A boatswain's mate, John Harrison, with a naval Lieutenant, Salvier, immediately attempted to follow, and succeeded in bringing the Indian down. For this Harrison and the Lieutenant were awarded the V.C. and eventually the soldiers were able to force their way into the Mosque.

Harrison died not very long after the engagement but William Hall survived to enjoy an active retirement. He had an interesting life. A negro, born at Avonport in Nova Scotia, he joined the Navy as an ordinary seaman and reached the rating of Petty Officer. When he left the Navy he returned to Nova Scotia and became a farmer at Avonport. His favourite recreation according to *Who's Who* was shooting crows. He died about 1900.

The third V.C. in the Indian Mutiny was won by Edward Robinson, an able seaman, also at Lucknow, but some six months later. The official citation reads 'For conspicuous bravery in having at Lucknow, on the 13th March, 1858, under a heavy musketry fire, within fifty yards, jumped on the sand bags of a battery and extinguished a fire among them. He was dangerously wounded in performing this service.' He recovered and lived until 1896.

The two naval ratings who won V.C.'s in the New Zealand War were also members of Naval Brigades. William Odgers of H.M.S. *Niger* won the first V.C. in New Zealand when on 28th March, 1860, 'He displayed

conspicuous gallantry at the storming of a Pa Lum Pah—(a defended
Maori stockade). He was the first to enter it under heavy fire and
assisted in hauling down the enemy colours.' The other was won by
Samuel Mitchell, Captain of the Foretop of H.M.S. *Harrier* at the storming of a Pah at Tauranga. This was an ill-conceived enterprise. The
Pah itself stood at the end of a promontory surrounded on three sides
by a swamp, which was assumed to be unsuitable for an attack. The
Pah was bombarded from the front for a time, and after some hours an
assault was delivered. The storming party, including a number from
the Naval Brigade crossed the ditch and entered the Pah. As no return
fire came, those outside assumed the affair was over; but the Maori
had taken refuge from the cannonade in underground chambers,
covered with turf and branches. Almost uninjured from the eight-hour
bombardment, the defenders waited until the attacking party was well
scattered round the enclosure and then opened up from their hidden
firing position. All the soldiers and sailors scattered and fled leaving
their wounded behind them—all, that is, except Samuel Mitchell.
Seeing Commander Hay, the commander of the first assault party, fall
wounded, he picked him up and, in spite of Hay's protests, carried him
under heavy fire out of the Pah. After the panic retreat no further
assault was made that evening, and the Maori escaped in the night
through the 'impenetrable' swamp.

Similarly in Japan, after the country had been opened up by
Commander Perry U.S.N., anti-foreign feeling led to war against
the invaders. In this war two further V.C.'s were won by seamen, both
during land operations involved in the foray of the Starta of
Simonozeki. Thomas Prute, Captain of the After Guard of H.M.S.
Euryalus won his award for supporting a Midshipman, Duncan Boyes,
in a rush made in advance of the main attack, until he fell wounded;
William Saley an ordinary seaman also from the *Euryalus* 'daringly
ascertained the position of the enemy, and afterwards, though wounded,
continued in the front of the advance'. As a result of the war Japan
accepted the foreigners and when a few years later two seamen from
H.M.S. *Icarus* were murdered, the incident was promptly investigated
and the perpetrators executed.

The seventh V.C. was won by George Hinkley during one of the
Chinese wars. In the autumn of 1862, some of the crew of H.M.S.
Sphinx were employed in operations against the Taiping rebels, and in
particular an assault on the city of Fung-Wha. George Hinkley, an
able seaman from the *Sphinx*, volunteered to carry a wounded officer
some hundred yards to a joss-house where the officer could be attended
to. The whole of the ground between the spot where Hinkley was
standing and the joss-house was being torn up by a continual fire of

musketry, jungals and stink-pots. Hinkley completed his task and returned to the safety of his post under the east gate. He then immediately volunteered to carry another wounded officer across and again returned to his post. Hinkley did rather better in the long run than most of the other winners of the V.C. Seeley was never promoted beyond Able Seaman, but Hinkley ended his service as a Quarter-master and lived to the ripe old age of 85, dying at Plymouth on 31st December, 1904.

It is not altogether surprising that all these awards were won ashore, since inter-ship actions were very few and bombardments did not often give much opportunity for outstanding valour. However, one V.C. was won by a boatswain, Israel Harding, at the bombard-ment of Alexandria. He was serving on board the *Alexandra* at the time when a shell entered the side of the ship but failed to explode. With great coolness and courage, Harding seized the shell, plunged it into a tank of water and extinguished the fire.

There is an account of this bombardment by Thomas Holman. He was not present himself but as he joined a Gun vessel on the station very shortly after the bombardment his account is broadly accurate. Though the *Speedwell* itself was an imaginary ship.

The *Speedwell* joined the Mediterranean fleet off Alexandria, just in time to take part in the bombardment a day or two afterwards. We all took up our positions for this real sailor's job on the morning of July 2nd. and followed the first gun from H.M.S. *Alexandra* with a regular fusilade at our several targets (i.e. the forts on shore.) The game was a very one-sided one from the first, and soon ended in our favour, without very much loss on our side, but with a much larger death role on theirs. So far the sailors had done well in their part of the work, for bombarding, and activities at sea, are, of course, pre-eminently sailors' work. But there followed the occupation of Alexandria by the blue jackets and marines. My readers will now excuse a little garb, but I am a British sailor, and I would draw their attention to the ubiquity and general utility, of the British Blue in doing so. I do not intend, of course, to argue that Jack is as proficient in all the branches at which I shall shew him at work, as are the particular corps of the army to whom such work is special alone, but I do claim that he has a sufficient general knowledge in each and all their branches, combined with a natural aptitude for adapting himself to any kind of work or environment, that enables him to do practically all that is required in the real test, viz., war.

Sailors and soldiers know too much of each other nowadays and have fought side by side in too many of our recent little campaigns to allow the old jealousies between the two services to arise again, and much to the detriment of each, for the army to take offence from the few remarks that follow. Our comradeship is sealed by a thousand grogs between, a thousand divided fowls from a thousand forages, and tens of thousands of common dangers in as many thousands of places.

After finishing the sailor's part of the business then, and giving Arabi's forts their quietus, we had to buckle on blankets and water bottles, and do what we could to prevent those skulking Arab thieves from looting the town. So, with a naval officer installed as head of police, we landed, and with machine guns, rifle and bayonets, and even fisticuffs if required, we beat and bullied those dogs into some sort of obedience and civility.

Then came the troops, who, with the assistance of 'Jack' and 'Joey' drove our friend Arabi and his Egyptian boats back behind a line of hastily constructed earthworks. Here he appeared likely to give some trouble, but was held in check and kept employed until, by a rapid movement, about which everybody knows, and in which the fleet was again utilised, he was dislodged by Lord Wolesley.

Meantime, behold the sailors. Here the General wants a gun, captured from Arabi, taken to the top of a neighbouring hill, between two and three hundred feet high, and there mounted in an exposed position to pepper the Egyptian right. No sooner do the sailors learn this, than a party of blue jackets commanded by a Gunnery Lieutenant are about the job. Hydraulic jack and tackle; out of the carriage she comes, and on to a waggon made for the purpose she goes. Up the hill climb the sailors; Crumpy Cringle, Frank Hansome and Ben Bonny all among the number. At it they go. Railway iron, by the ton, is dragged up from the foot to the summit, and buried in the sand, some straight, some horizontal, to form what the Lieutenant calls an anchor. This is backed up by another, similarly constructed by the laughing, chaffing, whistling, singing and very much exposed, jolly Tars.

Next a large pulley is attached; then from below is brought up the end of a large hawser, the other end of which is attached to the carriage containing the gun, this is rove through the pulley, and away dashes Crumpy Cringle with the end, down towards a couple of locomotives. To one of these he attaches it, and then hooks them both together. 'Go ahead' is the signal from the top of the hill. Off go the locomotives and up goes the waggon and gun. Unsling the gun; back come the engines; down goes the waggon. The carriage and slide are brought up the same way, each being received with a cheer as it reaches the top.

Royal Artillerymen, by jove! But she has to be mounted yet. A smooth-bore gun is sunk in the ground for a pivot, breech down, a good strong platform built with our railway sleepers, again most excellent adjuncts. The pivot bars are placed over the muzzle, and the pivot bolt dropped in; the gun mounted; and we are all ready for action with a first-rate arc of training, and close to the water fort at Ramleh.

The Lieutenant said we were all ready, and he ought to know, for had he not designed and superintended the whole business, but Crumpy Cringle demurred—in the lower octave.

'Shut up Crumpy,' said he of the wooden face.

'I shan't shut up, Frank,' replied Crumpy, 'this job will never be finished, nor no good done by her until we give her a motto.'

'The only motto she wants is well handling,' rejoined Frank.

'Well then, let it be said so,' bellowed Crumpy. Taking a bit of chalk out of his pocket, he then wrote on a bit of board, lying at hand, as follows:—

> 'Lay me true, and load me tight,
> And I'll play the deuce with Arabi's right.'

'There you are,' he said, 'you can call me an old fool if you like, but she'll do all the better for it.'

Whether this was so, or not, the old gun did very well, and threw a good many troublesome visitors into Arabi's camp.

Meantime other parties of British Blues are employed in other duties. Some mounted, some on foot; some in the fighting line of skirmishers that have constant brushes with the enemy; others with their nine pounders form a field battery, mounted on shanks' pony alone, and dragging their guns through the sand in grand style, even keeping pace with the less encumbered infantry artillery as they swing along to the strains of martial music.

Others are employed with gun cotton and dynamite, destroying gun, fort, and bridge, and assisting the engineers generally. Naval signalmen are to be found here, there, everywhere, flashing their lights by night and swinging their flags by day, passing and receiving messages in Morse as quick or quicker than the army signallers themselves.

Another party are to be seen, up to their waist in water, bridging a stream or building a breakwater—the latter proclaiming their handiwork on a large board similar to Crumpy Cringle's, on which is painted in large, if ill formed letters—

> 'This is the Breakwater
> That Jack built.'

All going ahead in this jolliest of moods, even the crustiest old ship growler among them forgetting, for the nonce, his particular function.

Yes, my brothers, here are some of your Tars at their work. nearly all the groups are interchangeable, and can change duties at any moment without breaking the continuity of their work, and can, tomorrow, all assemble on board their ships again ready for instant battle. You surely get your money's worth out of these tarry souls, do you not?

Tel-el-Kebir is fought; Drury rides to Cairo; and war in Upper Egypt ceases. The sailors pack up their troops, and return to their ships, to go on salt beef and biscuit again, and a large number of the soldiers to home, honour and roast beef. 'Twas ever thus.' The exigencies of the service are so exacting.

This account of the Navy at war is concluded with another passage by Holman, describing an engagement which took place very shortly after the defeat of the Egyptians. Again he was not actually present but the Gun vessel H.M.S. *Ranger* which he later joined was involved in the campaign. This was the Sudan disaster that included the death of General Gordon at Khartoum. Describing his own experiences Holman wrote:

We joined our ship at a port in the Red Sea, at that time alive with war scares day and night, and lay down the first night with accoutrements on, and our arms by our side ready to land at any minute; for the Arabs often came down to the shore and fired at the ships, their slugs frequently whizzing through the rigging or striking the ship's side with a sharp crack. Altogether, we opened our commission with a very merry six months, dashing about the Red Sea from one hot spot to another at top speed. Now at Suakin, sharing in the scares that nightly filled the air, causing the ship to send away armed parties for a sharp brush with the enemy in the darkness and back again by daylight; now running to and from Aden, to fetch and bring the mails; anon waiting on a mission to the 'King of Kings' i.e. the ruler of Abyssinia; and then assisting the Egyptians to evacuate one of their outlying posts as part of the Soudan evacuation policy.

Elsewhere, Holman gives a very dramatic account of an engagement that took place not far from Suakin. The object of this was an attempt to restore British prestige in the Eastern Sudan and an expedition was launched against the local ruler Osman Digna. They marched out of Suakin and reached a point called Tofric where they were to form three defensive squares. The Naval Brigade, which accompanied the expedition with four Gardner guns, was ordered to set up their guns in redoubts on the outside sides of the two outer squares, but the Arabs attacked before they had completed the defences.

We eventually found ourselves landed and under arms again, dragging, this time, our machine guns behind us. It looked more like real business now. Our enemy was more worthy our steel. Not half hearted pressed Egyptian troops, but real horsed Arabs, some of the desert, volunteers every one, and all primed with the courage of fanaticism.

'We shall have a tough job, in my opinion,' said Frank Hansome.

'Not tougher than we had at Majuba, I guess' put in Jim Martine. 'What do you think, Harry?'

Harry Mann thought we should 'find them tough customers; and it must come to a hand to hand fight, in which we must all stick together, back to back, if necessary'.

Harry was right, for when we at last came up to our bronzed antagonists, they rushed on us like infuriated devils. We were all at one gun in the corner of the square, and so fierce was the onslaught that they came right up to the muzzle, being mowed down the while by the steady pump, pump of Harry Mann who was number two at our gun, and was heaving around the handle of the Gardner machine, while Frank Hansome, with his face a little more wooden than usual, was, with perfect coolness and knowledge of his weapon, elevating and training it on that part of the coloured fanatic mass which was the most near and threatening. I was number three, and kept the feed going as well as I could. The gun was comparatively new to us at that time, but I had learnt a few of their weaknesses while on board the gunnery ship *Excellent*, before we left England.

Crumpy Cringle was bringing along the feeders, and playing a tune of encouragement upon the lower bars; and then also, close up to us, and encouraging us all, was our aristocratic First Lieutenant, a commoner now, using commoner's language, forgetting affectation, white gloves, and cosmetics, and acting as a British sailor pure and simple.

'Steady, steady, Hansome' he was saying, 'take that group to the right. Well done! Now this to the left. Good, good, that has cleared the devils; but look out, look out Mann, steady with the handle, don't jam us, or we're done.'

'Ay, ay, sir! I'll take care,' replied Harry.

'Fill the feeders carefully, Cringle; tell the men at the timber to take care, and be careful now, careful; there they are again. Let them

have it, Hansome. Well done, Mann; be careful but quick—look out
for the bullets, number three! Damn 'em; they're close upon us now.
Fire! fire! Let them have it; hit them; punch them; knock them ba—'
A dull thud and down he fell, poor fellow, shot through the heart by
a bullet. Here they were, the bronzed devils all around us by the
hundred, thrusting with spear, slashing with double-edged sword,
firing their matchlocks, led on by mad sheiks, mounted on swift
steeds; all utterly regardless of their comrades falling by the dozen
around them, every man among them appearing to think himself an
army alone.

On, on they pressed, a perfect avalanche; breaks in the front are
filled by hundreds in their rear and eager to depart to Allah fighting
for the faith; no square however solid, could stand such an onset.
British hearts behind British bayonets, clubbed musket, and even
bare fist, did their best, but were borne in by sheer weight of numbers.

What a time then ensues. Crumpy, wounded in the arm, falls down,
and is succeeded by Jim Martine, shot dead the next moment. With
teeth shut tight we cease to be human and become friends. The square
retires and there we are alone, too few to drag back our gun over
uneven ground and dead bodies, and too intent on our duty to either
notice the withdrawal or desert our wounded shipmates.

Ben Bonny has taken Jim Martine's place and stands beside us
with his filled feeder, but we are alone and surrounded, although the
square is not more than twenty yards in our rear, and has already
reformed; still there we are alone, and by mutual consent we get
between the wheels of our gun carriage for protection, as the
crooked fall of a cartridge jams our gun.

Pistol now, and sword are our only means of defence, as one of
our fanatic assailants makes for the wounded body of Crumpy
Cringle, just in rear of our gun. Crumpy aims a weak left-handed
blow at the approaching enemy, accompanied by a thunderclap
that sounds above the row of guns, and causes the Arab to pause,
but the little man misses, and is just about to have his skull cleft in
twain by a double-handed blow, from a huge double-edged sword,
when Ben Bonny springs from the shelter of the gun wheels, and
with a swing of his sea-service cutlass almost decapitates Crumpy's
assailant, and with a quick and powerful movement drags the little
man to the shelter of the gun wheels. Here we protect ourselves as
best we can against an infuriated onslaught of the Arabs, Henry Mann
receiving a spear thrust that partly disabled him, and Frank Hansome
a slug wound that destroyed two of his toes.

Ben Bonny fought like a giant, never hesitating to jump out and
have a square set to if opportunity offered, and freely risked his

life for the protection of his wounded shipmates. I had been placed *hors-de-combat* early in the fight by a prod in the thigh by a long spear, and could only use my pistol, and that of our fallen First Lieutenant's to pot at every copper-coloured skin that came within the zone of attack, or danger limit.

There we lay, an isolated and small party of Britons, infuriated and as callous to danger as the Mohammedan fanatics around us, who were calling on Allah to preserve them and deliver us into their hands, keeping them at bay from the shelter of the gun wheels, determined to sell our lives dearly, and encouraging each other to use such limbs as were not yet wounded for the preservation of those that were. Now our hearts would cease to beat as we curled up our bodies to evade, or stretched out our arms to ward off an impending blow; and the next moment it would go on at double speed and pump up into our heads, that throbbed and thrilled and maddened us, as with frenzied haste we hacked at our opponents with our swords or shot them with our pistols.

A mass of white, black and brown wounded humanity, mad with pain and excitement, slashing, hacking and heaving at everything around us; each cursing the other in a different tongue, and all determined to die hard, and endeavouring with their last breath and strength to hasten the end of their dying opponents. Panting, howling, bleeding, cursing, raving, praying, kicking, gnashing their teeth, biting the dust; it was sad, grand, bewildering, awful to view, to contemplate. Yet these things were as naught to us, our own life was all.

A chaos of noise encircles us, the whiz of bullets and slugs, the sound of exploding shell, the sharp crack of rifles, the shrieks and yells of anguish, groans of the dying, shouts loud and long of men rendered reckless by pain and excitement, the clash of steel bayonet and scimiter. The pulses are thumping as if they would burst, from nerves tried long in excessive excitement.

Thus we lay, at the cruel mercy of fanatical Arabs, waiting only for our ammunition to finish, for they, even they, dare not attack men at bay, so cool, so courageous as we were; and then they would sweep down on us and have the life out of our poor bodies with sword and spear. Eventually, however, the wild rush of the Arabs was checked, and our square reformed, advanced, and enclosed us again. We had had a terrible time of it, and were nearly dead with exhaustion. We had lost our gallant First Lieutenant, who had died as British officers have always died at the post of duty; his noble heart and aristocratic notions of the privilege of birth having left us for ever.

Jim Martine had also gone. Crumpy Cringle had a bad slug wound in the muscle of his arm, and Harry Mann a spear wound in the calf of his leg. Frank Hansome had suffered the loss of two toes. I was suffering from a lacerated wound in the thigh from the prod of a spear; whilst Ben Benny alone escaped scathless from that fearful environment of musket, spear, slug and sword; and he too, who had most exposed himself in our defence.

What mingled feelings of joy and sorrow filled our hearts when we were again within the square of British bayonets. The dead bodies of our First Lieutenant and Jim Martine were spared the atrocities we had witnessed and abhorred outside. It was enough, we were thankful; and as the din of guns, the crack of rifles and the clang of steel subsided, and we knew we were victors, we submitted our wounds to the care of surgeons, and were removed to the rear by the ambulance party, but not before our surviving shipmates had assured us that the dead bodies of our gun's crew should find burial in a common grave, where officers and men could be honoured and mourned alike by a grateful country.

The 'aristocratic' Lieutenant killed in the action was Montague Hamilton Marsh Seymour from the *Dolphin*, and in addition six blue-jackets were killed whilst bringing the Gardner guns into the redoubt assigned to them.

9

The Changing Navy

Of the three material changes which revolutionised the Navy during the century, the replacement of sail by steam probably affected the seamen most. The birth of the steam ship was a long process. In its early stages steam was thought suitable only for tugs, which might pull a line-of-battleship out of harbour if that was the only way the ship could move. Engines were considered (rightly at first) far too unreliable for men-of-war. Even the tugs were introduced only slowly. The first was commissioned into the Navy in 1821.

It was not until the 1830s that steam warships were accepted in principle, and not until 1843, when the screw steamship *Rattler* had towed the paddle sloop *Alecto* sternwise at $2\frac{1}{2}$ knots, that steam came to be regarded as the inevitable motive power for Her Majesty's ships. Even then it remained only an addition to sail. H.M.S. *Alert* in the Arctic in 1876 was a fully-rigged sailing vessel, as well as a steamship. The main reason for this was that coal was not available in Arctic waters. Even elsewhere it was not always readily procurable and when it was, cost money. Sail cost virtually nothing except the skill and endurance of the seamen. It was said that a fleet of seven sailing colliers were necessary to supply one of the large early naval steamships with coal—hardly an economic proposition!

Therefore, though after 1845 no large vessel was built exclusively as a sailing ship, all were rigged, the majority fully rigged, until 1869. Then there occurred the disaster to H.M.S. *Captain*. She was the first British steam turret-ship, and was fully rigged, but unfortunately her top weight was too great for safety. She was designed with eight feet of freeboard, and when she was completed this had been reduced to six feet. With a full set of sails she was grossly unstable and within the year she was caught in a gale off Cape Finistere and she simply turned turtle; only 18 were saved of a crew of nearly 500. Even then further steamers were built with sails.

The battle of sail versus steam was not fought solely on economic grounds. It was considered that a man could only learn the profession of the sea in a sailing vessel—and there is truth in this, as the Sail Training Association have shown today with the *Sir Winston Churchill*. In spite of disasters, training under sail remained an essential element in the Navy until at least the turn of the century. Many did not like the new-fangled steamships with their iron walls. At least one gunnery officer considered that 'the iron ships of today are not so comfortable to live in as the old wooden walls', and also that the seamen who served in the new steamships (in 1867) were a less able body of men than their predecessors.

Look how men used to strive and work that the ships they belonged to should beat the rest of the squadron; in that their sail should be first shifted, furled, or reefed as the case might have been; to be beaten at exercise touched their *amour propre* and they dared everything to excell. These are the sort of men we want, for a man who is a sound active sailor, holding his life as it were in his hand, and treating the risk as a bagatelle, so that he may excel others in ability and feats of smartness aloft, will be equally fearless and active at his gun. Contrast such a man, muscular, active, long winded, deep chested, fearless and daring to a degree, with a new steam man, round shouldered, relaxed, with no lasting powers, slow of mind and body, unused to danger and chary of himself; they bear as much comparison as a recruit does to a small colour-sergeant.

This was probably a common view while these changes were taking place, particularly among the officers, but there can be little doubt that the ending of sail greatly improved the seamen's lot. There was, however, a new class of seamen who, at least in the tropics, suffered considerable physical hardships, equivalent in their way to those of the top men of old. These were the stokers. Shovelling coal in the steamy foetid atmosphere of the boiler room of a ship in the tropics was not an easy task. For the seamen, too, coaling ship was a new and unpleasant occupation, but for the naval seamen in general the ending of sail was of considerable benefit—in spite of the glamour and in spite of all the skills that could be learnt by a smart topman. The change was welcome even if only because it removed the danger of losing one's life from falling from the rigging—a death that had occurred with depressing frequency. Before these changes were fully resolved there were inevitably many supporters of the old ways, and not merely among the Admiralty. Twenty years later, when sail had finally been abandoned and the third major change—the substitution of shell-firing turret guns for the old shot-firing broadside—also completed, no one doubted the value of these reforms.

Even in 1871 there were those who viewed the seamen of the new ships in a more favourable light, although with a touch of nostalgia. An anonymous gunnery officer wrote:

> In the old days sailors were full of frolicsome fun, with a possibility of mischief; a ship would come home and land a cargo of men ready to be fleeced to their hearts content, and well worth fleecing. The crew of the *Hannibal*, paid off late at night twelve or thirteen years ago, included men, each with 50 and 60 pounds in his pocket, who roamed the streets of Portsmouth the next night without a penny left them. This, however, was not so attractive a sequel to the cruise of the old tar as getting into Devonport and hiring all the cabs in the town for a short cruise around the place, all hands outside, and the inside reserved for any 'lubbers' who liked to take them. Happily, those days when sailors were the victims of crimps are well nigh over, and with them the old seaman has vanished; the old hands of 10 years ago are out of the field; the stoke hold has superceded the decks and rigging, and the courtesan holds a higher rank than the seaman in the Navy.

Ten years later when the Navy was fully committed to large steam-driven turret gun ships, in a pamphlet on the seaman's life on board a man-of-war a less nostalgic picture was drawn of the past.

> No leave to go on shore from the day the ship was in commission until paid off. No wages until paid off, but occasional prize money. The ship filled with prostitutes at every port, by permission of the C.O. Not many years ago (it was since 1840) the Captain of a frigate at a West Indian port (Barbados) gave an order to the First Lieutenant, that every man and boy was to have a black woman on board, and the order was carried out, but this was at that date, an exceptional case.
>
> The majority of able and ordinary seamen and many Petty Officers got drunk on every opportunity, viz. when their boats went on shore, or by smuggling liquor on board, or by saving their daily allowance. Flogging was a weekly, almost daily, occurrence. It was almost certain that somebody would be drunk at evening muster, and the punishment was flogging at 11.30 next forenoon. The men could as a rule neither read nor write. They were brave as lions and generous, if utter recklessness with their money when they got it, could be called generosity. After a three years' commission, men have received £60 to £100 of pay alone, irrespective of prize money.

As a general rule, they lost all their money the first night after the ship was paid off, and the pennyless men returned for another term of service. Such was a seaman's life but all this is now changed.

The pamphlet ends:

The sailors' positions in Men-of-War has immensely improved of late years and his conduct and character have benefitted largely in consequence.

Sailoring in the R.N. is now by no means a bad profession compared with that of other skilled workmen, the bricklayer, the stone mason etc. tyrannised over as they are by trade unions and with only the workhouse in prospect if health fails.

And in his book *England in the Sea*, W. H. D. Evans wrote of the seaman:

It is true, he is not what he was. Those of us who go down to Portsmouth or Plymouth nowadays do not expect to find any resemblance—there is none—between the Jack Tar of the Victorian Era, with his trim and decorous appearance, his decent behaviour and his wise thriftiness, and the quaint, queer characters, obviously drawn from the life, which utter strong oaths in Smollet, or those 'sea-salts' of Marryat and Chamier.

In truth the law of development has no finer example than the English Seaman, who, in the last five and twenty years, has undergone a 'sea change' very remarkable yet very natural. Happily he is none the worse for this; he is as brave and as faithful, as loyal and as ready as in the old days. While he has acquired not a few virtues which his predecessors could hardly boast of.

Undoubtedly the material changes were a major factor in the altered position and attitudes of the sailors but another significant cause was the direct action taken by the Admiralty to reform the Navy.

One of the major problems with the sailors was undoubtedly drunkenness—not that this was abolished by 1885 but it was considerably reduced and this was at least partly because of the halving of the spirit ration in 1825 and again in 1853. In addition, after 1850 other provisions could be swapped for the rum ration. Bechervaise has already pointed out how beneficial he considered the reduction in the spirit ration; but the change reflected at least in part a change in society at large. It owed much to the actions of abstinence societies and religious groups, and also to individuals such as Agnes Weston.

The Admiralty also stepped in to curb flogging. Here changes came slowly, and the practice was retained until 1871 owing to pressure from officers of the old school, such as the gunnery officer who in 1867 wrote: 'Corporal Punishment cannot I think be done away with. Some cases need its infliction. Discipline, I fear, is too lax at the present time.' Even in 1871 it was only suspended in peacetime, and then in 1879 it was 'suspended in wartime', and even this did not cover men in the second class for conduct. It was a long and sometimes bitter battle. The matter had been raised even during the 'Great War' but at first, abolition received little support. Writing in the *United Service Journal* in 1829 a naval officer gave full support to flogging:

> The navy's success has not been achieved by men of weak nerves or false philanthropy, but by firm gallant spirits who could give and by others who could take their three or four dozen whenever it was deserved (and that was not seldom).
>
> A few years back a man-of-war was considered by the generality of landsmen as differing totally from all others. Its inmates were represented to be as rough as the elements they combatted. . . . How is order to be maintained among five or six hundred men, most of whom are thoughtless to a proverb, many ill disposed and some as vile miscreants as any in creation. They are only deterred from committing crime by fear of punishment. Discipline is maintained by flogging and it is no argument that flogging is not necessary ashore. Transportation and imprisonment are impossible on board. The fact that men dislike flogging makes it a good deterrent. Solitary confinement is no solution because others have to do their work and there are no suitable places for imprisonment.

The *United Service Journal* acted as a platform for reactionary views though it also included articles by those who supported reforms. In 1830 it contained an article against flogging round the fleet 'the one blot on the navy'. Later the same year, it was suggested that, though 'too much laxness would undoubtedly be dangerous', the maximum number of lashes should be fixed. Yet many of the old officers bitterly opposed any kind of reform of the regulations for punishment and considered such new-fangled punishments 'like polishing shot and rubbing iron stanchions bright as silver were calculated rather to produce discontent and desertion than the legitimate objects of necessary punishment'. There was even James Toggle, a tar of the old school who had been at sea for the past forty years. To him:

> Everything gets worse and worse. Everything is iron; they have iron topsail sheets, iron bolstays, iron cables and iron ships. It is everyone for himself now, and God for us all: all hands are looking out for good berths.

8

When I first went to sea we used to have our quart of grog a day; now they serve out tea. It may do all very well in peace but it wont do in war. Only let them Yankees get hold of you, they'll larn you it.

He had been shipwrecked, in love and in action—at the Glorious First of June, at the Nile and in the *Temeraire* at Trafalgar. He was admitted to Greenwich Hospital and died there. Naturally, he supported flogging!

Until the old generation of naval officers had died, there was little hope of any real reform. The extremes of punishment were abolished and the serving officers became more humane. They did not flog a man for being last down from the rigging, and looked back on the discipline of the old school as 'Unsparing severity was its rule, the cat its instrument, the art of discriminating character was not thought of: to reason with a man was considered absurd; to modify punishment a useless trouble—the cat! the cat! the cat!' This was written in 1833, when they said of the contemporary navy:

The service has undergone a complete change; the interior of a ship presents a picture of health, comfort and satisfaction. The men have ample indulgences, little work and scarcely any punishment, are well fed and well clothed, yet we hear of nothing but the horrors of our discipline, and they want to abolish flogging for which no secondary punishment can act as a substitute and without which it would be hopeless to maintain effective discipline among large bodies of men, confined in narrow spaces, experienced to infinite hardships and many privations.

There is little point in repeating this same argument which naval officers were to use for the next forty years and more. It is even conceivable that harsh discipline, including the cat, was the only way to keep the sailor under control because Jack was that sort of person. But it is equally possible that Jack became that sort of person—or more accurately that only that sort of person joined the Navy—because of the cat. The sailor's lot had not, of course, suddenly become all sunshine, as some of the officers liked to imply—John Tilling will certify to that. But in time the reformers won. First flogging round the fleet was abolished, and then, most significantly, the captain's arbitrary right to punish was curtailed. Flogging in most cases was limited to sentence by court martial, and finally in the 1870s virtually disappeared.

Flogging, of course, was not the only target for reform. Lack of leave had been one of the major grievances of sailors of the old school. During the war the majority were pressed men and the dangers of granting leave were obvious, but even after 1815, when all were volunteers other dangers remained; in particular, the sailor's addiction for strong drink meant that the crew of five or six hundred released on the unsuspecting populace of a foreign port could do, and all too frequently did, untold damage. Bechervaise's friend who smashed the globe full of goldfish and was put in prison was probably exceptional only in getting caught. Tilling tells of the damage caused by the crew of the *Leander* on leave at San Lorenzo *—again largely attributable to drink. But it was not drink alone. The discipline on board remained extremely strict even if not harsh, and sailors on shore, temporarily freed from restriction even without drink, were liable to create havoc among the local populace. Thomas Holman tells the following story of a run ashore in Greece in the 1870s.

I was then Second Captain of the fore top on the *Lord Warden*, at that time belonging to the fleet of Admiral S——. We were sent to the Piraeus in Greece, to give leave, and as was usual in those days, one watch after having been a short time on shore got into bad bread with some Greeks.

Indeed so much friction had been set up between the grog primed British Blues and the excited Greeks, that it eventually became both prudent and necessary to land an armed party from the British ship to quell the riot into which the skirmish had developed, and with the view of catching as many of the violent tars as possible, and conveying them on board the ship again. About half a dozen of us, all fast chums, succeeded in evading these armed patrols, and eventually found ourselves in the suburbs of Athens.

Our scrimmage with the Greeks had been just sufficient to rouse a little bad blood in us, and we were on mischief bent. 'Here's a vineyard; a feed of grapes for me,' said one of our number as he entered the gate, and 'for me', 'and me', said the others as we followed and plunged into the place. There we proceeded to help ourselves to the choicest bunches the vines produced.

Presently our attention was arrested by the loud howls, and frantic gestures, of half a dozen armed Greeks who were brandishing their guns in the air, and bearing down on us at a good rate. Taking in the situation at a glance, I said: 'What say you boys, shall we fight or run?' 'We're British sailors,' said Tom Smart, 'and as such we ought to stop and have it out.'

'We should be darned fools,' said Bob White, 'if we do. It will be quite time enough for six of us, without as much as a hand-spike in our hands to fight six of them lubbers with loaded guns when we're obliged to; at present off we go.'

* See page 126

We all felt that the odds were too great, so by mutual consent we cut and ran, making tracks at top speed towards the opposite wall, which was about eight feet high and distant about two hundred yards. This we all managed to reach, and scale easily, and on landing on the other side felt we had attained comparative safety.

I said *all*: I must qualify that.

I meant all except poor old Jack Grant, who had drunk a tot or two more than most of us, being a man just a 'little fond'. Well, poor Jack had mounted the wall all right, and had nearly all his body, head and arm on our, the safe side, but, alas! his legs and feet on the other; and there he hung poised on the coping, without being able, for the moment, to move either backward or forward, and was thus in imminent danger of capture. Suddenly we heard a report; and Jack felt a stinging sensation on that important part of his anatomy which was at that moment the most elevated. The next thing we knew was that Jack had fallen on our side of the wall—the sting having imparted the necessary amount of spring to give preponderance to the head portion of his carcase. We immediately tacked ship and went to the rescue of our shipmate, for arms or no arms, we could not leave a wounded mess-mate to the enemy.

But the shot of the Greek at Athens was only the antidote to the bad grog of the Greek at Piraeus, for before we could reach Jack he had scrambled on his legs again, and was making towards us with a full head of steam, the ribbon of his torn breeks streaming in the wind, doing his level best to overhaul us, and cussing the blarmed Greeks in good strong Saxon.

After making good our escape, we bore up for a saucy wine shop, and there stretched Jack out to see what timbers were injured, and to decide if an operation was necessary—Jack declaring with charming earnestness that we might cut any part off we liked, so that it was out of sight and wouldn't betray us when we got on board. On examination, however, we decided that no operation was necessary in the cutting line, extraction only was wanted; and having started to remove the slugs by trying to hook hold of them by means of a part of one of our knives, with a thing attached for removing stones from horses' hoofs, we took Jack on board, and put him in the hands of the surgeon, who, in about a week, turned our friend adrift with us again, all sound in wind and limb.

Portsmouth might be able to cope but aboard there were very real dangers in granting leave. Desertion continued to cause concern and it even occurred among hand-picked crews, as Bechervaise recorded of the *Blossom* in South America. It became less common as the century progressed, though even in 1875 over 1,200 sailors, boys and marines deserted. There was also a real lack of things to do and places to go ashore. Gradually sport came to be widely encouraged. Football was played on the ice by the sailors of the *Alert* and the *Discovery*. Cricket, too, became increasingly popular.

This was no solution to the evenings. By the 1880s leave was almost thrust on men and night leave, probably quite rightly, was said to 'ruin so many of our young men who frequented low class public houses, with brothels attached.' That the situation was not worse, was due in no small part to a devoted spinster, Miss Agnes Weston, who dedicated her life to the service of the 'Blue Jackets'. Her major object was to spread Evangelical Christianity among the sailors of the fleet and, in so doing, encourage temperance. To further these aims she established 'Sailor's Rests', which gave seamen a home ashore instead of the pubs and brothels. She had her opponents at the time—she was opinionated and convinced of her own rectitude—and she has been sneered at since. Yet there is little doubt that her work did untold good. As well as providing the hostels she also produced Monthly Letters and *Blue Backs*, short religious pamphlets which proved very popular.

One of her devoted supporters, Adam Ayles, a Petty Officer, was on the Arctic expedition under Nares. Like many others he was a total abstainer. He had promised his mother never to touch strong drink and he 'warn't going to break his promise to her for all the snow and ice in the Arctic regions'. As Miss Weston put it, 'By his help the pledge-book and cards of the Royal Naval Temperance Society went farther north than any had gone before or since.'

Also on that voyage went Aggie Weston's *Blue Backs*. They were used to receiving them monthly, and so one bluejacket had the bright idea of having thirty-six letters, one for every month they were away, put in two boxes, one for the *Alert* and one for the *Discovery*, and they were served out on the first of every month.

One of the stories she herself told may seem too sentimental for modern tastes but it is worth recording for the light it sheds on the attitude of some of the sailors.

I remember a glorious summer afternoon; the Solent looked so blue, and the golden haze seemed to shimmer over our great iron ships, destroyers, and torpedo-boats—pictures of intellectual strength, swiftness, and power—and the white ensign, our grand naval flag, floating lazily at the stern of our battle-ships, carrying one's thoughts back to the time when Nelson, Collingwood, and a host of brave men maintained old England's supremacy as mistress of the seas.

My meditations were brought to an abrupt pause by a cheerful hail from a sunburnt bluejacket as he paced up and down under the white ensign that marked out the coastguard station. He was an old friend, and had served on board the *Temeraire* and many other of Her Majesty's ships.

'Beg your pardon,' he said, 'but I couldn't let you pass. Fine day, isn't it? The sight of that fleet warms me up, and makes me feel that but for the wife and children I should like to do a bit more sea time. They do look grand; and is it true, as I've heard, that every ship gets her *Blue Backs* and *Ashore and Afloats*? Well, times have changed since I was a youngster.'

'Yes,' I replied, as we walked up and down, 'we have circulated a large number of *Blue Backs* and *Ashore and Afloat* this year.'

'Bless me,' he cried, 'every ship in the navy has her parcel, and a fellow from the *Orlando* told me that the men came round like bees when the parcel was opened, and they wanted a hundred more every month. And then you send them to the American navy and the merchant sailors no end. I'm glad that Johnnie gets them as well as Jack and Joe and Uncle Sam.

'Do you know,' he continued, 'it's a sight of good them papers do. Wherever they go men will always read them, if they read nothing else, because they come from Mother Weston. You must want plenty of shiners to do that. I'll give half-a-crown. I know the good that they do at our coastguard station. I wish I could give more. I owe all my happiness to a *Blue Back*.'

He suddenly stopped and seized the halyards. The sun was just dropping in the west like a ball of fire; a puff of smoke, a report, and down fluttered the white ensign. 'If you can wait a minute,' said my bluejacket friend, 'I will tell you about the *Blue Back* and this here old flag.'

I willingly waited while he made all taut and trim, and then, his watch being over, he told me his story.

'Do you remember writing a *Blue Back* called *The White Ensign*? It was all about this flag of ours, and the lessons it taught, and how we carried the cross all over the world? The Union Jack in the corner, you said, taught Christian love; the white ground was Christian holiness, and the red cross was the Cross of Christ.

'I was on the coastguard then, near Hastings, and as I read that *Blue Back* in the watch-room, the words they just seemed to sink into my heart, for no one knew better than I did myself what a sinner I was: I kneeled down and prayed when I had read that *Blue Back*. Next morning I was early astir, for mine was the morning watch— it was as beautiful a summer morning as this is a summer evening— and I was just waiting to hoist the ensign.

'The sun showed out of the sea, and up went the flag; as she fluttered out in the morning breeze over my head there was the red cross on the white ground. I kneeled down on the beach, and I felt there and then that Christ was my Saviour, and His Cross my only hope.'

The westerly glow lighted up the rugged face of the bluejacket as he uttered these words; and, grasping my hand, he turned away. From that day to this I have never forgotten this story from real life.

Aggie Weston did a great deal to increase the self respect of a vast number of sailors. Copies of her weekly paper *Ashore and Afloat* found their way into almost every ship. Her evangelical tub-thumping may seem excessive; we may not condemn as she did the activities of the sailors after the ship had been paid off when they hired every cab in the town and drove round in cavalcade stopping at every pub until the only sober animals were the horses. Yet drunkenness was a terrible vice and for some at least complete temperance was the only solution. For a time Aggie Weston also provided a safe deposit for the men's money, and some £84,000 passed through her hands. It was partly thanks to her action that the Admiralty was persuaded to set up the Savings Banks system which enabled men to save money on board ship and then transfer it to the Dockyard Bank when the ship paid off—a far cry from the days when the men were paid only when the ship itself was paid off and the money had to be collected in London. For all her weaknesses, few did more than Aggie Weston to raise the status of the sailor.

A steady improvement in pay accompanied the rising status of the profession. In the years 1815–85 even the basic wages of seamen increased by almost half (though there were no increases after 1853), and this was a period when even at the most conservative estimate, the cost of living fell by a third or even half. The Admiralty also introduced inducements, first for the gunners. Those who qualified at H.M.S. *Excellent* as seamen gunners had an additional three pence a day added to their pay. Later a more significant inducement was introduced: good behaviour could bring the sailor good conduct badges, and these earned him three pence or even up to six pence a day. This was proposed by Captain Milne in 1848 and introduced in the following year, and in 1853 increases came for those who signed on for 'continuous' service instead of simply for the commission only. Also a host of new and specially paid ratings, for example Chief Petty Officer, were introduced so that the prospects for an ambitious and capable seaman were greatly enhanced. Thomas Holman who climbed the ladder to Warrant-Officer could do quite well for himself financially. (A Chief Gunner

earned £165 a year or 9/– a day as opposed to an Able Seaman's 1/7.)
But, and this was Holman's only major complaint, that was as much as
any sailor could earn. The upper reaches of the Navy (and the pay that
went with them) were closed to the lower deck. Milne who did a great
deal to improve the standards of naval ratings wrote in 1859:

> As regards promotion from the forecastle to the quarterdeck, I have
> no desire to see any but a *gentleman by birth* decorated in a Post
> Captain's uniform.

The change was to come but not until this century.

Taken together then, these regulations on pay did much to build up
a more responsible element on the lower deck, and together with the
regulations on manning they were responsible for creating a peacetime
Navy which offered a permanent and worthwhile career to naval seamen.

For the regular Navy there was a very successful change in recruiting
and consequently in recruits. Better prospects for older recruits encouraged men to join for longer periods. Continuous service was
introduced in 1853 but was not immediately successful. The *Renown*
for example as late as November 1857 was detained by lack of men for
172 days, and then sailed 62 short of her complement. As a result of
these difficulties a Royal Commission was appointed in 1858–9, and the
Admiralty subsequently introduced a number of improvements. The
scale of victualling was improved and boys and men joining for continuous service were supplied with kit and bedding free of charge.
Training ships were set up for the boys. As a result of this and of other
changes (such as the Naval Discipline Act of 1860 which firmly regu-
larised the punishments a Captain could inflict), the proportion of
continuous service men increased to nine-tenths by 1864. By 1870 only
a few hundred non-continuous ratings were still serving.

By that date a permanent regular Navy had been created. How the
seamen viewed it, will be shown later, but first a last look at the 'Old
Navy' which still existed in the eyes of Able Seaman John Tilling in
H.M.S. *Leander*.

10

A Sailor of the Sixties—John Tilling

April 4th. 1864. At 7:30 a.m. a grating was lashed to the main rigging. Williams took his 4 doz without a murmur. He writhed and trembled very much but after 3 doz he felt no pain. The boatswains mates flog them, the master at arms counts the lashes and gives the culprit water to drink after each doz. Baynes and Dunn cried out very much; the prisoners, after the flogging was over, put on their clothes and went below under the sentry's charge. No such thing as dressing their backs was ever thought of.

So wrote John Tilling in a journal he kept on board the *Leander* during a commission on the South American station. The men concerned had been sentenced by court martial for desertion. Williams had been absent for 132 days, the other two for eight weeks. In addition they received eighteen months' to two years' imprisonment and Williams was also dismissed the service.

Some months later another deserter Thomas Breedon, was caught.

March 24th. 1865. Thomas Breedon received his 36 lashes. All hands were sorry for him but it is no use commenting on the faults of others but I hope I shall never see such another sight. Although he never murmured the twitching of every lash told that he must have felt it acutely for he is a very fleshy man.

And again.

Nov. 6th. 1865. Ramsay and Reynolds received their 48 lashes; both took it very well. Reynolds groaned a little but Ramsay never uttered a murmur. I say why not flog an officer as well as a man? If it teaches a lesson to men why not an officer? What is good for the goose is surely good for the gander?

The *Leander* was not unique:

Nov. 13th. 1865. Commodore said he would try to get Hounsell off his imprisonment. The commodore is certainly anything but a bad man. When I was with Capt. G. W. Preedy in the *Liffey* I have known him to flog men for the same cause as the Commodore would give him seven days No 10 but this is not the reason why he is so interested in Hounsell's case. By getting him off it will tend to preserve order and prevent another mutiny for of course everybody will think of this before they rebel.

But this made little difference.

Nov. 16th. 1865. Robert Frederick Hounsell got his 4 doz this morning at 7 bells. I wonder if the society for prevention of cruelty to animals could not interfere and put a stop to these disgraceful floggings.

And Tilling himself did not escape.

Jan. 26th. 1866. Received 36 lashes this morning for mutinous language. The Commander turned as white as a ghost when the warrant was heard. Ralph gave me the first dose and sheeted it home too. Then came Master the left handed boatswain's mate and then Tyzill.

When reading the more optimistic accounts of some of the later sailors it is too easy to forget that most of the old traditions carried on, even into the eighteen-seventies. Queen's Regulations and Admiralty Instruction for 1887 carried the following passage on discipline:

It being requisite for the maintenance of the efficiency, discipline and even safety of Her Majesty's Ships of War, that the power of inflicting corporal punishment, when absolutely necessary should be continued; such punishment may under the following conditions, be inflicted under the responsibility and authority of the Captain, who is however to exercise the power vested on him with the greatest discretion and forbearance, compatible with the discipline of the service.

The crucial condition came at the end:

The power of Commanding Officers to award Corporal Punishment for any offences tried summarily under section 56 of the Naval Discipline Act is suspended until further order.

Nonetheless:

Nothing contained in the foregoing articles can be deemed to extend to the nullification or abatement of such powers as are vested in Naval Courts Martial.

In practice, though, the punishment was not awarded even by Courts Martial.

Who were most accurate—the men on *Leander* or the many more contented sailors? In one respect certainly Tilling's views were not typical; the Pacific station had a worse record for offences than most. In 1862 nearly 2½ per cent of the men deserted as opposed to less than 1½ per cent over all, though Australia did worse still with a rate of over 3½ per cent. Desertion was the main offence for which flogging was still the punishment. It is unlikely that these excesses occurred only in remote stations. They must cloud the rosy picture of a new humanitarian Navy no longer bound by the old conventions and brutalities. It seems likely that Tilling was not typical, but equally he was not unique. Certainly one event in the commission of H.M.S. *Leander* was unusual. This was recorded in the entry in the ship's log for 9th November, 1865.

> On calling the watch but very few men making their appearance and there being a riotous noise on the Lower Deck, the Pipe 'Clear Lower Deck' was made with similar results. Some minutes afterwards the Commodore ordered Lieutenant Cookson and Sub Lieutenant Pugh to go down to the lower deck to clear it and report immediately if assistance was required. The R.M.A. and R.M.L.I. who had fallen in were ordered under arms. Lieutenant Cookson returned to report that the men did not obey his repeated order to go on deck but shortly afterwards all hands fell in in the usual order to the former pipe of 'Clear Lower Decks', this being 10 or 12 minutes after the first pipe.

Tilling's account is more graphic:

> Nov. 9th. 1865. At 1:15 all the hands started shouting 'Money and Leave'. The order to 'Clear Lower Deck' was given but the fore ladder was unshipped. Marines and officers called but the men would not leave the lower deck. Lieutenants Pugh and Cookson finally persuaded them to go on deck but not complete until 2:00 p.m. The Commodore told them that if any one had a grievance to step forward and say so but no one was so foolish as to fall in the trap he was laying for them. During dinner time a hand from each mess went up to ask for the customary leave according to the Admiralty Instructions which is 48 hours each month which we have not had for nearly two years. In Callao there was only privileged leave because of the inhabitants and from fear of Shanghaing but here a peaceable sort of people. Asked him before and the commander said he did not see men in the dinner hours. This was the signal for us to show we would not be trifled with any longer.

What happened then and who was responsible is not clear. At the subsequent Court Martial a good deal of the evidence turned on the question of who unshipped the fore ladder which prevented the hands from going on deck. This point was not satisfactorily resolved. The immediate results of the mutiny for the ship's company were not all bad. A week later general leave was given for the first time for nine months, but inevitably a number of men suffered for the mutiny. Ten men were tried by court martial four days later and six were found guilty, but as the Lords Commissioners of the Admiralty recorded, 'Having carefully read the minutes of the Court Martial . . . it appeared to them that the most guilty had escaped detection.' Only one rating below Leading Seaman was found guilty of Mutiny and this was Robert Hounsell, who was condemned to two years' hard labour and 48 lashes, which as we have already seen, he received a week later. Tilling goes on to add:

> Nov. 13th. 1865. I was very sorry for poor Bob Hounsell as he is a nice sociable fellow but somebody must suffer for it and it is well that nobody else is yet implicated. It was Clerk and Gundry that split.

(The latter were two Petty Officers who were also found guilty, disrated to Able Seamen and given twelve months' imprisonment.) Clearly Tilling did not record all that he knew—it would presumably have been too dangerous. As Tilling was later sentenced for mutinous language it is possible that he himself was one of the ring leaders, but there is no evidence for this.

A mutiny—and a mass action of this sort is classed as 'mutiny'— was certainly unusual, and the officers and men of the *Leander* were involved in a considerable number of Courts Martial. Certainly compared to ships on the Home or Mediterranean station, the *Leander's* record was poor; but other ships on the Pacific station fared only marginally better. An account of the whole commission of the *Leander* puts events in perspective.

The ship had been built at Portsmouth some years previously. In 1861 she was then lengthened and fitted with engines. But although they provided 400 h.p., they burnt 50 tons of coal a day, and so the order 'Up funnel, down screw' was seldom heard. She was commissioned on 14th April, 1863 for service in the Pacific, and Able Seaman Tilling joined her on commissioning.

They left Sheerness on 17th June, calling at Madeira on the way, where they took cattle on board. However they did not reach Valparaiso until 11th September, having been driven 400 miles off course by a gale after rounding Cape Horn. By that time they were out of cocoa, bread and, worst of all, rum!

Their first Christmas, which Tilling certainly enjoyed, was spent at Juan Ferrados.

> Dec. 25th. 1863. Those men who did not go ashore amused them-
> selves dancing and skylarking on the main deck some of them
> dressed as clowns and in other ridiculous ways. A band played horn-
> pipes and other dance music . . . at 8 o'clock we went below and had
> a song. The lower deck being illumined by 1000 candles, some in
> chandeliers and others along the mess shelves. Lights were put out
> at 9 o'clock half an hour later than is usual.

But the New Year at Valparaiso was more appreciated in the Gun Room.

> December 31st. The midshipmen got the bandsmen's instruments and
> commenced making a frightful noise with them. The band sergeant
> got them away and restored them to their places. The midshipmen
> then commenced singing and ended the year with a fight.

They spent the next six weeks at Valparaiso.

> January 9th. Dance on board to which some of the crew dressed as
> clowns danced to the amusement of officers and visitors.
> January 25th. Ball on board. Seamen 'blacked' and dressed as
> niggers and sang 'Lady won't you marry.'

The officers were already beginning to feel the strain and one of the Warrant-Officers, Mr. Ryan, the *Leander*'s carpenter, was dismissed the ship for drinking. While they were at Valparaiso nine men died and seventeen deserted.

They then visited Coquimbo where they spent a month, and already Tilling's discontent was becoming plain.

> March 10th. Ball. 'Negro' entertainment, Hornpipe and song
> 'Tom Bucolic'. Not to be compared with what I have seen in
> London.

When they returned to Valparaiso at the end of the month a number of courts martial for desertion took place and Williams received his four dozen lashes.

A war was currently being waged between the Peruvians and the Spanish, but Tilling was less concerned than most with the lack of action.

> May 2nd. Almost mistaken for a Peruvian ship by a Spanish frigate.
> Men seemed rather disappointed that they did not have what they
> call a good wire in.

He was still prepared to say a few good words about the officers:

May 9th. The Spanish Minister took refuge aboard *Leander*. As did an Italian gentleman of the Mexican Army (Captain Seruti). A Lieutenant, McInroy, sent to fetch him from the drawn sword of seven Peruvians, 'In that bluff manner peculiar to British sailors' said he did not care. His orders were to take him (Seruti) on board the frigate and if the Peruvian officer did not like it he must come on board the frigate to make his complaint to the commander.

There was the occasional cricket match against the Lima club, which the *Leander* won. But there were minor disasters.

October 7th. Our rum is all consumed. Consequently we are all out of spirits.

And also,

July 27th. Hayward, Captain of Afterguard lost overboard.

For most of this time they were at Callao and only went to sea 'for the health of the ship's company'. Already, morale was beginning to drop. After Christmas that year (1864), twenty men who had brought spirits on board or hoarded their tots were disrated and lost their Good Conduct Badges. The steep decline began after the visit to San Lorenzo, a port not far from Callao.

February 19th. Shore leave. Some were brought on board in a very elevated condition after destroying a great deal of property.

Tilling, who presumably was among the defaulters, wrote a poem about the evening's adventures which he called 'The Siege of San Lorenzo'. Many of the crew got drunk on the local liquor 'Pisco', and broke the place up. As a result, all the offenders had their leave stopped and lost three months' pay and thirty days' grog. The damage was calculated at 15,000 dollars. It must have been quite an evening!
This coincided with the change of Admirals.

March 12th. Admiral Jackey Kingcombe left her at Panama. He was one of the old school rough and ready but not severe: it may be because he was once a 3rd. class boy.
Relieved by 'Hon. J. G. Denman' who was in the Royal yacht and this no doubt accounts for his early promotion. He has his wife on board which is not liked by the foremost hands for her word is law with 'Joey' and for this reason neither the Admiral or his wife are liked by the crew.

Tilling's later remarks were even less complimentary. And he was not alone. On the same day, 16th March, a petty officer, Thomas

Breedon, was sentenced to 48 lashes and two years' imprisonment for desertion, and Lieutenant McInroy was dismissed the service for drunkenness.

> March 20th. Admiral's inspection, gave us praise for our good conduct. Complimented Captain and First Lieutenant on manner in which crew trained. Spoke of desertion as one of worst crimes. Seaman who had completed his time asked for his discharge in this port but admiral told him that it was very possible we might go to war very soon. Tried to induce him and several others to join again but they all refused.

And Tilling has some yarns to tell about other ships.

> July 5th. Merchant men brought in three shipwrecked sailors who had been wrecked 14 months ago near Cape Horn. They ate their mess mates as they died. Built a boat and caught seals, and finally after 13 months picked up by merchantmen. One (Andrew Smith) went almost mad.

But the events on board were not yarns.

> July 17th. Chief Engineer died. (Through drink. He fell in a fire when drunk some years before.) Chased a spider out of his cabin saying 'here they come as large as lobsters'. The Paymaster in hospital and the Gunner under arrest—both awaiting court martial for drunkenness.

The first major complaint that was to lead to the mutiny then occurred:

> August 6th. Leave granted to those three months off defaulter books. According to admiralty order no man is supposed to be kept on board more than two months harbour time or three months sea time but there are a great many men who have not been ashore since we were in Valparaiso sixteen months ago.

They got to Valparaiso again on the 19th October.

> November 5th. Privileged leave today, the first since we have been in here except the officers who have been ashore every day since we have been in but as we are not flesh and blood the same as them we could not get leave so five of the marines and one blue jacket stretched it. We have asked for general leave but the commander told us we should have neither.

It was this, together with the flogging of Ramsey and Reynolds, which culminated in the mutiny four days later.

Surprisingly the immediate effect of the mutiny on Tilling was to make him a little less hostile towards the ship. And he still had some loyalty to his Captain (the Commodore) although at the expense of the Admiralty.

> January 27th. Admiral Denman was born the same year as the Commodore joined the service, was a midshipman when Tommy was Commander, has done no good to the service and yet is ahead all through being in the Queen's yacht. The Commodore is a hydrographer to the Admiralty and has surveyed the whole of this coast.

But the *Leander* had clearly ceased to be a happy ship.

> February 12th. A man named Birchwood (Cooper's Mate) committed suicide with poison. The foolish fellow thought a great deal of a girl of ill fame on shore and in consequence of one of our stewards having slept with her he intended to shoot him (the steward) and then the girl and himself and he carried a six barrel revolver all day for that purpose but he had no opportunity of doing what he intended so he took five grams of strichnine and died in her home at 7:00 a.m. the morning. (He went out riding the day before with the girl and the steward.)

The 'post-mortem' on the mutiny from the Admiralty seems to have helped no one.

> March 22nd. Admiral came on board to read letter from their Lordships. Their Lordships could not see reason for mutiny. Excused imprisonment for all except Bob Hounsell. He hoped we would continue so as WE had cast a certain amount of blame on the Commander. I was very glad when the mighty big Admiral with the nose took his departure.

But even without the Admiral he remained surly.

> April 23rd. Shifted Jib Boom. Maintopsail yard and mizentop gallant mast. This is what the Commander calls Drill. I call it the best of hard work and gives a fellow an appetite for his dead horse and potato broth. Such a beautiful dinner. If the casuals what we read about in the papers were to have such a feed there would be very few in the workhouse the second time.

Tilling's bitterness continued to grow.

> May 17th. The Commander and Mr. Briggs (Lieutenant Warrington) had a Parrot each in a cage and they both got away. A bottle of grog was the reward for their capture and Levitt caught Mr. Briggs',

but the Commander's, had it been seen, would not have been caught, for while we were in Valparaiso, he saw a canary belonging to Nick Andrews and wanted to know whose wild animal it was, then called the jolly-boat away to land it. This is a very good specimin of his kindness to the ship's company.

And Tilling noted that so far during the commission nineteen men had died, sixty-two had run (i.e. deserted) and fifteen had been discharged by Court Martial. And it was not simply the officers and men who were feeling the strain. The ship, too, after three years was showing signs of wear though Tilling probably exaggerated.

May 28th. The necklaces went on passage. The clew of the mainsail snapped out of the sail; stormsails Halyards, tacks and sheets gone at different times in our passage, the caulking in the seams is all working out. If I could leave the service I would never go home in her as I do not think it is safe.

And after a survey on the ship

May 28th. If she works like this on a short peaceful cruise, I wonder what will become of her on the passage home. The safety valve is defective and unless the pumps are manned she would sink in nine hours.

And not surprisingly

June 6th. *Topaze* our relief has arrived and was to leave on the fourth for this port. Such a commotion was never raised since or before the mutiny . . . Everybody is so overjoyed that they are capering like mad.

Thirty hours' leave was given, and three more men deserted, making a total of sixty-five for the commission.
Tilling also disliked Douall, the new captain for the voyage home.

July 3rd. Rating who deserted (A. B. Murray) got seven days solitary and whilst in cell broke down. Given thirty-six lashes. So much for Captain Douall.

His resentments towards the officers became even more bitter:

July 14th. Still wet below and on deck very squally. Decks leaking very much. I am very happy that the officers get their share of it as it is the first time anything has been equally divided during the commission.

But his deepest loathings were reserved for the Commander.

9

July 19th. At muster Captain asked why we did not wear mitts and shirts. I cannot say whether he was told the truth. This is, the Commander will not allow us. Mighty cold—thermometer 40°.

And again.

July 23rd. Our noble Commander is humbugging us as much as he can. Ports triced up, all hatchways uncovered and windsails down on the lower deck. The maindeck guns secured inboard so as we shall have nowhere to walk about. He knows he will not be anything more than what he is for some years to come. Captain Douall does not like to interfere.

After rounding Cape Horn on 31st July they ran into very heavy weather.

August 3rd. Wind increased and O.O.W. Briggs would not shorten sail. Captain ordered to reef topsail and furl top gallants. Snow falling very fast and thick. Could not tell whether I had hands or not for the cold. After breakfast further reefing seven to ten. Every man and boy on the ship wet through and freezing. Captain said he was sorry he could not see the junior officers in their stations as they ought to be and mentioned something about the mainbrace. There is a midshipman stationed in each top and crosstrees whenever anything is being done aloft. They are supposed to see the orders of the Commander's officers on deck properly carried out and answer whenever the top is hailed from deck, but this morning not one of the midshipmen went aloft. It was too cold for them but in moderate weather they will often exceed their duty and cause men old enough to be their fathers to get into trouble perhaps for answering back. No matter what an officer says in the navy you are supposed to obey whether right or wrong. It is often the case—not in this ship only, but in all others to put a mid, or quite a boy about fifteen years old in charge of a lot of men who have been to sea all their lives who has never seen a ship or blue water till they joined this one. Spliced the Mainbrace again; not, however, with our NOBLE Commander's consent.

Tilling's complaints about the officers continue.

August 17th. John Pillar, blacksmith, invalided from the *Shearaton* (probably *Shearwater*) died or rather was killed by Doctor Clarke at 5:30. Doctor told him there was nothing the matter though he could hardly speak or move and ate nothing and indeed a man must have a constitution like a horse to eat navy rations. So his messmate went and stated his case to the Captain who ordered sick rations for him and his hammock in the sick bay, the only dry place between decks. He is the seventh he has killed in the same way.

One with three fingers knocked off could not get on the list.

He had a little more time for the Chaplain 'Who is, I think, a good and pious man'; the paymaster, was less popular.

August 18th. 1866. I could not help noticing Old Honesty—how sanctified he looked when he is the wickedest old sinner in the ship, and paid us in the new Peruvian money when in Valparaiso so as to pocket the odd cents and cheat us in such a clever manner over the check money by paying it in a different country coins so that he drives a fine old trade.

They did call at Asencion on the way home, that was from August 24th to 28th, but they did not finally arrive at Plymouth until 29th September, which Tilling called a voyage of '90 days at sea arriving out of coal, rum and cocoa'.

Not a very happy commission. How often conditions were as bad as Tilling suggests is hard to judge. But he left the Navy as soon after the *Leander* paid off as he could. He joined a merchant vessel, the *Daphne*, and his journal tails off after 1866. There is one entry worth noting:

Nov. 12th. 1870. Captain drunk. 8th. time since leaving. It wasn't only the Royal Navy that was wrong!

I I

A View from the Lower Deck

A fashion at present obtains of trying to make the lower-deck uniform and this is often done at the expense of comfort. What advantage accrues to the Service by having all the mess-traps of an uniform pattern, and insisting that the men should provide and keep the stock up to a certain standard out of their own pockets? Why should each man's ditty-bag be required to be of the same size and pattern? or why is it essential that the ungainly hats should be stowed in a particular way? Why should certain officers insist on bringing their friends around the lower-deck at meal-hours, and pointing out the curiosities of the table, as though they were in a menagerie? Why, when in a foreign country, is anyone and everyone, white or black, allowed to visit, but on her arrival in a home port after a long commission, a man may not even see his wife, mother, or any other relative? Why should everything, no matter how frivolous, be done in a hurry; and why, in the name of common sense, should the hands always be turned up in the middle of the night to do work which could be sooner done if commenced at a proper hour? Why can we not get rid of that irritating system of going to breakfast at about 5 a.m., and then keeping men hard at work till noon, when they are piped to dinner; and all these eight long hours on a basin of cocoa and biscuit? We hasten to admit that the Lords of the Admiralty discountenance such proceedings, but so, also, do their Lordships prohibit holy-stoning; and yet we much doubt if there is one single ship in the Service in which it is not done, and often too. Why do so many officers construe Circulars in such a manner as to bear as hardly as possible on any one wearing a blue shirt? And why are men not allowed to advance in their behalf any Circular bearing favourably towards them, without being told they are impertinent and d——d sea lawyers? Why should officers who are continually in the habit of dining over freely, be allowed to punish a man who may have transgressed the strict Service rule of sobriety? Or what is of still more importance, why should those officers who are notorious swearers be ordered by Queen's Regulations to read prayers, and thus bring discredit on religion? Why should superior officers speak to their inferiors (gentlemen) in language which would cause their names to be removed from the books of any club of gentlemen? Why do the officers who speak thus demand that these same junior officers should be respected by the ship's company? Why should those officers who are so sensitive about a mere touch of the cap be the only ones who seldom (or never) return such salutes when given?

Is it reasonable to expect, that where all or part of the foregoing, combined with bullying, is the chief code of discipline, and where a man is never safe from punishment or abuse for two consecutive hours—we repeat, is it reasonable to expect that comfort should find a resting place in such a ship?

These complaints come from a pamphlet, *The Seamen of the Royal Navy, their Advantages and Disadvantages as viewed from the Lower Deck.*
The anonymous author particularly attacks the disciplinary relaxations in the training of boys.

In the training-ship did not the instructor have to wash his clothes, and even hang them on a line for him? So that now his troubles really begin, they seem to be severe, and discontent follows. Why should he render obedience to a man of the same rank as his late instructor,—a man who wears the same device on his arm in worsted as he himself wore when a boy in gold, and further, a man who may at the present moment be his messmate? Discontent is succeeded by impertinence, and impertinence is insubordination; that which in the training-ship would have been passed by as not worth heeding is now considered and treated as a crime. From small offences to large ones the road is very short and easy, and thus we soon find him striking the petty officer for whom he has learned so little respect; prison follows, and now his character having been blackened for the remainder of his Service-career, what can we expect but that he will continue in the same course until brought to a court-martial and turned out of the Service, having succeeded in costing the country £95, and disseminating his bad example amongst those of his companions who may as yet be not altogether irreclaimable.

This hardly seems the case for the sailors whose memoirs follow and not *every* seaman ended up in prison!
The author voiced complaints against leave and pay, and also about

the food. The quality of the food was not good. But it was the cooks who came in for the real blame.

In the cooking lies the gist of the whole matter; even the portion of the allowance pronounced good is entirely spoiled in the cooking. Men are trained for this purpose, and one part of their training consists of putting meat into boiling water thus at once rendering it hard and tough.

The ship's cook being responsible for the good order of the galley is generally much more anxious that there should be no spots or marks on the deck surrounding it to offend the eyes of any officer passing that way, than he is about the food for the men. If ships' cooks were liable to be dismissed for faulty cooking, then a vast improvement would certainly follow, as so much depends on this one man.

Another source of conflict was the dress the seamen had to wear.

The opinion is strong in the Service that the dress is ungainly in appearance. It is known to be uncomfortable to wear, and if medical testimony is a criterion, injurious to the health, in exposing the chest, and hindering the circulation of blood by means of its tightness around the hips; but it would seem that nothing will produce a change in that direction.

Shortly afterwards a Circular was issued by the Admiralty directing the flannel of seamen to be cut square and close up to the neck.

His major complaint about uniforms, though, was one of cost.

Do officers ever reflect that possibly the new pair of trousers represents so much bread from the man's children and that the man looks on them in this light.

One wonders quite how true this really was. Certainly any seaman who 'got on' was not too badly off though an able seaman on 1/7 a day cannot have had much to spare.

His most telling remarks concern the attitude of the general public towards the seamen. This most definitely was to change in the eighties and nineties, even if in the seventies there were still people who remembered the seaman as he had been and treated him accordingly.

What man possessing the faintest tinge of manly feeling would dare to walk through one of the public streets in any of our naval ports, in uniform, having his wife or any respectable female in his company? One might just as well try to pass through Petticoat Lane in the same dress without being asked to purchase something, as to perform the first feat without being insulted; and this is the chief reason why our petty officers and seamen prefer any dress, when on shore, to the objectionable one they are called upon to wear when on board; but a few facts are worth any number of suppositions, and we will now give a few. Want of space necessarily limits the number, but instances are of daily occurrence; let these few facts suffice to illustrate the amount of respect shown to petty officers when in uniform.

The writer of this, in company with another petty officer, went on shore at Malta. There was to be a performance at one of the regimental theatres, and invitations had been sent to the ship. In due time we found ourselves in the barracks, but as it wanted an hour ere the performance would commence, we strolled into the non-commissioned officers' mess. Judge our surprise on being informed by the mess-servant that we were not allowed in the mess; that no Blue-jackets were permitted within, and, therefore, we must leave. We asked to see the serjeant-major; the senior serjeant present came forward, corroborated the statement of the servant, regretted the order, &c., and told us we were at liberty to enter the canteen, i.e., mix with the privates. Of course we declined the offer and left the mess, our tempers not at all improved by the fact that, at the billiard board stood the Schoolmaster and Captain's Steward of our own ship, playing a game with two serjeants. (N.B.—They were not Blue-jackets, being non-executive.)

Instance No. 2. The same two petty officers in course of time arrived in England (Portsmouth), and being strangers, on a night's leave, thought of whiling the time away by going to some place of entertainment. The theatres were closed, so there was nothing for it but the Music Hall, St. Mary's Street; thither we went, purchased a ticket for the stalls, but on presenting it to the functionary presiding at the entrance, we were rudely told that Blue-jackets were not allowed in that part of the house. Whilst standing there, a soldier, and what appeared to be a half-drunken navvy, passed us and entered. We were offered seats farther back, but this we declined, preferring to quit the place altogether. (The same rule holds good at the present moment (Feb., 1877), with reference to Blue-jackets entering this place of entertainment.)

Instance No. 3. A petty officer, desiring to avail himself of the privilege of travelling double journey for single fare (as granted by several Companies during the Christmas holidays) started in uniform, and was speedily reminded of the fact by the uncouth treatment, coarse language, and impertinent familiarity of a fellow-passenger, who eventually quitted the carriage, with the offer to send him (the sailor) 'a gal'. Finding matters so unpleasant, the sailor thought it were the better plan to try plain clothes. The effect was magical; the porters offered to find him a carriage; to place his carpet-bag in safety; enquired kindly after his luggage, as though it had recently been in a delicate state of health; in fact, they were all suavity, and overflowing with the milk of human kindness, where but a short time previously they had been begging a 'chaw of baccy' whilst a gentle-man suffering from 'stopped watch' very politely asked, 'Can you tell me the time, Sir?'

There was some truth in this, as indeed there was about the pensions and the treatment of the ex-sailor ashore:

It will be found that the Naval Pensioner has very little chance of obtaining anything that will raise him above the condition of a labourer, and that is hardly the future a man will look forward to when he has, perhaps, served the last ten years as a petty officer.

Again, tradition dies hard and the sailor had not got a good record for sobriety and reliability.

Instructions in furling and sail reefing, in H.M.S. *St. Vincent*.

Musketry drill in H.M.S. *St. Vincent*.

The Slave Trade

H.M.S. *Vulture*.

Aboard H.M.S. *Vulture* at Mozambique, August 1873.

12

Training the Boys

The Captain was anxious to reach his anchorage before dark, for the already low barometer was still falling, probably a Southerly gale was brewing, and the fine Northerly wind might chop round to the South-east; moreover the ebb-tide was making strong round St. Catherine's point, and although the ship was bowling along through the water at the rate of 9 or 10 knots, she was not going more than 5 or 6 past the land.

It was half past three; the wind was freshening; as the ship passed out from under the lee of the Island the wind would freshen more; there were hard edged clouds of dazzling whiteness passing swiftly overhead, but the high land off Dunmore was dead to windward, so they could not be seen far off. The wind off the shore was sharp and cutting; the Captain ordered the watch to be called to shorten sails, the ropes were manned, but not a ropeyard must be started till the order is given. He sees the merchant vessels in the offing shortening sail betimes to the freshening gale, as shorthanded vessels must; but the *Eurydice* with her numerous picked crew can well afford to wait till the last moment; his men have never failed him yet, and they will not fail him now; it is no rash or foolhardy spirit that makes him wait to give the order, but the experience and self reliance of some thirty years of seafaring life.

The first puff of the coming squall is seen and the order is given to take in the royals; the royal-yard-men are in the rigging on their way up to fold their sails when the Captain calls them down; the squall is already increasing with dangerous rapidity, and at once the order is given to shorten sail; already the studding sails are coming in when a terriffic blast strikes the ship on the port bow, and without a moment's warning throws her on her beam ends. A blinding snow-storm envelops the ship; the furious gale howls through the rigging, snaps off the mizen topmast, rends to ribbons the now loosened

sail and lashes the ropes in a hundred directions; the poor hull
staggers and strains; the water rushes in through the lee main-deck
ports along the lee gangway and over the lee hammock netting;
the men are washed away from their stations and carried overboard;
the fore and main sheets are let go to ease her and the Captain's
order is 'if you can't let it go cut it'; the topsail haulyards and the
topsail sheets are let go. A gallant young Sub-Lieutenant rushes to
the wheel and helps the steersman to put the helm hard up and then
he is seen no more.

The Captain climbs on to the weather side of his ship, whence
he sees her keel level with the water. The lee boats have, of course,
been washed away: in vain he directs an effort to lower the port
boat, bravely supported by his first lieutenant. The two doctors
having reached the deck, are now seen struggling in the water. The
sea is rushing down through the hatchways, and above the howling
of the blast are heard the roaring of the escaping air, and the confused
cries of the men on the lower deck; and as the vessel fills she slowly
rights herself, gives a slight plunge forward, and sinks to the bottom,
barely five minutes from the time the squall struck her.

We know but little more; our last glimpse of the Captain is
standing on his sinking ship; for others there might be life-belts,
or boats, or floating spars, but no thought of self could cross the
Captain's mind at such a time. The depth of that moment's sadness
his brother-officers alone can realise, but as he remembered his
young wife and two baby daughters he would commit them to
God's mercy and to England's sympathy, while for himself he would
know that his Country's verdict would be that the Captain of the
Eurydice died striving to do his duty.

In ten to fifteen minutes the dense snow-storm clears away as
rapidly as it had arisen. The wind falls to a keen stiff breeze, and the
sun again shines out brightly upon the sea. In eleven fathoms of
water, off Sandown Bay, and little over two miles from shore are
visible the mast-heads of the ill-fated ship; the strong tide swiftly
sweeps away to the southward all wreckage, and such drowning
men as are clinging thereto; one by one they drop off, benumbed
with the fierce cold, and disheartened at finding themselves swept
out into mid-channel. Still as anon, one passes another, comes a
cheerful shout to hold on, and to be of good courage, for who
could doubt that in so great a thoroughfare and so near the shore
help must be at hand? Alas! the thickly falling snow-cloud had
hidden the sight from every eye, and as yet none realised their peril.

Captain William Langworthy Jenkin, of the schooner *Emma*,
bound from Newcastle for Poole, first saw the wreckage and the

royals of the ship above water. Being somewhat further from the land, and under reduced canvas, he had not felt the extreme violence of the squall. He at once steered for the spot, and hoisting out his boats, succeeded in picking up five men, of whom only two survived; —Benjamin Cuddiford, able seaman, and Sydney Fletcher, ordinary seaman. The other bodies brought on shore were those of Lieutenant Tabor, the first lieutenant, Captain Ferrier, of the Royal Engineers, and George A. Bennett, a first-class petty-officer.

Benjamin Cuddiford was saved by a life-buoy which he found floating in the water, and which brought him again to the surface after he had been sucked down by the sinking of the ship. He did what he could to save others by taking them pieces of floating wreck. Sydney Fletcher was also saved by a cork life-belt. From the mouths of these two comes all we know of the loss of a splendid frigate, and her living freight of some three hundred and fifty souls.

Among those who went down with the ship was Petty Officer First Class, Daniel Harley, late of H.M.S. *Alert*.

The *Eurydice*, commissioned by Captain Hare in February 1877, was a frigate fitted out for the purpose of training young seamen just off the training-hulks. During the summer she had been in the English Channel and in November had sailed for a cruise round the West Indies. She left Bermuda on 6th March. She was lost because the main deck ports were open (as they commonly were in fine weather) and the exceptional squall forced the vessel so far over that the sea had flooded on to the main deck over the coamings round the hatches and so below, filling the ship with water. No real blame was attached to Captain Hare, but the loss of a training ship with so many young men on board inevitably shocked the nation.

Two years later it happened again. On a similar voyage the *Atalanta*, employed on the training service, sailed from Bermuda to England on 1st February and was never heard of again. On 29th June, a reward was offered by the Admiralty for information concerning her, but it was never claimed. In her were the Captain, Francis Sterling, a crew of 113 officers and men and 170 young seamen under training. A committee appointed to inquire into the vessel's efficiency reported that the *Atalanta* was thoroughly sound when she left England in November 1879 and on the whole was a very stable ship. The Captain, officers and crew had all been carefully chosen. All that was known was that exceptionally violent storms raged at that time in the part of the Atlantic she would have to cross.

Inevitably, there was a public outcry, but the Admiralty was reluctant to abandon the principle of training the young seamen in sail. However, the disasters were ammunition for those who wanted a more 'scientific' Navy. A better-organised sail training squadron was set up, but it was not until 1899 that square rigged ships were abandoned. Up to that time every seaman was trained in sail, even though after 1880 few sailing vessels served with the fleet.

This was the final stage of a seaman's training as a boy. Before then he spent some time—generally about a year—in one or other of the training hulks lying at one of the major naval ports. For example there was the *Impregnable* at Devonport where Patrick Riley went, Charles Humphreys' *Boscawen* at Portland or the *St. Vincent* at Portsmouth in which both Thomas Holman and Sam Noble served. The anonymous seaman of Chapter XI has described only somewhat exaggeratedly the changes that took place in the training of the boys. Charles Humphreys, the earliest of the four was much the most critical of the training he received.

We arrived at Portland the next day and then I was transferred to the *Boscawen*. She was to be my home for 12 months and I arrived on board on November 14th. 1870.

I cannot describe those 12 months of learning discipline. We were often very short of food and many a rope's end did I feel. Our instructors were very cruel, but I suppose it was mainly because we had a very stern captain. Life in the Navy was not thought much of. Our instruction comprised:- Sail drill, knots and splices, boat rowing, school, gun drill, rifle and cutlass drills and everything that goes to make a sailor. We were taught to make and mend our own clothes and to wash them every Thursday. That day was known as 'Rope yarn Sunday'. We were paid the large sum of threepence per week and if we liked and our character admitted, we were allowed to go ashore for a run every Sunday afternoon until sunset. At midsummer those who had homes and parents who could afford it, were allowed to go home for three weeks. Those who stayed behind, had to clean the ship and do other work, but no drills took place during the holidays. The same thing happened at Christmas. Being a long way from home and my parents very poor, I had to remain on board. This seemed very hard when I saw other boys go on leave and enjoy themselves. At Christmas, we who remained on board, had extra plum duff and we thought we were very well off. We were very glad when the holidays were over for they were no holiday for us.

Thomas Holman also suffered from the rope's end, but had fewer complaints.

Here I was then, at last, my wildest dream realised: I was installed on board one of Her Majesty's ships, and advertising it to the world by a suit of blue serge, which I fondly believe gave me all that look of picturesqueness that I had so often admired in others similarly clothed. I soon found, however, that I had not come there to dream; my life became one of never ending excitement, accelerated at times by a sharp cut from the Corporal's cane, which sent me bounding up the ladders between decks, three steps at the time. I remember the first time I became acquainted with this same cane was by a cut at random from one of the ship's police, who, out of pure fun or devilment, was dealing out quite indiscriminately, and in the most liberal way, slashes, both right and left, to any of us poor hapless youngsters who happened to be in the sphere of his operations.

This state of affairs existed twenty years ago, and, I have no hesitation in saying, it was a scandal and disgrace to the authorities that such men as those Ship's Police and Petty Officers—the majority of whom was then largely, or totally, uneducated, and with no sense of judicial fairness—should be free to wreak their own sweet will on the boys, who were without a chance of appeal or redress, placed under their care. Those days are however gone, relegated to the limbo of the past, and to-day we are verging on the other extreme; for so rigid are the regulations, that should any of the instructors on board our training ships strike a boy, even though under aggravating circumstances, he is at once reduced from a Petty Officer to an Able Seaman, and sent out of the Training Service. This is placing dangerous power in the hands of the boys, who are sometimes not above using it in combining to ruin a Petty Officer; still it is, in my opinion, the lesser evil of the two, and the Instructors are certainly much more able to look after themselves now than we boys were then.

The weeks floated past, and I felt myself becoming more and more a sailor. I could splice a rope, make all sorts of pretty and useful knots, had learnt to reef a sail, could run aloft fairly well, and was early promoted to be 'An Upper Yard Boy'—an honour I am proud of to this day, for there was a great competition amongst us boys, in endeavoring to be the most agile.

Looking back on those days brings many pleasant reminiscences, from which I even now derive much pleasure. We were well fed, and generally well cared for in body and mind; the schooling we received laid the foundation of a desire to seek after a knowledge that afterwards bore fruit in many ways advantageous to ourselves and the service.

Another seaman's introduction was more dramatic. This is how Sam Noble fared.

The ship's sides were snow white; the mess tables, stools, traps, and everything sparkling, and the whole place smelling as sweet as a dairy. The great big deck was deserted: nobody at all on it but ourselves. But overhead there seemed to be plenty of life. We could hear loud voices giving orders and hurrying feet, and heavy bodies being moved about, causing a tremendous thumping. Twice a whole broadside of guns went off—the first so suddenly that Peter and I knocked our heads together. We were still sitting rubbing them when a Sergeant of Marines stepped briskly up and blew a loud peal on the bugle. We then heard four or five different voices shout: 'Still!' Another order in a lower key was given and a movement made, then—' 'Tention! Dismiss!' and down the boys came trooping through the hatchways like a fall of snow.

It was 'spelloe'—what is known at school as 'minutes'.

What a crowd! and of all sorts and sizes—big boys, little boys, fat boys and thin boys; the stream seemed never-ending. They were all dressed in white duck. Some went dancing into the messes and took down their ditty-boxes from the shelves running parallel with the edges of the beams; some ran past without taking any notice of us; some merely gave us a glance in the passing and dived into the lower deck; others, again, put their fingers to their noses, made faces at us, and then disappeared, grinning. A dozen or so gathered round the form, and after staring for a minute or two, as if we were creatures of another world, began to joke and sky-lark as boys do everywhere with newcomers. One asked where we came from; another, 'did our mothers know we were out?' a third, with his arms round the necks of the two in front of him, and his head between their shoulders, squinted at us fearfully and squeaked, 'Poo' sings!' which set them all laughing.

And so they went on. I see their mischievous faces now.

A few more joined the group, with hunks of bread in their hands, which they were busily eating, and pushed and jostled those behind to such an extent in their eagerness to see what was going on, that the ones in front were almost driven on top of us.

They shoved and pushed and wriggled about us; some sat down on the form and squeezed us together; some mimicked our northern accent and laughed—but not very loud, for they knew the corporal wasn't far off, and they were afraid of him, and of a cane, which, I forgot to mention, lay across two brass hooks just above the desk. My cap was knocked off, and when I stooped to pick it up, the boy nearest me on the form stuck a pin about an inch into the very tender spot and caused me to shoot forward so suddenly that my head plunged into the stomach of a boy in front with such force that the shock nearly killed him. I jumped up wild with pain and indignation to catch the one who had jabbed me, but the imp was away along the deck laughing like a hyena. But I knew him again, and I'm glad to say had it out with him by and by. I saw the other one, however, crawl over to the nearest mess and sit doubled up on the stool, and that was some satisfaction.

Peter, too, came in for his full share of the badgering, but I must admit he came through the ordeal with more glory than I did, and, what was better, made good his boast in the train. I sat down again, feeling miserable, and leaning as much to one side as possible, for a pin-stab, as everybody knows, is pretty troublesome. I didn't mind that so much. My feelings were hurt, and I was cold and hungry, and do what I would I couldn't help my eyes filling. This only made things worse. One of them cried:

'Oh, I say, look; 'e's a-going to pipe 'is eye; fetch a swab somebody!'

The words were no sooner out of his mouth than he was pulled back and another boy—a fat, bullet-headed one, took his place and made us an elaborate salaam. He chucked Peter under the chin and said:

'Hullo, Joe, 'ave ye come to git yer 'orns clipped?'

'Ay, cud you dae't? retorted Peter; and before he knew where he was, the fellow got one in the chops that sent him spinning almost through the entry-port.

The row that followed brought the corporal out of the cabin. He rushed forward and made a grab for the cane, at which the whole tribe disappeared as completely as if a magician's wand had been waved over them.

It would be tedious to detail further my first appearance on the stage of naval life. Let me simply say, then, that shortly after this, Peter and I were taken below and given our first meal at the Government's expense, and did full justice to it. Then we were given a mess number, and a boy was told off to take us round the ship and explain the different parts, and instruct us how to sling and unsling a hammock, and also how to get into it—the crowning event of a most eventful day, and not accomplished till I had a couple of bumps on my head as large as eggs through falling out.

In a day or two my kit was served out, and mighty proud, I tell you, I felt when I put on my new Jolly Jack's uniform. I found, too, that the life was going to suit me 'down to the ground', as the saying is, and wouldn't have gone back to the mill—no, not for the price of all the jumble of stone and lime, machinery, jute and all the rest of it in the whole town of Dundee.

Another seaman Patrick Riley remembered his first days in the *Impregnable*.

Our pay as Second-class boys was sixpence a day. We received only threepence, or a 'Holy Joe,' as spending money each week. Should we break a basin or plate, there was no 'Holy Joe' that week. The other three shillings and threepence was placed to our credit in the paymaster's books. In consequence, I seldom went ashore, but remained on board roaming about and taking stock of the various things.

I well remember the first Thursday I spent in the *Impregnable*. It being a fine day, the liberty boys had gone on shore, while I, with other boys, climbed aloft. I went up the fore-rigging, getting up as far as the cross-trees, this being my first attempt at climbing aloft. I stood up on the cross-trees, and holding fast to the rigging, I had a good look round and marvelled at the splendid panorama with the different ships moored in the harbour. It was a glorious sight. Saltash Bridge could be seen quite clearly, the Torpoint Ferry crawling along towards North Corner. The training ships *Lion* and *Implacable* were moored together between Torpoint and Saltash on the Cornish side of the Tamar. Yes, it was grand! As I was about to make my way down again, I saw one of the boys standing on the other side of the mast, shivering and holding on to the rigging like grim death. His eyes seemed to be standing out of his head and he was shaking all over. I saw it was a case of what may be termed 'stage fright.' I told him not to look down, but to look up at me or in front. I then took hold of his arm in order to steady him a bit and let him recover himself. Most of the other boys having gone down, I said, 'Now, you follow me, I'll show you the way.' He followed me through the crosstrees on to the topmast rigging; I waited for him there and we both came down to the top, i.e., a platform for setting up the topmast rigging, where I thought it wise to step inside the rigging for a while so as to enable him to pull himself together. I then guided him through the 'lubber's hole' into the lower rigging both of us then going down together until we reached the deck. Taking hold of my hand with both of his, he gave it a good shake and said he could not think what had come over him to make him so nervous. He added, 'And when I saw a little chap like you looking so cool, it helped me to recover myself.' I told him it was only a case of 'stage fright,' and that he would soon get over it, and would knock spots off me in going aloft. He told me his name was John Jack, and that he came from Belfast. He had been in the service a couple of months and this was the first time he had been so high. He was a man in comparison with me. I have often thought of that time since; both of us standing under the fore-rigging in our white duck suits, he so tall and I so short.

Holman gives a good description of daily life on board the training ship.

A day on board the *St. Vincent* was exceedingly bright and cheerful, and, so far as I can now remember, was somewhat after the following description. At 5:30 a.m. in summer the reveille would sound on all decks on which the boys slept; this was followed first by the shrill notes of the Bosun Mates' pipes, and then by three deep bass voices—at least three notes below the bellow of a bull, with a noise that came rolling along the deck from its after part like a great cloud—fairly stupefying the new boy, who, however, was soon brought to his senses by a rap with the Corporal's cane if he tried to get what we used to call 'cunshaw,' i.e. an extra minute or two in his hammock. It took me exactly six months before I could make a connected and coherent sentence out of this great cloud of intensified bass, which sounded like 'nourousou, rousou, rousou, shoaleg, shoaleg, shoaleg, orurerskin,' but I at last interpreted it into the following—'Now, rouse out, rouse out, rouse out, show a leg, show a leg, show a leg, or a purser's stocking.' It was then intelligible, as a leg is the first part of a person's anatomy that is seen over the side of a hammock on getting out, and this was not, especially in the winter time, infrequently clothed in a stocking obtained from the Purser. Once out, the next thing was to lash up one's hammock, as quickly and neatly as possible, and hurry on deck. The last boy up was generally assisted by the corporals. Happy boys! this is all over now. The next duty was to scrub and wash the decks (on Saturday holystone them); this was generally finished by 6:30 when all the boys that could swim were allowed to bathe overboard. How delightful that used to be, how invigorating, and how late we often used to be to breakfast, which was begun at quarter to seven, and finished at 7:15. Half the boys then had to dress for going on deck; in summer time in white clothes, and white they must be, or woe betide the lad that was dirty. The other half, who remained below, cleaned out the messes and scrubbed the mess deck. At 8 o'clock there was what was known as 'morning evolution,' which meant, for the most part, drill aloft in loosing and furling sails, and crossing the upper yards. This was really a very important object lesson to us all, and much pains used to be taken to impress us as much as possible at these times. The boys stationed on the upper yards were considered great swells.

This evolution finished, the watch (or half) for cleaning mess decks went below again to dress in 'whites,' like the remainder, and clear up 'tween decks. At 9.0 a.m. the bugles sounded the 'assembly,' and all the boys fell in, in rows, on the upper deck for inspection. The Instructors each had a section of from twenty to thirty boys to look after, clothe and keep clean; four of these sections composed a division, to which was attached an officer for inspection and super-vision. After most close scrutiny by the instructor and officer, in which a dirty boy was soon spotted and warned, or, if necessary, awarded some minor punishment, the boys were all marched on the quarter deck, and prayers read by the Chaplain or Captain. This over, the boys were 'told off' and immediately proceeded to instruction—one half going to school, and the other to seamanship or gunnery instruction. The seamanship instruction consisted of swimming, boat pulling, knots and splices, monkey topsail yard—i.e. a yard close to the deck on which the youngsters were taught to get in and out, and loose and furl sails, before they were allowed aloft—then bends and hitches, and, as a boy advanced, all the hull and rigging of the ship, compass, helm, lead, etc. The gunnery consisted of working the guns, and rifle, and cutlass drill. What men we used to think ourselves, slashing about with our cutlasses—especially after reading 'A fight with the Pirates' the night before. All these instructions came in perfectly easy and graduated stages, accommodated to the intelligence of the slowest of slow boys. The brightest lads were always selected for instruction in signalling also; but this was a shame, for in those days the signalmen, although the most intelligent men in the fleet, had much the smallest field of promotion. It is different now, but not so good as it ought to be.

At 11:30 a.m. the instructions ceased, and the decks were again swept up for dinner. A number of the boys called 'cooks of the messes' together with the 'caterer' went below, fetched the food from the 'galley' where it was cooked, and allotted it out in plates—one for each boy in the mess. A basin of fairly nourishing soup, not less than half a pound of cooked meat, three or four potatoes, and one-fourth of a loaf, or a large slice of plum pudding, was the usual fare. One day each week we had pea soup and boiled pork. This was certainly not a bad dietary for a lad of fifteen to seventeen. The oldest boys somehow always contrived to get the largest shares. At 12 o'clock, when all was ready, the bell struck eight and the boatswain's mates piped to dinner, and every boy rushed below to see what the plates contained. The first there stood up beside the plate that looked to him to contain the largest share. Then the bugle sounded 'the still,' and an officer passed around the mess deck to see if there was any complaint; and the caterer at the end of each table said grace as he passed. If a boy wished to complain, he stood at the end of his table, plate in hand, and invited the officer's attention to either the quantity, or the quality, as the case might be, of the food. The officer usually got out of any difficulties of this sort by calling for the plate of the boy who had portioned it out, and exchanging it for the one complained of. This was a healthy check on unfairness, and kept things pretty level. When the officer had gone round, he ordered 'carry on' to be sounded, and we fell to.

At one o'clock the 'assembly' sounded again, and we all fell in on the upper deck; and, if any boy was to be punished, we were all marched aft and saw the culprit, mounted on another boy's back, receive the number of strokes (from a cane) allotted him. From this we went to instruction again; the watch that had been to school in the morning going to seamanship and gunnery, and the other watch to school. At 3:30 the instruction again ceased, and, if washing night, we were ordered to put on blue clothing and bring our whites up. Washing tubs, ready filled with water, were placed along the deck, and the boys arranged on either side of them, four or six to each tub; the bugle sounded, and we each made a rush to the nearest tub and began to lather up. Instructors usually came to the assistance of the newly joined.

At 5 o'clock we went to tea, and at 5:30 hung up our clothes to dry, on lines provided for the purpose. We next washed down the upper deck; and the remainder of the evening was our own. Bathing was allowed, and indulged in, as also was climbing aloft and running in and out on the yards; and mightily we used to enjoy ourselves in racing each other up and down the rigging, each trying to excel the other in gaining the fore or main top. At eight o'clock the hammocks were 'piped down,' and hung up ready for 'turning in'; and at 8:30 the decks were finally cleared up for the day. At 9.0 p.m. all lights were extinguished, and every boy had to be in his hammock. The first Lieutenant then went 'the rounds,' to see all correct for the night. After this silence should prevail, but seldom did, as the liveliest among us generally had a good story to tell, which would set all the others laughing, and this sometimes led to a whole 'tier,' or row, of boys having to turn out, lash up their hammocks, and stand with them on their shoulders on the quarter deck. This usually cooled both our heels and our ardour, and we were glad to go to sleep when allowed below again. This was the ordinary day's routine. On Thursdays we all received threepence each, and were allowed the afternoon on shore for a stroll, or for a game in our recreation ground at Haslar, where much trouble was taken to provide for our amusement.

Saturday was given up entirely to cleaning the ship; when we were all shoeless and stockingless, and either up to our elbows in soap-suds scrubbing, or to our knees in salt water washing the soap-suds away; which was glorious fun, especially in the summer. On one evening each week we had an entertainment, lasting about two hours, and consisting of singing, dancing, reciting, etc.; and some-times a conjuror was hired, to give us a special treat.

Sunday was, of course, the best day. The reveille at quarter past six—long after the sun had commenced to peep through the port-holes. How we used to enjoy that extra forty-five minutes in our hammocks! Then there was no cleaning decks; simply to bathe and breakfast. After breakfast we dressed in our very best and cleanest to go on decks; a few only remaining below to clear up 'tween decks. 'Divisions' was at 9:30 on Sunday, and the Captain used always to come around and inspect both the boys and ship. I was on these occasions the most envied of boys, for he would occasionally ask me how I was getting on, and if I liked it. After 'divisions' Church; which I must confess was the first divine service I ever cared for—there seemed a dash of romance in it. Church was followed by the best dinner of the week, and this again by a run on shore for those who wished, a few only being compelled to stay, and these only for the purpose of pulling the others on shore, or in case of fire on the ship. We used to land at 1.30, and come off at 6.30. The evenings on Sundays were much the same as other evenings, except that we were not allowed aloft.

Sam Noble describes some more dramatic events on board.

I was only about seven or eight weeks in 34 Mess when I was shifted to 24, on the middle deck, among the Petty Officer boys. This mess was the Park Lane of the *St. Vincent*: the P.O. boys being considered—or considering themselves, which is the same thing—the aristocracy of the ship. The reason for my early promotion was that I soon learnt to use the 'bo'sun's call'—that is, the whistle for regulating drill—and was lucky enough to attract the attention of Mr. Phillips, the chief boatswain, who promised to speak to the captain, and get me made a bo'sun's mate-boy.

Accordingly, one day I was sent for by the mess corporal, and told to get my bag and in future to stow it in the rack belonging to 24 Mess on the middle deck.

Here another rumpus took place. As I have said, 24 was the Petty Officer boys' mess, the 'upper circle' of the *St. Vincent*, and I was not a Petty Officer boy—was merely a novice, in fact. The caterer, a slim slip of a lad, named Browning, belonging to Houndsditch London, was a Greenwich school boy, and as full of pride as a young bantam.

Those Greenwich schoolboys, being trained in seamanship before joining the Navy, easily outran their mates and won distinction early. That made them a bit cocky as a rule. There were two of them in 24: Browning, and another London boy, Charlie Calman by name, a bright-faced, sweet-natured lad, who was further distinguished by having an uncle who was a Beefeater in the Tower. This latter boy, Charlie, and I became chums afterwards, and I spent two or three gorgeous week-ends with him at his home in the Minories, and roaming wild among the gloomy dungeons in that grim old fortress.

Nice enough fellows they were, those Petty Officer boys I mean; you found them so after you had impressed your niceness on them in the old, old boy way, by knocking it into them. Not that I was much of a fighter. Never was. But neither were the boys I happened to be up against. And luck was usually with me—a tremendous asset in a boxing bout.

However, I did as I was told: put my bag and ditty-box alongside of the aristocrats, and went through the forenoon's drill and lessons with a heart as light and as high as the pennant at the masthead.

At dinner-time, my first meal in the mess—(I remember it was 'Sea pie' day and the deck was full of delicious flavours)—I hung around rather diffidently till all the others were lined up, not wishing to be thought cheeky; and then, seeing a vacant place about the middle of the table, lifted my leg over the stool and stood waiting for 'Grace' to be said.

It was amusing to hear 'Grace' said at dinner-time—the only meal, by the way, that was considered worthy of such a distinction. This was quite a ceremony, often a very trying one. The 'still' was sounded; then the officer of the deck (there were two mess-decks in the *St. Vincent*) walked slowly round the messes, where the boys were lined up, each in front of his plate, asking as he passed: 'Any complaints? All right here?' etc., etc. Then, having made the circuit of the deck, and got back to the main hatchway where he started, he would wait for his opposite number either above or below to arrive. Sometimes there would be a hitch somewhere, and then we all had to wait, as a rule ravenously hungry with the flavour of the dinner filling our noses, and making our mouths water, till the hitch was adjusted. You daren't take a bit on the sly, for if you did, and got caught—! I had a mate called Archie Smith, belonging to Perth, who once sneaked a nugget of Christmas pudding, and had just plunked it boiling hot into his mouth when the captain and officers came along. He daren't chew—that would have given him away—so he bolted the hunk whole, feeling it scorch his gullet all the way down. But never a murmur! Eyes front all the time! It set up some trouble that was the means of his being invalided, and eventually carried him off altogether—not very long afterwards, either, poor chap.

Sometimes, when the flavour was special, or Mr. Bennett was in a particularly good mood, he would rub his knob with a pleased twinkle in his eye, and preach us a little homily on how grateful we should be for having such nice grub to eat, and what a grand profession the Navy was, and what a fine country we lived in, and a lot of balderdash like that, while we, with the slaver running down our chins, stood squinting at our plates. Then he would shout:

'SAY GRACE!'

and a thousand boys would immediately yell:

'What we are about to receive may the Lord double it!' In less than five minutes every plate would be emptied! Of course, the correct 'Grace' was:

'For what we are about to receive may the Lord make us truly thankful,' but we hadn't time for all that.

This day, however, I wasn't interested in the 'Grace' or the dinner either. As I took my place they all looked at me, but nobody spoke. I saw the fellow at the top of the table next Browning give him a nudge, which he answered by a nod and a jerk of the head in the direction of Mr. Bennett, who was starting on his round of inspection, and a meaning glance passed between him and the fellow opposite.

I thought it was all right; that the caterer knew of my coming and had the place kept for me. But I was mistaken. When 'Grace' was said, and I made to sit down, the fellows at the top and bottom of the stool jerked it back, and down I went with a bang that almost rattled my bones out through my skin, and nearly knocked my brains out besides with the bump I gave my head on the stool. In my descent I grabbed the table cover and brought half-a-dozen dinners along with me, broke the plates, and scattered the grub all over the deck.

The mess was the first one forward, next to the sick bay, and there was a wide gangway between it and the bulkhead. Many a time we danced in it when the band played 'tween decks during the officers' dinner hour.

But it was a different dance this time.

I got up dazed, not knowing whether it was Christmas or Easter, and felt myself all over. Then, collecting my wits, I made a dive at the fellow at the top of the table, Ikey Bean, by name, who wasn't expecting me, and landed him right on the nose—a fine soft, juicy nose it was, too!—and he had blood for dinner that day, I can tell you. Down he went. Then I rushed for the one at the foot; but he wouldn't stand—sprang right out of my way he did, and got mixed up with the mess-gear—so I took the first that came and, with a lightning punch in his empty stomach, he followed Ikey.

Then arrived pandemonium!

In the turmoil I heard Browning's voice say: 'Leave him to me,' and there was I in a whirling circle of excitement sparring up to him like a windmill. He let fly, and got me on the side of the neck—a blow that sent me careering up against the sick bay with a force that nearly put me into it. But I bounced off again, and at it we went, hammer and tongs, with the whole middle deck and part of the lower as spectators.

Browning was about my own size and weight, but he had the advantage of me in his bouts with the Greenwich schoolboys; and I believe would have handled me roughly had luck not come my way as it did in my first scrap.

In one of his plunges he stepped on a potato, and his heel slid about four feet throwing him off his balance. His arms went up and he came down with his head thrown back, like an acrobat doing a leg-stretching feat on the stage, and with all his guard open. Seizing the chance, I flew at him and got one in under his chin that sent him rolling into the corner like a ball.

I looked wildly around to see who was coming next, but just then a cry of 'Wa-a-re-o' behind, like the long quivering note of the loon, signalled the arrival of the corporals with their canes, and the crowd vanished like smoke in a wind. Next minute it seemed an octopus had gripped me. It was Tubby Molgan, the mess corporal. Tubby was a little round barrel of a man, with a greedy-eyed, hairy, rat face, and the strength of a gorilla. He was also punishment corporal. It was he who lugged the defaulters up before the skipper, and if anybody had a dozen with the cane or the birch ladled out to him, it was Tubby who laid them on. He nearly squeezed my life out. Then he jerked my head up so that he could see my face, and gave a great start.

'Hallo!' he exclaimed, 'why, you're the boy I sent here this morning, aren't you?' I let my head drop as if it had the weight of a mountain. 'What's the meaning of this?' he cried, facing round. 'Where's the caterer of the mess?'

Browning, who had unrolled himself, and looked a proper battle-scarred veteran, came crawling over, with his head in his hands as if he were holding it on, and said, 'Here, sir.'

'Oh, you're there; are you?' said Tubby, his harsh, menacing voice like a dog's growl. 'And what's the meaning of this 'ere? What have you done to this boy? I sent him here this morning by the express order of the Captain and Mr. Phillips; and now look at him. . . .'

Browning mumbled that it was all the result of a joke. That it was merely intended I should pay my footing as a new member . . . but —His voice trailed away to a wheeze, and he put up a weary hand and lifted his head a bit and looked at the corporal.

Tubby was furious. A joke! By heavens, a capital joke . . . Browning had no idea! . . . He would see what sort of joke it was before he (Tubby) had done with him! That he would! . . . 'Here's a pretty picture!' he fumed. (I agreed with him. It was a lovely picture of a battlefield. Beef, duff, potatoes, onions, and all the other ingredients of sea pie trodden into the deck. Knives, forks, broken crockery, and what not, strewn all over. Ikey Bean's blood, which had flowed freely—rich, thick blobs of bright crimson— adding a lovely realistic touch suggesting carnage. Calman told me afterwards that he envied me my luck in bringing it about.) 'Here's a fine state of things,' cried Tubby, bending his heavy beetling brows upon Browning in a terrible frown. 'You are supposed to set an example to the other messes and look at this! . . . Whoever saw such a mix-up? And you call it a joke! . . . we'll see what the Captain has got to say about it.'

He brought the whole mess out amidships, whipped out his notebook and took every one of our names, bullied everybody, threatening Browning with disrating, ordered the mess to be scrubbed out, and dared one of us to so much as put a crumb in his mouth till he gave permission—kicked up a proper shindy, in fact, and then went off in a blaze of fireworks.

Such a how-de-do!

The first thing Browning did when Tubby was out of sight was to hold his hand out to me, which proved him a thoroughbred, and made me love him. I gripped it heartily, and one of the fellows on the starboard side cried, 'Bully for Browning!' which raised a small cheer; but this was soon doused by Jimmy-the-Fog at the desk who held up both his hands, crying 'Hush!'

Then we all set to work to get things into ship-shape order again. It was 'off jumpers, up trouser-legs.' Some rushed to the galley for buckets of warm water, others for brushes, squeegees and swabs. Calman ran to his ditty-box and fished out a big hunk of soap, and into the work we went 'Like brothers in a common cause,' and all enmity forgotten. By the time Tubby came to inspect the mess you wouldn't have known anything had happened, beyond the deck being wet and some of our faces a bit askew.

After the inspection we had another thriller. Browning stepped up to the corporal as he was going away and asked permission to say a word. Tubby said: 'What was it?' frowning like an angry chimpanzee. Browning said he was sorry for the row, also for the trouble it had caused, but he hoped the corporal would be kind enough not to report his messmates, as they had nothing to do with it; the blame was all his, and he was willing to bear the consequences.

Tubby glowered at him with his hang-dog face, gave a shrug to his shoulders, saying: 'That's for the Captain to settle'; threw a scowl around, which took us all in, and departed, growling in his beard.

A proper curmudgeon.

But we all thought it grand of Browning. It showed him a true sport. Down we sat to what was left of the dinner, as cosy as peas in a pod, eating it as happily as though it had been the finest fare in the world, instead of cold, tasteless hash—very little of it, too, and some even trampled. I couldn't help smiling over to him in an admiring sort of way as he sat at the head of the table, and he smiled back, telling me there was no ill feeling. The whole crowd were as decent as could be, some giving me bits off their plate though they hadn't much for themselves. Ikey sat opposite; and though his nose was a bit lumpy and high-coloured from the bash it got, geniality flowed from his eye. Charlie Calman threw me a grin which warmed my cockles, and was the start of a chumship which lasted all the time we were in the *St. Vincent* together, and afterwards, and would flame up as brightly as ever in a moment should we happen to meet one another again. My left eye was bunged up, my neck twisted, and my tongue bitten through; but the day was mine, and I felt like an admiral back from a tough, totally unexpected engagement 'with all his blushing honours thick upon him,' and hugged myself to think I had got off so easily.

I don't know what happened—perhaps Mr. Phillips heard of the racket and put in a word—but nothing more was said about it. After that, things went as smoothly as clockwork.

Browning, poor fellow, shortly afterwards was drafted to the *Eurydice*, and went down in her on that fateful day in March 1876.

Certainly the boys were brought up in a hard school, but the instruction was generally good and a high standard was required before a boy passed out. He had to be able to read and write well from dictation, know the first four rules of arithmetic and 'simple and compound proportion, practice, vulgar and decimal fractions'. He had to learn the names of all the parts of a ship and be proficient in squad drill and arms drill. Finally a high standard of seamanship was required that included knowledge of all the bends, hitches and splices used in the Navy, be able to pass an earring and reeve running gear for making plain sail and pull in a boat. The food on board was adequate and generally enjoyed. But afterwards, according to an 1877 pamphlet:

> When the training ship is left, and the pampered boy has really to face the fare provided in sea-going ships 'A change comes over the spirit of his dream' and he at once finds himself deceived and disappointed.
>
> A few years ago the system of training boys might be simply and fitly described as one of cruelty; the most trifling offence met with a severe rope'-ending, whilst anything approaching a crime was certain to bring the offender to the breech of a gun and the cat. Boys just shipped were mustered (often in bitter cold weather) almost naked on the upper deck, their hands blistered with a cane, and they were then ordered over the mast-head; petty officers concerned with their training were armed with a stout cane, and reprimanded if they did not use it freely; but a change became necessary, for the matter had not merely reached the public ear, but had actually become notorious, and parents hesitated to send their children to sea in Her Majesty's Navy. A change was accordingly made, not a modification of the old system, but a revolution from cruelty to pampering. A boy in the present day has no conception of discipline until he is rated ordinary seaman; the utmost latitude is permitted him, punishment is the exception, in order that the books may bear a favourable comparison with those of other training-ships, and so far from the petty officers being ordered to carry and use canes, they are now not allowed (on pain of great displeasure) to even speak harshly; but should a petty officer so far forget himself as to wound the feelings of a boy in the latter particular, he is certain to be reported by the boy and punished by the commanding officer; and in our training-ships instances are of daily occurrence in which a petty officer is publicly reprimanded in the presence of all the boys for some real or imaginary offence. Under this system

(or, no system) the instructor loses all control over those beneath him; the boy reaches the age of eighteen, is rated a man, has forgotten even the mild discipline of going to bed supperless, and sees no reason why additional restraints should be placed upon him, now that he is, in Service parlance, and in his own opinion, a man; the punishment sheet is kept almost a blank, favourable criticisms are made, someone is promoted, and all goes on happily as heretofore; but this cannot last, the discipline of a sea-going ship brings a change, the man begins to feel the screw being put on, his petty officers do not cuff him, but they expect him to do his work, and even this he has not been accustomed to.

Too much credence should not be given to these views of an old seaman from the lower deck but changes had taken place that made the training of the boys softer. These can even be seen from a comparison between the description which Charles Humphreys gave of his training and those given by Tom Holman and Sam Noble.

One particular change was the growing emphasis on academic achievement, but as both Holman and Noble show, life was not particularly soft! Still, the problem of the change from Training Ship to the fleet was a very real one and in this respect, too, the loss of the *Eurydice* and the *Atalanta* was a disaster of the first magnitude.

From the training ships the boys were drafted into Receiving Ships where they remained for several months and often unlearnt what had been taught them, and became 'initiated in the vice of a port, instead of learning their sea duties'. The old seamen may have exaggerated the problem, but it existed and was not solved until a satisfactory training squadron was developed. Even this was only a partial answer.

Holman, though he himself made the 'change' successfully was well aware of the problem. He had the advantage of being a Good Templar, and did not drink. He wrote:

It is at the age of from eighteen to twenty-one that all the dangers of a young man's career in the navy confront him. Recently let loose from the close supervision that used to be, and still is, exercised over boys, and becoming entitled to be rated as a man on the ship's books, together with receiving different treatment from all the men around him, and being allowed his grog, it is seldom indeed that a young man has sufficient ballast on board to steady him in such a sea of excitement . . . If a lad can but tide over his first two or three years of manhood, without getting into serious trouble, his position is comparatively safe.

As a result of his experience Holman was convinced that temperance should be encouraged though as he himself admitted 'I like my grog now as well as most'.

Sam Noble also made the change successfully. Summing up his life in *St. Vincent*, he wrote:

Altogether my days in the St. *Vincent* slid along as happy and full of events as any boy could wish. I was eighteen months aboard of her, and passed out of my classes creditably. The days were employed in instruction in everything that can make a man useful, the evenings in play or study, or writing home. I loved the life, there was a flavour and a tang about it as sweet as the sea itself. It was full of interest, full of adventure, full of possibility, full of change.

The last words on training the boys of the Navy are from Patrick Riley.

In looking back after so many years I feel like the old waterman who first took me on board the *Impregnable*, and told me that he had served his time as a man-of-war's man and would do it again if he were a boy. 'It's a fine life,' he said, 'but hard, sometimes very hard.'

I would go through it again if I were a boy, especially under the present altered conditions of service, with improved diet and a first class boy's pay, which amounts to nearly as much per day as I received when serving as an able seaman and trained man. With all its drawbacks and hardships, it is a good life, and a fine way to see the world, as I have done in nearly every port, helping to keep the flag flying.

13

Sailors of the Seventies—Sam Noble

Your reference to my life at sea awoke many pleasant memories, and I felt a whiff of fine salt air playing again on my forehead. How I liked the Navy! The discipline was always strict, and the life some-times hard, but there was a fascination about it that agreed with me immensely. I remember when I saw the X go on my medical sheet in Melville Hospital, Chatham, which intimated that I was dis-charged from the service as an invalid, I went back to my ward and cried like a child. I did not know what was to become of me—the whole world seemed to be a blank. The life I had hitherto led was free, careless, and (while you did your duty properly) happy. It suited me entirely, for I had found many friends in the service, and had always been treated with consideration and kindness. The officers I had sailed with were, without exception, gentlemen, and the men true, hearty sailors, rough, it may be, on the outside, but true and tender within. What a free-and-easy, happy-go-lucky life it was!—no count, no care, grub and pay-day always sure, and the benefits of a sight of the world without having to pay for it.

So wrote Sam Noble of his career in the Royal Navy, and a very different view he has from that of Tilling or the anonymous seaman who wanted to tell the Admiralty how to run the Navy. Is Noble more typical? It is hard to tell. One significant detail is that he joined in 1875 'when trade was bad'. The Great Depression certainly encouraged recruiting for the Navy and the increase in applicants brought with it a better standard of recruit. Yet Noble was obviously not an outstanding person—indeed he never rose above Able Seaman although he shows this was no hardship to him. He was born at Arbroath in 1859 moving to Dundee while he was still very young. There he received a basic education—at that time probably considerably better than the one he would have received in England—and at fourteen went to work in a jute mill. He was more or less talked into joining the Navy by the local

recruiting sergeant and was sent to H.M.S. *Vincent* where some of his
early career has already been noted.

After he completed his training his first sea-going ship was the
Swallow, where he spent most of his active naval career from 1877 to
1881. He paints a very cheerful picture of life on the lower deck:

> Altogether the lower deck of the *Swallow* was as tidy and cheerful a
> sea parlour as you could have afloat, and when we all got into it at a
> meal hour, say, or when both watches were off in harbour especially
> on Saturdays, which was 'scrub and wash mess-deck' day, and we
> started to sing—then we made the rafters ring. There were seventy
> odd common Jacks in that choir, and every one did his little bit,
> or tried to.
>
> Sometimes an argument would crop up, bringing twenty or
> thirty into it all trumpeting their opinions at the same time. Talk
> about a shindy. It was like W. S. Gilbert's politicians in the street,
> or Burns's scene in the pub at the 'Holy Fair.' Boys weren't allowed
> to take part in these debates. The tradition was that nobody could
> argue or sit on the mess-table till he could show hair on his breast.
>
> Sometimes a quarrel took place, and then you would hear a few
> pithy sentences, fairly well flavoured with salt, regarding one or
> other of the contestant's fathers or mothers or grandmothers.
> (Isn't it queer how men always drag the ancestors of an opponent
> into the argument and sneer them out of all shape and form?) It was
> amusing to listen to them. If the dispute took a bitter turn the
> other fellows usually slipped quietly on deck, if the weather was
> fine, and left the two to worry the bit out between them; if it were
> foul, then they rose in a body, put the foot down and stopped it.
>
> Sometimes there was a real fight: a regular downright bout of
> fisticuffs. This was usually settled on the fo'c'sle, and the captain
> winked at it, believing that the men would be better friends when it
> was over. And he was right. I don't remember any of these scraps
> leaving bad feeling behind them.
>
> But this did not happen often. We were a happy crowd as a rule,
> and rather fond of one another. Really, I don't recall much unpleasant-
> ness on that little ship. And after all, it is only the pleasant things in
> life that ought to be remembered. There is enough dirt about
> without storing it up. That's my philosophy.

Obviously Noble was temperamentally fitted for service in the
Navy but he was also lucky in his ship and particularly in his Captain:

> The Captain, John Borlase Warren, was one of the finest men that
> ever breathed. Strict on duty, but an honest, fair-minded gentleman

for all that. He never punished a man on the day he was taken up before him, but always delayed sentence till the day following, so that he could think the 'crime' over and give the man fair-play. If there was any doubt, the man got full benefit of it.

And he hated toadying—simply loathed it. He dismissed a whole batch of defaulters one day—I was one of them, and mighty glad I was about it—because the bo'sun's mate, who had a man up for some breech of discipline, adopted a wheedling tone and used too many 'yes, sirs' and 'no, sirs' and 'd'ye see, sirs?'

The skipper looked at the P.O. with his lip curling. Then he snatched his cap from his head, dashed it on the deck—a habit he had when irritated—and burst out:

'Silence, sir! How dare you speak to me in that fashion! Go away! Dismiss everything! I'll have nothing of that kind in this ship'—and off he stumped to his cabin, the ship's corporal running after him with his cap.

He was sharp as a needle at an evolution or at drill and saw everything. He had only one eye; the other had been lost in some scrap in the Baltic, I heard, but we used to say he had four; two in front, one at the back, and one at the top of his head. He was quick to notice a flaw in a man, and to point it out to him in a sensible way, and just as quick to see a good point and praise him for it.

Talk about faithfulness to duty! I have known him keep the bridge during a storm that ran its miserable length into weeks; when the galley fire was washed out and life was Desolation itself. Hardly ever going below, but just having a bite brought to him by the steward. At such a time, if you were inclined to grumble or think yourself ill used, a glance at the poop would steady your nerves and set you right in a twinkling.

Certainly very different from Tilling's *Noble Commander*. But a less amiable man than Noble might well have complained especially about the food.

We used to have salt beef ('salt 'oss' we called it) twice a week at sea for dinner. Some of this stuff was so old that nobody could tell its age. On one occasion a cask of beef was actually discovered in our hold, whose mark and tally dated back to Trafalgar! At another time, one of my messmates cut a half model of a frigate out of a piece, sandpapered, varnished, and then glued it to the ship's side above the bread barge. You couldn't have told it from mahogany.

Sam Noble said that its cooking smell was 'the kind of flavour you would expect an Egyptian mummy to give off if it were boiled'. But the major point was that when the men complained, the Captain showed them that he was eating the same food as they were.

The cruise covered 60,000 miles and both sides of the South Atlantic and was everything that Sam Noble hoped. One of their major tasks was to patrol for slave traders off the West African coast. But there were plenty of other incidents. One, off the west coast of Africa, underlines the superiority which the British Blue Jackets felt over any foreigner.

It was in December, and we expected to spend Christmas at sea. One of our fellows, Nobby Clark by name, a quiet methodical sort of chap—a married man, too, by the way—had gone ashore to buy the provisions for all the four messes, but had been drugged by the storekeeper, a vile-looking Portugee, robbed of the money, stripped of his clothing, and then carried inland and left among the rocks. When the search party found him, eighteen hours afterwards, the poor soul was lying unconscious, with froth oozing from his mouth, and almost dead from exposure and the effects of the drug.

That Portugee was brought aboard, pretty nearly flayed alive by the bo'sun's mate, soused in the sea so that the brine would tickle him up a bit more, and then taken ashore and handed over to the authorities.

We heard afterwards that they had hanged the brute. Whether they did or not didn't matter to us, but I'll wager none of that cinder heap of an island ever wanted to interfere with a British bluejacket again.

Among the ports they visited were Kabinda, at the mouth of the Congo, where they called several times, Cape Town, Monte Video, the Falkland Isles and Buenos Ayres. Noble thoroughly enjoyed these visits:

One of the pleasantest features of the cruise that I love to recall now, when sitting by the fireside of an evening, is the entertainments that came off during our long trips at sea—very often in the harbour, too, especially Monte Video, where we had big audiences of ladies and gentlemen to hold forth before.

One of the turns of which he especially approved were those of the author's grandfather.

Mr. Baynham, the Navigating Master, had a humorous turn. Two of his songs I remember well—perhaps because of both the tunes being Scotch!

Life was not always as placid.

One afternoon, Tom Carter, belonging to the 'side-party', was slung over the bows in a bo'sun's chair, giving the ship a touch up, when he lost his balance and fell into the water. Three or four of us were working in the waist washing down. I had just flung over the bucket for another dip (a breech of the side-party's rules that Carter himself would not have been slow to make a noise about, but a providence for him then!) when the skipper, who was walking the poop, cried:

'Waist there! Look after that man.'

We all sprang to the side, and there was Tom's head bobbing in the fast moving current. Dolly Brown, who had hold of the line, pulled up the bucket, jerked it empty and swung it forward to meet Tom, then gradually drew in the slack, saying to us:

'Stand by to hoist him up.'

All of a sudden the skipper cried excitedly: 'Pull, men! Up with him! For God's sake, quick!'

Automatically we fell back on the line and up came Tom's head over the entry port, like a Jack-in-the-box, followed by a splutter in the water alongside. We bundled him in and looked over. There we saw a beauty of a croc. pawing the water, in the attitude of a dog 'begging', with a mouth like a jail door, his jaws working for all the world like a pair of gigantic scissors.

Dolly cried 'Damn your eyes!' and flung the bucket right down his throat, and the brute made off with it, carrying away the lanyard. Then the skipper cried from the brake of the poop:

'Carter! Down on your knees, sir, and thank God for your deliverance. . . . Down with you!'

Never, surely, ascended to heaven from a ship's deck a more fervent expression of gratitude than when poor Carter, in a voice trembling with emotion, ejaculated 'Thank God! Oh! Thank God!'

The Captain came down and congratulated him on his escape—which you will admit was a narrow one—patted his shoulder, and then he told him to go below and shift, and after that to go to his (the captain's) steward, and a glass of grog would be waiting him, and altogether carried through this rather exciting business in a manner that endeared him to the whole ship's company.

Not long after they were ordered home and Noble was very glad to set sail for England. Finally:

We dropped anchor at Spithead, and were inspected by Captain Seymour. Then it was out powder and shot; into dock; dismantle, and—hey for Bonnie Scotland!

All about coming into Pompey Harbour, under steam, and with the long-commission pennant with a gilded balloon at the end of it streaming far behind us; The *St. Vincent*'s band playing us in; the making fast to the buoy—the same buoy we had left from four years ago exactly to the day—the fortnight in the dockyard; the yarns around the galley fire; the high jinks in the town during that fortnight—for your Homeward-bounder in from a long commission is always sure of a warm welcome!—the journey to Dundee—these are memories that will never fade, but would almost need a book for themselves.

I brought home a parrot (in a gorgeous cage which I had bought in London), a Spanish cardinal, two love-birds, a piece of the True Cross (purchased from a lying Maltee in Cape Town), a pair of horns from Uruguay, and some other little knick-knacks.

As the train drew up at Dundee the first face I saw was my mother's. And yet I hardly knew her, she had altered so much and seemed to have grown so small! She was the only soul I knew in all the crowd. I nearly jumped through the carriage window to get hold of her! . . . Ah, these mothers!

At the station gate (the railway landing-stage wasn't the elaborate thing then that it is now), standing by the kerb, a blind fiddler was scraping out 'Home, Sweet Home' on his crazy old fiddle. I put my hand in my pocket meaning to give him tuppence. But happening to look at the coins before I dropped them in his little tin, I saw they were two two-shilling pieces. I hadn't the heart to draw back. I said to myself—

'Ah, well. Poor old chap. If they do you as much good as your wheezy old tune has done me—we're quits!'

Having bundled my belongings to the street, we were surrounded by cabmen yelling for custom. But there was to be no cabs for me that day. I was for marching home in state! So I hung the horns round my neck; swung my bag and ditty-box over my right shoulder, with the other trophies done up in a black silk handkerchief in the crook of my arm; hooked my fingers in the ring of the cage containing the cardinal and the two love-birds, and, my mother having taken the parrot to carry, I tucked her right under my left, and out we set.

It was a glorious June day, and there were lots of people about, and we had 'more spyers than buyers', as the saying is, but a happier pair than my old mother and I would have been hard to find, you may take my word for that!

And so ended half a dozen of the most helpful and happy years a young man could live, and practically finished my career in the

Navy, for within little more than another year I was hurt and—but that's a different story.

He had been drafted to the training ship *Unicorn* in Dundee harbour. Here he fell from the roof between the pier and the ship and received very severe injuries, internal as well as external, and lay several months in hospital. He was granted a small pension, but not enough to live on. He then started a small but successful confectionery and bread shop. Like many other sailors he was a keen Good Templar, and he married in 1888. He was still alive in 1925, although largely confined to a wheel chair.

14

Sailors of the Seventies—Patrick Riley

During the first dinner hour spent in England—visitors being allowed on board—the ship was surrounded with watermen's boats bringing off mothers anxious to see their sons; and wives with their children anxious to see their husbands after being parted for four long years; some of these kiddies never having seen their daddy before.

But it was not such a joyful homecoming for Riley.

It was quite lively on the mess deck with the joy of reunion; I and others who had no one to meet them cleared out as soon as we had had our dinner, and went on deck to look round.

Thus Patrick Riley gives the lie to at least one of the old sailor's complaints—that no one was ever allowed on board at home. Like Sam Noble, Riley held a rosy view of the Royal Navy. He was brought up near Plymouth and was at an early age attracted to ships and the sea. When his father moved from Plymouth to South Wales, Patrick remained with his Aunt so that he could join the Navy, as he said, to see the world. This was in 1872 and he recalls,

In looking back after so many years, the main thing which comes to my mind was the kindness and encouragement I received when joining as a sailor boy.

His experiences on board the *Impregnable* have already been told. After serving on the training ship for over a year he spent a time in the training brig *Squirrel* and then after gunnery training in H.M.S. *Campbell* and another brief spell in the *Impregnable* he joined his first proper sea-going post—H.M.S. *Amethyst*—a square rigged ship carrying fourteen guns—and he was to have his desire to see the world gratified to the full.

They called first at Rio de Janiero, where he had a narrow escape.

A few days after arriving at Rio de Janiero some of the younger officers took it into their head that they would like a swim away from the ship after such a long trip. They had the dinghy called away. I was one of the dinghy boys, so we climbed over the boom and brought the boat alongside the starboard gangway. When the officers arrived, one of them, Lieutenant Reeve, said: 'Can any of you boys swim?' I said, 'Yes, sir, I can.' The other boy said he could swim a little bit. Lieutenant Reeve then told me to get my towel if I wanted a swim. I very quickly nipped in board, down to my locker, got my towel and back in the boat again. Needless to say, I had no bathing costume.

After pushing off, the boat was steered to a spot just outside, and to the left of the island fort, which we had passed coming into the harbour. It lies in a direct line with the entrance and is about three-quarters of a mile inside.

The four officers undressed and jumped overboard, swimming around and having great fun with each other. Rio being in the tropics, the water was nice and warm. I quickly undressed and was over the side as well.

I said to the other dinghy boy, 'Jack, don't forget to give me the tip when you see the officers returning to the boat.' I naturally kept away from them, swimming and paddling on my own.

While enjoying myself, I saw a crowd of Brazilian sailors, dressed very much like our own blue-jackets, standing on a kind of platform, which ran round the fort and above the guns. I supposed they were attracted by the unusual sight—to them—of seeing naval officers swimming about near the fort.

I saw that the officers were enjoying themselves, so very foolishly, I swam closer to the fort, so as to get a better view of the men, not thinking of any danger. I kept on swimming towards the fort until I saw the Brazilians waving me back. I stopped swimming and turned away from the fort, but found myself being carried by the silent, heavy ground swell, which was coming in from the Atlantic, closer to it. I struck out with all my might, but found I was not strong enough, so I turned and swam with the swell, working myself around to the side of the island as far as I could before being caught by the waves and dashed up on the rocks surrounding the fort.

I tried to grab them, but failed to hold on, the receding wave carrying me back again like a piece of cork, but I kept my nerve and presence of mind, endeavouring each time I was carried by the inrushing surf, to hold on. I sometimes came in feet first, at other times I had to put my hands in front of my head for protection. At last I must have been carried between two rocks in a kind of gulley-way, where I was able to hold on and pull myself up clear.

The shouting and gesticulations of the Brazilians attracted the attention of the officers, who at once swam to the dinghy, got on board, and pulled in as close as they could with safety. Seeing that I was safe they told me to go round to the lee side of the island, where they would pick me up.

The Brazilian sailors on the platform about thirty feet above me, were jabbering away in their own language, and were pointing out the way for me to go, but I could hardly walk as some of the sea eggs had penetrated the soles of my feet when I returned 'feet first'.

I saw the dinghy could not come in very close as there was a lot of jagged rocks in her way, so that it was necessary for me to swim out to her. I was very glad when there was sufficient water to do so as my feet were very sore.

After I was dragged into the boat I got a good lecture for being such a confounded young fool, and for going so close to the island. When the officers saw the state I was in, both my thighs bleeding from scratches, some of them deep, which had been cut by the rocks, also the lower part of my body bleeding from the same cause, they took pity on me and cheered me up. The salt water caused the cuts to smart so much that it brought tears to my eyes, for I was only fifteen and a half years old. I still carry the marks of the cuts on my thighs, and I suppose I shall keep them until I cease to draw my pension.

The officers were very kind to me when I got on board, and had me taken to the sick bay, where my cuts were dressed and bandaged up. It was a fortnight before I was right again.

Ashore, things had not changed much from Tilling's time. But the men seemed to cause less trouble.

There were no such places as Institutions or Sailors' Homes at that time; we either had to go for a long walk—which was not attractive in that climate—or spend our leave in a dancing place. Sailors went on shore for a bit of fun and they usually had it.

Very few of the men broke their leave on this occasion nearly all returning on board at the proper time, some of them in a 'semi-sober' state but quite happy! Those who did not return would be hunted up by the police for the sake of the reward which they received for bringing a man on board. They were known as 'vigilantes'; funny looking little chaps they were, with copper coloured faces, rather short, and with long swords hanging down to their heels.

As a man breaking leave lost only a day's pay for every twenty-four hours he was absent, he generally used to give the vigilantes a run for their money.

So much for the old sailor's view that the punishments for leave breaking were too severe! But very shortly afterwards harsher punishments were imposed.

After Montevideo, where they spent Christmas, they went north to Rio, also paying visits to a number of places on the coast including Buenos Aires and Maldonado. At Rio, he was rated a 'man'.

The next day, September 14th., 1875, I passed for Ordinary Seaman, the bo'sun taking me on the fo'c'sle, where I was questioned about the fittings of the spars and sails that had been carried away and was also examined by questions about other parts of the ship. I then had to appear before the Captain to be rated. What a change from the present day! My pay was increased from sevenpence to one shilling and a penny per day. Shortly afterwards I passed for trained man in gunnery, making my pay one shilling and twopence per day. Shall I ever forget the feeling of shyness that came over me when I arrived in my mess for dinner as a 'man'? I had finished with the drudgery of a mess-boy and all that it meant, and in future I would have more time to myself. I was entitled to all the privileges of a Man in Her Majesty's Navy; being allowed to take up one pound of tobacco each month from the purser. I never smoked until I was thirty, so I had no use for it. I was also allowed half a gill of rum each day. I had that! Although rated as a man in the service, my real age at the time was only sixteen years and six months. I was gradually overcoming my handicap of age, and was growing a fine, upstanding youth.

In November they sailed from the east coast of South America and through the Straits of Magellan (where parties of men landed at each anchorage to cut down sufficient wood to eke out their coal supply!) and so into the Pacific and on to Valparaiso where they spent the next Christmas.

They visited Coquimbo and Juan Fernandez, and then took part in the one serious action of the commission.

The ex-President of Peru had persuaded two Lieutenants of the Peruvian Navy to gather a crew for their country's finest fighting ship the *Huascar*—a formidable vessel armed with two ten-inch guns. They then proceeded to stop and search any vessel they came across—including British mail boats—and take off coal and stores, giving in return a receipt chargeable to the Peruvian government. This was indeed piracy, and in company with the flagship, H.M.S. *Shah*, the *Amethyst* set off to capture the Peruvian vessel. They sighted her near the town of Ils at 2 o'clock in the afternoon, and even after a damaging bombardment of three hours the *Amethyst* was unable to board the *Huascar*. In the dark the Peruvian vessel stole away. The following day she was discovered between the lines of the Peruvian fleet. Much to Riley's (and his Captain's) disgust she had surrendered. Riley adds

> Wherever we went ashore, and got into conversation about it, the impression was that the British had lost a certain amount of prestige in failing to capture the *Huascar*.

Yet the *Amethyst* remained a happy ship to the end of her commission. Riley describes their last Christmas at sea:

> The men were pleased when they heard that the Captain and officers intended going around the mess decks to sample the nice things the men had provided for their last Christmas in the *Amethyst*. The Negro Minstrels assembled with their full orchestra, the sweepers in their grotesque get ups, sweeping away old Father Time for the last time before paying off. The day was spent in the usual fashion with the added consolation that the next Christmas would be in England.

Finally their relief arrived but they had one sad task to complete:

> Everyone seemed anxious to be off but we were delayed a day to embark a human cargo, for in these far off days it was customary for a ship returning to England, which had sufficient accommodation, to take on board all court martial prisoners who had been sentenced to long terms of imprisonment to complete their sentence in a naval prison in England; those sentenced to penal servitude were sent to Portland Convict prison on the ship's arrival in England.

There were excitements to come in the straits of Wallington:

> When the ship was brought up with a sudden jerk and a grating sound; the men on their knees were thrown forward on their faces, and the spars and rigging shook like leaves, but nothing came down.
>
> The engines were reversed to full speed astern, but it was no good; we were hung up on an uncharted rock, with our bows well up and the stern low down in the water.
>
> The navigator, having two of the Quartermasters in the dinghy, took soundings all around the ship, and it was found that the ship was aground on a ledge of rocks, but with plenty of water all around. As the Straits at this spot were fairly narrow, two officers went on shore to select a large tree, as near in line with the keel as possible. It was no use trying to kedge her off owing to the depth of the water.

An eleven-inch cable-laid hemp hawser was taken on shore and secured to the tree selected, the inner end brought off to the ship and led over the stern, and the screw purchase used for hoisting the propeller out of the water when under sail, was secured to the inner end of the hawser, which was then brought for'ard to the capstan.

While preparations were being made for getting the ship off, parties of men were detailed to throw overboard the whole of the shells and stores we had taken on board at Valparaiso. It was fortunate we had them to throw and thus enable us to lighten the ship!

As most of the shells were stowed for'ard in the cabin lockers it was a great help, as it would, of course, make the forepart of the ship much more buoyant when they were removed. I was down in the locker for three hours passing those 20-lb. shells over my head until my arms were fit to drop off, but I was young, and soon got over it. Several of our own 64-pounder shells were also dropped over the side; in fact, anything moveable of any weight was thrown overboard to lighten her.

The captain was afraid the ship would break her back, as the after-part of the ship was in deep water, and while we were passing up the shells the captain and first lieutenant were down on the lower deck examining the iron stanchions between decks to see how they were standing the strain. I remember hearing the captain ask the question, 'Where was the ship built, in a Government or private yard?' He seemed satisfied when told the *Amethyst* was built at Devonport Dockyard.

When all surplus shells and stores were thrown overboard, and the purchase fall ready, every man Jack manned the capstan bars—there were no steam' capstans in those days—spinning around the capstan until the purchase fall was taut, and a strain brought on the hawser. The critical moment had arrived: engines reversed, going full speed astern, the men with their chests bearing hard against the bars, legs straight and bare feet pressing on the deck, using every ounce of strength in their bodies. Officers joined in with the men on the swifter, heaving and cheering, as with the heave ho! all together, we felt the ship move. Around flew the capstan to take in the slack of the purchase, as the ship gradually glided into deep water, bringing intense relief to us all; the ship then steamed over to a spot where we could anchor. Bill Jane, our gunnery instructor, was the diver who went down to ascertain the damage. He reported that the fore-foot and keel were torn off as far as ten feet abaft the foremast.

They managed to lash the bows of the ship together with a chain cable, although the pumps had to be manned for an hour every watch to reduce the water level. They reached England safely with the home-coming already described, and Riley was soon able to go away to Ireland.

In time Riley became a gunnery instructor, and he retired from the Navy in 1895. He rejoined briefly during the Great War.

15

Sailors of the Seventies—Thomas Holman

Thomas Holman has left us a graphic description of daily routine on board a ship in the tropics:

We start at 4 a.m. when the stillness is broken by the shrill pipe and hoarse voice of the Bosun's Mate calling all the 'Starboard Watch and Idlers', who have to 'rouse out—rouse out—and lash up', and take their hammocks around the capstan, where the Midshipman of the watch calls out their names in turn. They walk or stumble past the officer of the watch, according to their degree of wakefulness and stow their hammocks in the netting. The 'Watch and Idlers' may then smoke till 4:30, at which time they are, in most ships, piped to scrub and wash the upper deck. The 'Idler's'—a misleading term applied to the mechanics, who are usually the hardest worked men in the ship—man the pumps below, and supply the water, while the sailors proper, with their trousers rolled up to their knees, scrub and wash most thoroughly every plank, and corner of the upper deck. The 'washing down' over, the Idlers come on deck again and assist in drying up the decks, coiling down the ropes and resetting sails, if there are any set.

The sun by this time has appeared above the horizon, and the fresh morning air is most enjoyable. A huge canvas bath is generally got up and filled, in the lee gangway; and at 6:15 the other watch is again turned out, and all hammocks lashed up and stowed. Then the hands are piped to bathe, and those who choose can revel in a salt water bath to their heart's content, except that, as room is limited, one must have a little regard for one's neighbours. At a quarter to seven the hands are piped to breakfast, usually consisting in those latitudes, of cocoa and bread or biscuit, or such other luxury in the way of butter etc., the individual may care to treat himself to. At 7:15 the watch coming on deck for the forenoon dress themselves in white duck clothing, and the watch remaining below starts to scrub the mess deck, and any decks or 'Flats' below, and also clean the steerage. At 7:30 the forenoon watch falls in, and are employed in polishing up all the wood and bright work on the upper deck, and spreading the awnings. At 8:15 the watch below also dress themselves in white, and at 8:30 the bugle calls every one to quarters to 'clean guns'. For this, half-an-hour is usually allowed, and as clean guns and gun gear are usually the ornaments of the ship, and a source of pride to the men, this duty is performed with great zest, each gun's crew trying to excell the others—polishing and burnishing their respective parts up to a high standard of excellency. The operation is usually superintended by the Gunnery Lieutenant and Gunner; the first Lieutenant and Boatswain always seeing the upper deck cleaned in the morning. After 'quarters' the decks are again swept, and the bugler sounds 'division' at which nearly all the officers and men assemble. The men fall in, in rows, and are inspected by the officers of their divisions, and spotless must be their clothing if they wish to escape being found fault with. A ship's company dressed in white and fallen in at divisions on Sunday morning under the awnings, in a soft subdued light in the tropics is a sight worth seeing by any man and is a distinctive feature of a British man-o'-war . . . Divisions inspected, prayers are read by either the Chaplain or Captain, and the men are then dismissed, and a quarter of an hour allowed for coffee. After this the forenoon watch is piped to fall in, and are told off, by the Boatswain and Gunner to perform such work as may be necessary.

The following picture would nearly represent a typical man-o'-war at sea in the latitudes I have mentioned (i.e. the tropics). Plain sail would be set, with studding sails on one side, and the awnings spread as best they could, to shade the men and decks from the sun. The Yards, braced a bit forward on one tack, would require the fore and main sheets to be steadied aft, which would send a pleasant current of soft air in over the lee nettings—circulating throughout the ship, on deck and below—sufficient to keep the bodies of all, except those engaged in violent exercise, at a very comfortable temperature. The sails now fill with wind and belly out to the breeze, and give the ship a fresh impetus through the water, quickening the turns of the little musical waves at her prow, and now flap lazily against the mast, fanning the whole ship with a big current of air as they do so.

Aloft, at the fore topmast head, on the shady side of the mast, would be seated the mast-head man, on the look out for other ships or sails; while seated here and there on the yards or in the rigging on tops, would be seen sailors engaged in repairing such ropes or sails as were in need of it, the motion of the ship rocking them to and fro, and making the soft breezes for their sun brown faces in compensation for an occasional momentary exposure to the sun, which the rocking entails. Down on deck, under the awning, peeping wistfully aloft now and again from some steady spot, would be the officer of the watch, responsible for the time, for the safety of the ship and crew.

At the wheel would be found an Able Seaman to windward, assisted by an ordinary seaman or boy to leeward, keeping the ship to her course, superintended by the Quarter-master and generally the oldest and most trustworthy petty officers in the ship—who would give the compass an occasional rap or two to prevent its getting sluggish, and also, when all was going on correctly, impart a little advice and instruction to the 'lee helmsman'.

Around the upper deck, the sailors of the watch would be employed in splicing ropes, strapping blocks, refitting or mending sails; the ordinary seamen and boys being either at work with the able seamen, assisting at some practical job, or under the tuition of the Bosun's Mate in the lee gangway; where also would be found the sail-maker and his crew, doing the heavier jobs of repair to the sails.

The Boatswain in charge of all this would be strolling from place to place, advising and controlling, and occasionally hailing, from some vantage ground on deck, instructions to the men aloft, regarding the repairs or alterations they are making or instructing the midshipmen on the forecastle. The midshipmen of the watch would be strolling listlessly up and down the weather side of the quarter-deck, preventing any but officers passing aft on that side, and also causing all those who passed about the lee side to salute the quarter-deck, as they stepped by the main-mast on to the holy ground; breaking this monotony by running an occasional message for the officer of the watch, and heaving the log every time the bell struck the hour; also dealing out a little mild abuse, if the mariner or youngster who held the reel were a little slack in responding to the peculiar call of the Bosun's Mate's pipe—which denoted their being wanted.

On the quarter-deck also would be seen a squad of men at rifle or cutlass drill, or exercising with one of the heavy or machine guns under the tuition of the Gunnery Instructor, and the supervision of the Gunner or the Gunnery Lieutenant. Under the forecastle would be found the carpenter's crew, their benches rigged and they at work, superintended by the carpenter; and surrounded by hen coops full of cackling fowls, sheep pens with what occupants they might have (depending largely on the number of days the ship had been from port), and 'harness casks' containing the salt beef and pork, which require to be frequently visited and opened by the ship's steward and butcher. Yet with all these difficulties Chips and his crew are working merrily away, and keeping the ship and boats in sound repair. The First Lieutenant would stroll around the deck occasionally, to see that all the work is going on as it should be, and to consult with the Gunner, Boatswain or Carpenter, on work connected with their departments.

Sitting about on the upper deck forward will also be found the men belonging to the watch below, who would be, for the most part, making their clothes, or some fancy articles for wives, sweethearts, or mothers at home. They are usually seated in couples, the youngster picking up 'wrinkles' from the old sea dogs, either in making a piece of clothes, or in learning some 'seamanship,' in view of their presenting themselves for an examination for the rate of A.B.

Below on the mess deck, the watch below would be similarly employed, perched on mess stool and table, stitching or knitting away with great zeal. The snowy white cap of the ship's cook would occasionally be seen popping up the foremost hatchways covering a perspiring head and face that betokened the warm quarters in which the owner worked. 'Come up for a breath', he would assure you, 'The thermometer in the galley registers 160 degrees'. 'Incredible', you would say; but the ship's cook reasserted it—and that is sufficient. A ship's cook on board a man-o'-war is the fountainhead of truth and information. As you pass the stoke hold hatch you might see the head of a leading stoker up for a breath. You ask him if it is warm below. Through the grating you might see the stokers cleaning up the engines and boilers under the superintendence of the Engineer. 'Hot below?' you say again. 'Not very, quite a nice breeze today'. You tell him what the ship's cook says about the galley. 'Well, I wouldn't have believed it' he declares, 'if it had not come from such an authority.' Chortles, and darts off down below to give the latest from the ship's cook. Passing on to the quarter-deck you might perhaps meet the Paymaster and Doctor, both come up from below to enjoy a ten minutes blow on deck. You repeat the ship's cook's story. 'Well, I never,' they say, 'but the authority is unimpeachable'. And that night it is told at dinner in the wardroom. Small things assume big proportions in the isolation of a long sea voyage, and the smallest jokes are acceptable. At seven bells this calm peace ceases, and noise and bustle begins. All the jobs are put away, the Bosun's Mates' pipes 'Clear up decks', and the watch on deck are busy in seeing the ropes clear and everything ready for shortening sail during the dinner hour, should necessity arise. Below there is a clatter of plates and dishes, and a savoury smell comes up the fore hatch which informs us that the 'Solomon' of the lower deck has taken the cover from the copper containing the pea soup. Everybody seems to have suddenly woke up; the corporals are shouting out the names of John Smart, Arthur Silence, William Wideawake, and Tom Hopeful, who are to appear on the lee side of the quarter-deck, to go before the First Lieutenant. They are found at last and fall in; the 'Master-at-arms' reports the fact to the First Lieutenant, who appears, telescope in hand, to investigate the charges brought against them. John Smart comes first; reported by the captain of the fore-top for being late in falling in after coffee yesterday.

'What is this, Smart?' says the First Lieutenant.

'Please sir, I was as quick as I could.'

'But all the rest fell in at the pipe, why not you?'

'Cause sir, I was trying to cadge a drop of milk from the cook's mate, as owes me ten bob, for my coffee.'

'This is the third time Smart, for the same offence; that yarn won't do. Let him stand on the lee side of the quarter-deck tonight for two hours, in the first watch.'

Next man—Arthur Silence; the gunner's mate reports him for talking at drill.

'What excuse for this, Silence?' asks the First Lieutenant.

'Well sir,' says he, 'a marine trod on my toe with his boots on, and I swore at him.'

'Can't allow swearing anyhow,' says the First Lieutenant. 'Damme what next, I wonder! three days, ten black list, Master-at-arms.'

Next comes William Wideawake; reported by the officer of the watch for being asleep while on the look out last night, in the middle watch.

'Very serious charge, Wideawake.'

'Yes sir, but I wasn't asleep sir! I went on the look out, sir and just closed one eye, sir, to try and see if there were any lights about sir, when the midshipman of the watch pushed me, and said I was asleep, sir.'

The midshipman of the watch and the Bosun's Mate both testified to the fact that Wideawake was sitting down, and snoring so loud that they could hear him on the other side of the forecastle. Moreover, a lantern had been held to his face and a large block dropped on the deck beside him without the slightest effect. It was the first offence, and William Wideawake was sent away with seven days black list; protesting that he had only shut one eye to look around. Tom Hopeful then appears.

'Well, Hopeful, you here again? I'm afraid you are going to the bad! What is it this time, Master-at-arms?'

'Drunk on the lower deck yesterday afternoon, sir, and swearing at me.'

'Hm! I must report you to the captain, Hopeful.'

The man is marched to the other side of the deck; the Captain is acquainted with the case, and presently appears followed by his clerk, carrying the Queen's Regulations and Minor Punishment Book, together with the man's parchment certificate, showing his former services and character. The Master-at-arms again states the case.

'Anything to say, Hopeful?' asks the Captain.

'Yes, sir, I wasn't drunk.'

'Can you prove it?'

'Yes, sir.'

'Where are your witnesses?'

'Haven't got any sir, but I know I wasn't drunk 'cause when I woke up, I was lying on the mess stool, sir, and when I am drunk I always rolls off, under the table.'

The Captain cannot consider this conclusive evidence, and having regard to former offences, sentences Hopeful to ten days cells on board, stops his grog for a month and also promises him imprisonment the next time he appears for a similar crime. Hopeful is moved below, by the ship's police, a prisoner.

By this time it is nearly 12 o'clock, and the Navigator is to be seen on the bridge, sextant in hand, taking the sun's altitude; presently he stops, reads off, makes a brief calculation, and speaks to the officer of the watch; this officer immediately approaches the Captain, salutes and reports:–

'Twelve o'clock sir, please, lat.—degrees—minutes north.'

'Thank you, make it so,' says the Captain.

The officer holds up his hand, the sentry strikes 8 bells, and the Bosun's Mates make the ship ring with their pipes—piping the hands to dinner. The Quarter-master, Helmsman, Mast-head man, and the Boatswain's Mate are all relieved by men of the after noon watch who have already had their dinners. Spitoons are placed, and smoking commences. At 12:30 grog is issued by the Ship's Steward, a Petty officer, and Sergeant of Marines as officer attending. Each man is allowed half a gill of spirit, mixed with a whole gill of water; this is called two water grog, and is, as I have said, the fruitful source of many evils. The officers of the forenoon watch is also relieved at one bell. At one o'clock the bugle sounds 'Clean Arms,' and the men clean their rifles, swords, and pistols, and return them to their

Training a gun. 12th April, 1873.

Dinner in the lower battery.

Morning Service in H.M.S. *Caesar*. 14th July, 1855.

Hands to dance and skylark. 1st June, 1889.

proper places at 1:15 when the watch on deck is piped to 'fall in', and the 'watch below' goes below.

The afternoon's routine resembles that of the forenoon, except that the majority of the 'watch below' go to sleep instead of sewing. At 4 p.m. the watches are again changed, the watch from 'below' coming up in blue clothing. At 4:30 the Bosun's Mates' pipes 'Tea' and all the remainder change their white for blue clothing. At 5 the bugle sounds to 'evening quarters'. The guns are seen secure for the night, the men inspected, and a half or whole hour's smart drill aloft usually follows. After that the watch is again called, and both watches allowed to smoke and employ themselves as they choose. On two evenings of the week, water is served out, and the men wash their clothes, hanging them in the rigging to dry. Once a month hammocks are changed and the dirty ones scrubbed. When the sun gets below the horizon, a very short twilight intervenes, and the lights are lit and put in their places, look outs placed, and night begins. Between 7 and 8 o'clock the men usually have some supper but this meal is not recognised by the Admiralty; and unless something remains from dinner, the men have to provide it at their own expense, from the canteen, sometimes at enormous prices—a thing that needs looking into and requires speedy redress.

At eight o'clock the first watch goes on deck, musters around the Capstan, and remains till midnight. The look out over, the helmsmen are taken from the A.B.'s and ordinary seamen, each going on in turn. At midnight, the other watch comes on deck, musters around the Capstan, takes over the duties of helmsman etc., and remains until 4 a.m. when the first watch men are again turned up. Thus ends 24 hours in a man-o'-war at sea. Such a day's duty closely resembles the duties in more northern or southern latitudes, though the work would be somewhat harder owing to frequent storms etc.

Thomas Holman's early days in H.M.S. *St. Vincent* have already been described. From a very early age he had been bent on joining the Navy in spite of the objections of his mother who tried hard to dissuade him with terrible stories of disasters at sea and shipwrecked sailors, which not surprisingly only encouraged him further. At the age of eleven he ran away to Portsmouth, a distance of some sixty miles, and endeavoured to join the Navy though 'Her Majesty was not in want of such giants to man her fleet just then, as the Russian war was concluded'.

Shortly after though, he got his first chance of going to sea as a Cabin Boy in a local gentleman's yacht, and though he was thrown out of his bunk and though the owner tried to talk him out of it, he remained insistent on wishing to join the Navy. Eventually his parents gave way and with a certificate of character from the clergyman—'The only real badge of respectability in those days'—he went to Portsmouth and said goodbye to the yacht owner and his wife. The owner, an acquaintance of the Captain of the *St. Vincent*, gave Holman a good start, which he did not waste.

From the *St. Vincent*, Holman went out to join the North American and West Indian squadron but was in six ships in as many months. However, he was finally drafted to a large sloop and was taught a great deal by a Negro from Barbados who took great delight in instructing him.

One of Holman's most pleasant achievements was becoming bowman in the Captain's boat.

This brought me many enjoyable little trips in the way of picnics and excursions on water and land and gave me many chances of accompanying officers' shooting parties up the lagoons in central America after alligators, or on shore hunting.

Sometimes the excitement came a little too close as on the occasion when he was hit in the neck by a bullet watching a rebellion in 'one of those republics'. However he enjoyed the life so much that when the time came for the sloop to return to England, he volunteered to stay out on the station and joined a smaller ship, in which he was made captain of the foremast cross trees, and, again, bowman of the Captain's boat.

Previously he had been a Good Templer and when rated a first class ordinary seaman and allowed grog and tobacco, at first he did not take up the former though he adds 'I like my grog now as well as most'. Unhappily it landed him, like many others, in trouble.

One of Holman's tasks as bowman of the Captain's boat was to carry the Captain 'pig a back' through the surf when they landed on a harbourless shore. On this occasion the ship's officers and men were playing a cricket match against the Europeans of one of the smaller islands. Holman brought the Captain ashore and during the game the Captain offered him three brandy and sodas. On the way back Holman was unsteady on his pins.

'What the deuce is the matter with you?' asked the Captain.
'Nothing, sir, nothing,' I said as plainly and steadily as I could.
'Trod on a pebble sir, that's all.'
'Pebble be hanged, sir,' said he. 'Look out; what *are* you about?'
'Nothing, sir, nothing; another pebble.'
'Pebble, sir, you're drunk, sir. Turn back; go back this instant.'
It was too late, I had advanced too far; a wave broke at my knees,

then gave way, and staggering two or three paces to the front, and leaning well forward, I fell; and in falling plunged my rider head first into an incoming roll of surf that broke over both of us in the fullest and most complete manner possible. I next remember being grabbed by a pair of strong hands and hearing in the distance, shouts of 'Bring him here, coxswain, bring him here; he tried to drown his captain. I'll flog him, I'll flog him.' I was taken on board in the bottom of the boat between the thwarts, and on arriving alongside, ordered to be placed in irons.

After the Captain had changed into dry clothes, and had his dinner and wine, I was released, put in my hammock, and a messmate placed to look after me until I went to sleep. The next day I was had up, severely wigged, and suspended from the Captain's boat for a week in lieu of receiving four dozen with the cat.

The Captain's language certainly showed how hard the idea of flogging died. In 1874, strictly, the Captain had no right to inflict corporal punishment for bad conduct on men in the first class such as Holman. Holman was later reinstated in the Captain's good graces, but he never again accepted liquor on trips ashore.

The ship soon received orders for England and Holman was now anxious to return home. His aim was to transfer to H.M.S. *Excellent* but for this he had to pass as a leading seaman. He put his name forward to the First Lieutenant. His examination consisted of one question:

When we are stripping this ship, if you should be by any means the last man at our main mast head, and the last rope was to slip through your fingers so that you could not use it to get down, tell me, what would you do?

The answer Holman had learned from the Barbarian negro:

Take off my stocking, unravel it, and let the end of the wool go slowly down to the deck, where they would fasten on a piece of twine, whose weight would not break it, for me to pull up, and when the twine came to hand, something larger would be fastened at the bottom, and so on, until I got a rope sufficiently large to lower myself down.

He was passed for leading seaman and the First Lieutenant said he would be glad to have him in any future ship in which he served. He also put him up as a candidate for the gunnery ship.

When his ship reached England, Holman went home on leave and was reunited with his family. He had managed to save £40 some of which he gave to his mother. Not a fortune after seven years, but he was very content with his lot.

I had been absent between six and seven years, and many of my companions had, of course, gone out into the world to earn their own living. Some were doing better than I, some worse, but I felt confident no one among them was so happy or more thoroughly in love with his own profession, nor had they the same stock of stories about lions, sharks, elephants, and sea serpents.

After six weeks he returned to Portsmouth and started on a course of gunnery instruction in H.M.S. *Excellent*.

I class the twelve months I spent in the *Excellent* as among the happiest of my life; the days were only just half long enough to squeeze all the good things into. True, we were at instructions all day long, but then it was being instructed among so many young men of my own age and temperament that made it so delightful; always a keen competition among us to be first at our drills and always a keen competition also as to whom could play the biggest joke.

While in the *Excellent* one very unfortunate incident occurred to Holman. At the Officers' Annual Dance, the ship and its boats were spread with canvas and during the dance the wind blew some of the canvas adrift. Holman went aloft to secure it, but while descending, he slipped into the awning. There was no hand hold on the canvas and he slowly slipped down, quite unable to stop himself and finally 'Calling for mercy, I slipped over the edge and went whistling through the air'. He fell forty feet on to a boat below, but fortunately the boat's awning broke his fall, and though he was knocked unconscious, he suffered no other injuries.

At the end of the course he was passed a Seaman Gunner and promoted to Leading Seaman—then he proudly adds: 'I had in twelve months increased my pay by three shillings and sixpence a week.'

From the *Excellent* he was sent to assist in teaching the Royal Naval Reserve at the Lerwick Battery in the Shetland Isles which he thoroughly enjoyed though he found it cold. However,

There was plenty of skating and lots of exercise and good food. I rapidly improved in health which since my return to England had been somewhat shaky.

He remained there five months, and on returning to the *Excellent* he was fortunate enough to be selected to join H.M.S. *Bacchante* which was to take the two sons of the Prince of Wales (later Edward VII) on a cruise round the world—the two sons were, of course, their Royal Highnesses Princes Edward and George. There is no point recounting the full cruise in detail. They visited the West Indies, South America, the Falkland Isles, South Africa (where they just missed the battle of Majuba Hill), Australia, China, Singapore, Ceylon, and then back through the Suez Canal and the Mediterannean and so home.

When the Prince came on board.

Their racy voices caused many of the old tars to shake their heads and say, 'Prince or no prince their jawing tackles would have to be choked afore they sailed far in that hooker anyhow.' But this was not so, for as a matter of fact they were soon the most popular middies on board.

On one occasion Holman dropped a jemmy on to the deck from aloft after the rope securing it had given way. It might have hit Prince Edward who was near by, but fortunately it missed everyone. Holman was only lightly punished because he immediately owned up.

His greatest achievement in the voyage was passing the selection board for Gunner's warrant. When finally they returned to England he therefore joined *Excellent*, and after a twelve months' course passed 'on top of the roster' aged twenty-six after eleven years of service. He was promoted by warrant to the position of Gunner and appointed to a gunboat in the East India station.

The remainder of his career lies outside the scope of this book. Despite his earlier strictures on the service for the barriers against promotion from the lower deck to commissioned rank, Holman himself was promoted in December 1906 to the rank of Lieutenant. This firmly underlines the changes that had taken place in the Navy.

16

The Slave Trade

One of the greatest tasks and achievements of the Royal Navy in the nineteenth century was the suppression of the slave trade. From the West African trade alone, 150,000 slaves were liberated between 1810 and 1864, yet this represents only a fraction of the total. At its height in the 1830s, in spite of the fact that the United States had officially prohibited the entry of slaves, it has been estimated that over 100,000 slaves were carried each year across the Atlantic—the infamous 'Middle Passage'. The Royal Navy's success in suppressing the trade would have been less than complete without the support of other countries. But endless jealousies and diplomatic bickerings accompanied this war of attrition and even when diplomatic support had been obtained, it could not always be enforced. The mixed commissions set up to try slavers proved less than effective and for a long time the United States, among others, refused to allow the Royal Navy even to search American merchant ships for slaves.

All too often national pride appeared more important to an offended power than the lives of the human cargoes their ships carried. The Navy had to tread a complicated path among the multifarious regulations and agreements drawn up by various countries which sometimes meant that once across some parallel of latitude the offending slaver could go free. Even when a slaver had been captured and brought to justice, the courts, and especially the mixed commissions, could delay a case until the naval officer concerned could no longer be present and the case would then go by default. At times, too, the Navy got less than full support from parliamentary and diplomatic circles at home. On more than one occasion the commanding officer of a naval vessel engaged in hunting down the slavers was fined heavily by one of the mixed commissions for an error in administrating one of the highly complex regulations, and the naval officer concerned had to meet the costs himself with no redress. In fact it was not until America abolished slavery that a final conclusion to the struggle really became possible. With the closure of the American market after Lincoln's decree abolishing slavery in 1863, the major market of Cuba was forced to cease business and the task became largely a 'mopping up' operation.

For the officers and men of the Navy it was throughout a thoroughly disagreeable and dangerous duty. In the worst year, 1829, over a quarter of the men in the West African Squadron died from disease. This compares with an average of less than one per cent on the home station and less than two per cent on the other most unhealthy region, the West Indies where so many of William Richardson's shipmates died. There was also the monotony of the task, which probably accounts for the absence of memoirs. There was little chance of any pleasure ashore and even the coastline itself appeared from the sea to be a featureless, unbroken line. The occasional chase and capture was little enough compensation.

The slave trade continued for some years after the American Civil War, and the one really detailed lower deck account of a slave chase in fact comes from the 1870s. The action itself was similar to the thousands of chases that had occurred before, and the description brings out clearly many of the problems that faced the naval vessels throughout the period. Like a huntsman waiting for a fox to break cover, the Navy frequently was not allowed to attack the slavers in African ports but could only capture them in mid-ocean. Even if a slaver were caught, some international agreement or some set of phony papers could protect him from capture. The difference between this chase and those that occurred forty years previously was that the naval vessel was equipped with steam. Here it proved decisive, as Sam Noble's record shows:

We were heading for St. Paul de Loanda at the time, and Mr. Hopkins, the British Consul, was aboard. In the afternoon we sighted a brig which looked so suspicious that the captain determined to watch her. She was making for the land.

The news went through the ship that she was a slaver, and certainly when she came nearer she had all the appearance of one. A long, sinister-looking craft, with tall, tapering masts, raked aft, and covered with canvas. The telescope revealed crowds of black people aboard her.

We got steam up, took in sail, altered our rig by housing topmasts, shortening jibboom and such like manoeuvres, and passed her flying the American colours. She was a Portuguese brig, named the *Pensamento*. Her deck was full of black, woolly heads, which bobbed over the rail from every part of her.

We went by, taking no notice beyond the usual dip of the flag, then slipped into a little cove where the land was a trifle lower than our mastheads, rigged up a crow's nest on the main-royal mast, and there we lay, with a man on the lookout day and night, watching her. Two nights she kept us there in a fever of impatience; then on the evening of the third day, just after sunset, the lookout man reported her out under full sail.

Then the fun began! Down came the crow's nest, up went the sail—stun'sails, stay sails, trysails—everything that could draw, and off we went after her what we could pelt.

A fine spanking breeze from the land sent us along in grand style. At first we couldn't see the brig, but when the moon gained her splendour and turned the sea into a glory of molten silver, *then* we saw her—although not so much her in reality as the black velvety shadow she threw on the glittering surface over which she went like an ominous bird.

My word, couldn't she sail! Bending over so that sometimes we could have seen her bilge-boards had we been nearer, she simply flew over the water. Her people had seen us, knew that we were after them; guessed, I daresay, our stratagem of three days ago; and the Portugee skipper, knowing the qualities of the little vessel under him, and confident of out-sailing us before morning, determined to pull us after him—gave us a nice little outing, in fact, and himself the joy of beating a 'Johnny Anglesh, damn him!' and tell his cronies all about it when he got into port.

Well, sport is dear to the British heart, and as it was a fine night we had no objections. But, I tell you, the excitement aboard our hooker was something to keep the blood warm. Our fellows danced about the deck rubbing their hands and chuckling 'Go it old bird! After her! Fetch her in, little girl!'

But it was soon seen, that the *Swallow* was no match for the *Pensamento*—not in that wind, anyway. She easily went one and a half knots to our one. She bounded over the silver wavelets like a thing of life, clothing herself in glittering sparks from her forefoot, like the girls in the African village with their fireflies, leaving a wake behind her like the steam of a railway train; and seeming to laugh at our efforts to catch up with her.

We admired that little brig. Admired, too, the fine sailorly way she was handled, but we meant to have her all the same, ay, if we sailed to hell after her to do it.

Steam was up, the push of the screws was added to the sails, and now the little *Swallow*'s heart began to beat in earnest. We looked over the side to see the effect, but there wasn't much difference; she seemed to be almost doing her utmost under the pressure of canvas. But she dipped her beak in the wave, bent over to the race, flicking the spray as high as the fore-yard, and sending her wake boiling away astern like the wash of a river over rocks, and behaving as lively as her nimble namesake.

But it was no use. The brig gradually edged away.

A shot from the 7-inch gun was sent after her. Her skipper answered this by setting his stun'sails. Another, a little nearer this time. A loud shout of laughter, which went from the fo'c'sle to the poop, where the officers were all gathered watching the brig with their glasses, followed this second messenger.

We could still make out objects on the brig, and distinctly saw her skipper jump on to the taffrail, his figure twinkling under the glowing moon like a mannikin, smack his breech energetically and twiddle his fingers at us in contempt, twisting himself side-on to let us see him do it.

'By God, he's a plucky one!' somebody bawled. 'But we'll have you yet, you ruddy old pirate!'

Another laugh greeted this prophecy, and with a note of derision in it, however, for on the face of it it looked silly to hope for anything of the kind. And yet it worked out all right as events turned, proving the truth of Scott's remark about the shaft at ramdom sent.

Meantime, the additional thrust of her stun'sails put more life into the brig than ever, and she began to leave us hand over fist— melt away, in fact, before our eyes—till by and by all we could make out was a glittering pin-point on the horizon.

We thought we had lost her, and were cursing our rotten luck and calling the ship bad names, when suddenly the wind lulled and hope revived. Feverishly we took in the stun'sails, trimmed the yards to catch every breath—for it had changed a little—and after her we flew, saying our prayers again like true sailors.

The way we lifted the brig now showed that she had hardly any wind at all. We overhauled her as an express does a goods train. Soon she began to show up; then to take shape; then we could distinguish her individual sails; then out popped her black hull, and she laid broad to view just as we had seen her at first.

Our fellows went dancing mad about the t'-gallant fo'c'sle, shaking hands and telling each other about the prize-money that would line our handkerchiefs by and by, crying 'Good little girlie!' 'Pretty little swallow-tail!' 'Catch her, pussy; there's a mouse ahead, dear!' and Buntin, whose watch below it was, began to carol:

'When the swallows homeward fly.'

Oh, we were the happy crowd!

Aft on the poop the officers were just as excited as ourselves, although, of course, they wouldn't show it. They never do, these people. Their dignity won't allow them. They stand as glum as undertakers, even on the most whirling occasions, and yet they must have their happy moments like the rest of us.

Our boys aft tried to make believe they took this business all in the day's work. But their manners betrayed them. The way they fussed with their glasses, clapt them to their eyes, took them away again, and fidgeted about the deck, showed that the blood was running as warm aft as it was forward. Routh, I'm sure, would be boiling. He was a rare sport. The captain, with his cap 'on three hairs', as they say at sea, meaning stuck right on the back of his head (a sure sign that he was pleased), was standing beside Mr. Hopkins, sending his glances everywhere at once—at the sky, the sails, the brig ahead, the smoke pouring from the funnel—everywhere at the same time, and all the time as dignified as a bishop. Mr. Hopkins himself, a terribly grave gentleman on duty, though an irresistible comic when off, stood on the poop as straight as a pole, with his hands behind his back, and his fingers twitching as if he would give the world to have them at somebody's throat. And the gleam of the chase in their eyes they couldn't hide, not they! Westwater, who was signalman on duty at the time, told me afterwards that he would gladly have forfeited his grog for a whole week just for the privilege of letting out one yell. That'll tell you how things were aft.

All this time the moon was flooding the sea with silver light. Soon we came up to within a mile of the brig, and then we saw three hang-dog, miserable-looking figures standing aft by the helm. The skipper himself—a proper-looking sea-jackal he!—stumping athwart-ships in front of them like a pendulum.

The first cutter was ordered away, and as this was the boat I belonged to, I was in her waiting to be lowered. She hung on the starboard quarter, and as the brig was to starboard of us, I had a good view of the proceedings.

Everything was ready: the crew lined up in the gangway; Mr. Hopkins, in his ordinary wearing clothes, the first lieutenant and the paymaster, the former wearing his sword-belt, standing by to go with us when—hanged if the wind didn't freshen again and off went the brig!

You should have seen the stampede aboard of that little hooker! Her people sprang into life as if somebody had set fire to them. Up went the stun'sails, which had been taken in. A sharp shower came on, just heavy enough to soak the sails and give them a better draw— as if to help her, you would have thought!—and away she went like a racehorse.

It was like snatching a bone from a dog! If you had heard the remarks on the *Swallow*, you would have thought sailors a rum lot—which they are, really.

However, it was only an expiring puff. It didn't carry us more than two miles, although the brig did about four, when it dropped altogether and went dead calm.

Then the hallelujahs started again!

'Hands furl sail!' 'Down, gallant yards!' 'Loose fore and main trysails!' etc.

In half an hour we were lying within a couple of cable lengths of her, on a sea like a lady's mirror, just dimmed occasionally by the clouds crossing the moon, as her breathing does when she brings the glass too close. In five minutes more the boat was in the water, and, with the three officers in the stern, was making towards her in fine style.

We smelt the brig as we came nearer. By the time the bowman got hooked on alongside we felt almost suffocated. What a stench! The paymaster, who was a delicate-looking young gentleman, had his handkerchief to his nose as he crossed the gangway, and whenever the three left the boat we dropped astern a bit to get away from it. One of the fellows remarked: 'It'll take a lot of prize-money beer to wash this down, hearties.' I never came across a smell like yon in all my life.

The Portuguese captain, a swarthy, beetle-browed ruffian, with two other yellow-faced beauties—his mates, I daresay—was waiting for us, and there were a good few more lowering heads sprinkled along the port bulwarks. As our officers stepped aboard we heard the skipper say in a gruff voice: 'Vell, vat you vant? Vat you mean by intervereing mit mee? Firing shotts at mee—on de high seeass! By Gott, you catch it for dis!'

Then we dropped out of ear shot. There seemed to be any quantity of blacks aboard, judging from the woolly heads that kept popping up and disappearing from every quarter. Big heads, little heads, some of them belonging to girls by the look of them, some to mere children, all black as soot and staring at us with big, wistful eyes.

The officers were gone only about a quarter of an hour when back came Billy and beckoned us alongside again. As they got into the boat we saw by the grinning faces of the Portugee and his mates that all our hopes of prize-money had gone by the board.

Mr. Richmond, the paymaster, with his handkerchief still at his nose, implored us to put our backs into the oars; to get away from that floating cesspool as quick as ever we could. But he needn't have minded; we were just as eager to get away as he was. The three officers conversed together while we rowed back, but all I heard (for I was pulling second bow), was part of a remark by Mr. Hopkins about 'caution being very necessary in affairs of that kind'.

However, when we got the boat hoisted, and dropped aboard again, the ship's head was turned towards St. Paul de Loanda, and the brig left a good couple of miles astern.

Then we heard the result. It seemed that although there were over 700 negroes—men, women and children—on board that brig, we couldn't touch her skipper because he had papers certifying every one of them to be labourers going to South America to be employed in the rice and cotton fields. Not a manacle or an iron was aboard her—I believe they got rid of these things during the last lap of the chase. She was a slaver all right only the brutes that commanded her were too cute to let themselves be caught.

Anyway they got clear. It was a terrible disappointment to us; it took the splicing of the mainbrace and a sing-song under the glorious moon to cheer the way back to port and make up for it.

This incident occurred towards the end of a tragic and bitter progress. Fortunately only a few slavers continued to run the gauntlet to the still open ports of South America. The 'Anti-slavery' Squadron itself had been disbanded and vessels no longer spent a whole commission of three, four, or even five years off the fever ridden coasts of West Africa. The *Swallow* spent merely a short part of her commission there, visiting in addition Montevideo, Cape Town and the Falkland Isles among other places.

But it was not only across the Atlantic that this human traffic was carried. A longer standing and just as terrible trade carried slaves from the East African coast to various countries of the Middle East. At Zanzibar alone an average of over 20,000 slaves were imported annually before 1875, mostly for re-export to all parts of the Middle East and India, and these figures do not include the thousands who must have died on the way to the coast or on the passage from the African mainland. As Christopher Lloyd has written: 'If the European trade transported six million negroes in three centuries, who knows what numbers must have gone east during eighteen centuries of Arab rule?' The Zanzibar trade was a well-organised business that does not seem to have altered much down the centuries. On their way to the coast the slaves were either roped together or had their necks wedged into forked sticks. If any fell ill on the way, they were shot and left to die by the side of the path. The crossing to Zanzibar though briefer was probably almost as frightful as the 'Middle Passage'. As the journey normally took only twenty-four hours, the slaves were fed before they embarked and no food was carried on board. If the dhow was becalmed or otherwise delayed, the slaves would die of starvation or suffocation.

Those who survived were marketed in Zanzibar and sold either directly to merchants from the Middle East or even the East Indies or more generally to intermediaries who would transport them to various centres—for example Bahrein—and there sell them to suitable clients. The trade itself was quite as illegal as the West African one but the problem of suppression was, if anything, even more complex, and it was not until the 1860s that any real progress was made.

As in the West African trade, diplomatic problems were a major stumbling block. In particular the Portuguese refused to limit the slaving activities of their nationals (it was of course a Portuguese ship which the *Swallow* attempted to capture) and Portuguese interests in the Indian Ocean were greater than those in the Atlantic. Relations between England and Portugal were traditionally very close. In addition the French badly needed labour in the Pacific colonies and allowed a free labour emigration system to deteriorate all too often into a Slave Trade. Though Napoleon III agreed to end this in 1861, smuggling continued.

A problem which the Admiralty or more truly the government could have solved was that the Arab dhows which were used to transport the slaves were generally faster than the naval brigs sent to capture them, at least until the coming of steam. The dhows also had a very shallow draft and they could often escape along the coast.

Thomas Holman strongly disliked this penny-pinching policy.

> If England continues to do this (i.e. attempt to suppress the slave trade) she should not be afraid to spend a thousand pounds a year to do it well, and give, by a better arrangement, her brave sailors the maximum amount of protection and comfort and the minimum amount of danger and exposure—in the shape of faster boats better armed. The increased cost would be largely met by the decrease in the expenses of the many men now invalided.

Holman's estimate of the cost may have been rather on the conservative side but the principle involved was unquestionably true. Holman spent most of his time in the anti-slavery squadron cruising in the Persian Gulf, whither many of the slaves from Zanzibar were taken. Here is his description of an anti-slavery patrol.

> A fleet cruising in the suppression of this trade usually does so in the following way: each ship is assigned a few hundred miles of coast-line up and down which she constantly cruises, dropping boats at

all the principle sheltering places or anchorages. These boats establish depots at these places, and from them patrol a certain amount of coast on either side, usually meeting the boats stationed at the depots above and below them. In this way 700 or 800 miles of coastline can be fairly well looked after; the boats forming a continuous line of inshore patrols, while the ships steam leisurely to and fro in the offing.

The ships suckle their boats' crews in turn, i.e. supply them with food and water, the latter being in some cases extremely scarce and not infrequently got at much hazard or danger—in extreme cases fighting with the coast Arabs, who are of course the bitter enemies of boats' crews lying in wait for the incoming slavers, so much desired by these lazy gentlemen. The Parent is sometimes absent longer than is expected, and the boats' crews get on short commons. The life lived in boats on this duty is exceedingly hard and the amount of exposure extremely trying. It is nothing but the characteristic good temper under all circumstances that brings so many of our Tars successfully through the trying ordeal of six months of this service, where they are exposed to the sun all day, to the dew all night, and to discomfort and danger continuously.

Imagine a thirty-foot whale boat with four men, an officer and interpreter, and a week's provisions, leaving the ship for detached duty, and remaining absent for a month or six weeks on a wild coast during the south-west monsoons. The vessel is never steady, food has to be cooked and eaten under the most difficult circumstances, and the quick motion of the boat at night renders lengthened sleep impossible. The constant chafing of men's bodies against some projection or corner, impossible of escape in so small a compass, renders constant changes of posture necessary to the keeping whole of men's skin.

The danger also of cruising in so small a boat touches the maximum. The instructions direct the boats to cruise in pairs, so that one may lie off while the other boards the dhows. Thus, should the crew of the slaver overwhelm, or by some device sink, the boat alongside, there is still the other to reckon with. But in busy water, this plan is next to impracticable, except by letting at least half of the vessels pass your boats without being overhauled at all; for they generally come in twos and threes, and with any breeze at all, two would escape while one was being searched.

This the British sailor would not allow. No matter what dangers the disobedience of such restrictions may entail, he will most certainly break through them and send a small boat to overhaul one of the escaping dhows. This leads to the danger that the smaller boats might be allowed to get alongside, and, on a part of the crew going in board to search, one of the large stones, which are carried for ballast in these vessels, let drop from their gunwale would inevitably find its way through the bottom of the searchers' boat, and place the entire crew at the mercy of the slavers. It will thus be seen how hazardous is the present method of slave cruising.

Charles Humphreys has left a more personal record of an anti-slavery patrol in the Persian Gulf. He was at the time he describes a boy seaman in the *Vulture* a small gun vessel which is illustrated opposite page (137). He was fifteen years old.

One morning about dawn, we saw a large sail in the opening, so we furled our awning, weighed our anchor, and pulled out to the fishing fleet. They knew what we were after, so they got away from us and tried to make signals to the dhow, which had been making for the shore.

Our officer told the interpreter to warn the fishermen that if they did not stop making signals they would be fired on.

When we got clear of the fishing boats, the crew of the dhow saw that something was wrong, but did not know we were men-o'-war boats until the gun was fired from the first cutter. Then they saw that they were in a trap, so we went round, as it meant a loss of time to put about. As we got farther out the wind began to blow and the sea rose.

We knew now that she was the dhow that had been expected, so another gun was fired with shot, but we were too far away.

By this time she had got round and was making for the sea, so we were in for a hot chase. We put on as much sail as we could; the sea was getting rougher, and we began to ship a lot of water, as the gun in the bows was heavy and put our bows down. The dhow was getting further away from us, so war began in earnest.

Our gun by this time was useless, so we had to revert to our rockets. Orders were given to fire a rocket, and as we had everything ready beforehand, this was soon done. The first rocket was fired and went over. However, we had got our range, fired another rocket, but failed. It was very difficult to fire straight and the boat was jumping about a good deal. We began to lose sight of land, but would not give in now that we had started, so another rocket was fired, but with the same result.

By this time the dhow was getting farther away from us and we were shipping a lot of water. However, another rocket was fired. We could see that everything was being done on board the dhow to get away from us. Our rockets began to get short as we only carried eleven. Another rocket was fired and went very close. The next one to be fired proved to be the winning one, for it cut the parrel that held the yard to the mast, and down came the sail. That, of course, brought the dhow to a standstill and we closed on her. When we got closer we could see that the Arabs and crew were getting ready to repel us, so we had to get our rifles to work and started firing. We knew full well that we could never overcome them, unless we killed some of them.

We could see the captain standing over the helmsman with a scimitar in the act of plunging it into him if he dared alter the helm. Our officer (Sub-Lieutenant Hendereon) had to take great precaution, knowing what we had to contend with, and out of sight of land. So we fired and closed on the dhow.

One of our shots killed the helmsman and he fell dead at the captain's feet. The dhow then swung round into the wind. Our interpreter told us there were slaves on board as he could tell by the smell that came from her. As we drew closer, we could see that they meant to show fight and the interpreter asked their captain what they had on board. Of course he said he was a legal trader, but when he was told he had slaves on board, that we were British men-o'-war's men, would make him a prisoner and it would be better to give in, he very nicely invited us on board.

Of course, we were not to be caught like that, so orders were given for the second cutter to run up on his port side while we ran up on his starboard side. We drew our cutlasses and the bowmen made fast to the dhow. With three British cheers we made a rush for the dhow, despite the fact that a heavy sea was running.

This movement took the Arabs and crew by surprise and they looked dumbfounded. We boarded the dhow and soon made prisoners of the Arabs.

The crew seemed to realise that it was to their advantage to keep quiet, especially as they had seen one of their mates killed. They were afraid and could not understand how our rocket had cut the parrel and brought the sail down. After we had captured them, we started to make things a bit ship shape.

The slaves were dumbfounded because they had been told that the white men would ill use them. The wind began to drop, and in the excitement we had lost our reckoning. A heavy sea was still running, so we dropped the boats astern.

In doing this, the boats collided and a big hole was made in one. Before the boat keeper could get into the other boat, she filled with water and sank like a stone. We lost everything that was in her, e.g. Rifles, gun, clothing etc. That left us with one boat. We had to

Serving out rum, H.M.S. *Edinburgh*.

The Ship's Band, H.M.S. *Edinburgh*.

H.M.S. *Caledonia*. Scrub hammocks, wash clothes.

H.M.S. *Alexandra*, Watch Below.

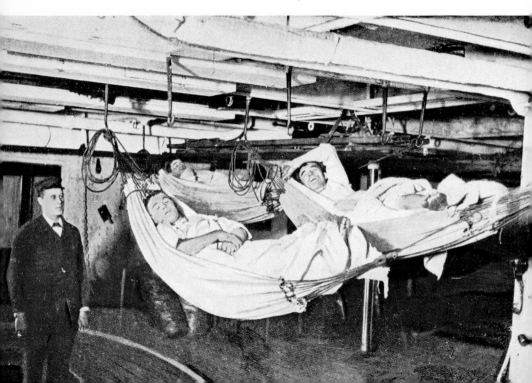

keep a good look-out, in case the Arabs and crew tried to overpower us.

Night was coming on, the sea was going down, but nothing happened. Next morning there was a dead calm and the heat was intense, but we had to make the best of it.

We managed to get some breakfast and got some rice for the slaves. We could not tell how many there were at the time and could not get any information from the captain.

The next thing to do was to get in sight of land and find the ship, so the cutter was manned and the dhow towed. The sun was too hot for that to be continued, and danger stared us in the face. We were running short of water and rice for the slaves because they had come to their journey's end and the slaves would have been landed that day if we had not stopped them.

We lay becalmed all that day. The next day was Sunday and the officers consulted as to what should be done. It was arranged that the cutter should be manned and go towards land and see if anything could be seen of the ship, so off the cutter started with a British cheer from the remainder.

It was thought that the ship would be cruising about looking for us, as she had been away over a fortnight.

It appears that the ship had gone up the gulf to chase a dhow, but she, not drawing much water was able to escape as the ship could not get in close enough. The captain then decided to make for the boats to see how they were getting on and, knowing that our provisions were running short, was getting anxious about us. When he arrived at the place where he expected to find us, he thought something had happened to us as we were not there. A good look-out was kept from the masthead. In the meantime, the crew in the cutter had been pulling a long time and had got out of sight of the dhow. Things began to look very black indeed.

It was about 2 p.m. when the masthead man reported a boat or a sail in sight. At the same time the men in the boat saw smoke in the distance and it gave them fresh courage, but their strength gave out, as they had nothing to eat in the boat and the sun was so hot.

The ship at once steered towards them, and as she got closer, the captain and crew were alarmed at only seeing one boat and nothing else in sight. The men in the boat were exhausted, but as the ship drew near they managed to give a cheer as they got alongside.

Lieutenant Drewey was in charge (the junior officer of the two boats). All the officers and men were on deck with fear in their faces thinking that the crew of the other boat had been massacred. The first question the captain asked was 'Where is the other boat?'

The officer answered that the boat's crew was safe on board the dhow but the boat was sunk. At that news the ship's company gave a hearty cheer and the boat's crew responded as well as they could. They were taken on board as quickly as possible and placed under the doctor's care and their boat was hoisted. The ship then headed for the dhow with full speed. After an hour's steaming, the dhow was sighted. There were great rejoicings in the dhow when the ship came in sight and as she came close to the dhow another cheer went up.

The slaves could not understand it. Some thought their end had come. The Arabs began to fear. The captain seemed unconcerned, although he knew he would be punished.

At about 4 o'clock on the Sunday afternoon our work began. The ship made fast to the dhow; the boat's crew went on board and had a good meal as we were very hungry. The Arabs and crew of the dhow were made prisoners and the slaves transferred to the ship. Some of the men and women were in an awful state. Some of the men were buried up to their chins in sand and had to be dug out. It was a terrible sight to see some of them. They were rotten and suffering from a disease called 'scuffuld' and had to be put in the boats.

By nightfall we had them all on board and found that, all told, the slaves numbered 169. We took the dhow in tow and steamed towards Muscat.

The next morning the dhow was cast adrift, our gun loaded and fired into and sank her. The captain watched her sinking, but said he did not care as it was the fourth one he had lost and would soon get another.

After arriving at Muscat, we took the captain on shore, and after going through the prize court, his dhow was condemned and he was awarded 6 months' imprisonment. This was a very light sentence.

The successful release of slaves from their captors was not always quite so straightforward an affair. Generally the slaves could be relied on to help in their release even though their Arab captors often attempted to persuade them that the white man would maltreat them. Sometimes they were too much on the white man's side as the following story of Holman shows:

I had charge of a steam cutter and dingy, and was stationed off one of the most famous slave marts on the coast of Arabia. We had heard from one of the domestic slaves in the fishing fleet that a number of slaves had just been landed by one of the boats belonging to a neighbour's village, owned by one of the Sheiks of the town, who, having a cargo of slaves coming across in one of his own vessels, just then due, had sent three of his boats to sail along the coast to meet them at a point where they would first strike the Arabian shore. There they were to warn the captain of the position of the boats along the coast, take the slaves on board the fishing boats, which would run them into port with much less chance of being searched, and allow the dhow to remove all traces of having recently had a human cargo on board. This they had contrived to do by landing their cargoes at separate spots along the coast—one at the town we were watching, the day before our arrival.

The Seedie boy (Holman's interpreter) was himself an ex-slave. We arranged that he should go on shore on the pretence of seeing a brother darkie—all of the same tribe call themselves brothers—and find out if the slaves had been sent up country, for sale to the Bedouins, or were still in the town. He landed in the morning and in the evening came off to say that they were still in the town, locked up in a house near the beach, and closely watched. I asked him if he thought he could persuade them to break out of the house— which, according to his description would not be a difficult thing to do—and he said he had no doubt he could, so after dark we landed him again. That night I took the coxswain and one of the crew in the dingy and pulled to and fro for a couple of hours after midnight, the time arranged that they should appear on the beach, and show a light at a spot I had indicated. At three we returned to the cutter without our cargo. The Seedie appeared in the morning to say he could not manage it that night but would the next. The next night the same arrangement was made and ended in the same result. Again our Seedie appeared in the morning with the same tale. On the third night also we were disappointed, and I began to think that Seedie was fooling me. I, however, decided to give him one more chance. As he begged me so hard and assured me their master would be away at a wedding that night, I yielded and he went on shore.

This time Holman decided to go on shore himself.

I was rewarded; for when about fifty yards off the light was displayed, and I could see a group of human figures running along the beach, squatting for a moment about every twenty yards like so many rabbits.

Fearing that the Arabs had caught my Seedie and set a trap for me, and knowing that I dare not touch the shore with my boat to rescue a slave without breaking our treaty with the Sultan of Marcut, whose nominal dominions these were, I kept my boat about twenty yards from the shore and hailed, in my best Persian, to ask if my Seedie was there. He answered, and I directed him to bring the slaves into the water to the boat; they all came, and as they became submerged to the neck I knew I was safe, and that they could have no dry guns without my seeing them over their heads. They tumbled into the boat, fourteen altogether. Thus with Seedie and myself we had 16 aboard a boat not more than large enough for half the number, which submerged her to within six inches of the gunwale. With the cargo packed under the thwarts, and everywhere each on top of the other I started to pull for the middle of the harbour to find the cutter. For at least half an hour did I pull about, without finding a sign. I dare not fire, for Seedie told me the Arabs were aroused on shore, and any of the fishing boats then passing out to sea, might contain a rescue party.

Our position was getting perilous, for a crack in the dingy's planking ordinarily out of the water and of no consequence was now submerged and letting the water in sufficiently fast to gradually increase the weight in the boat and thus decrease the already small amount of free-board. We had not more than three inches or so remaining between our gunwale and the water so that the slightest roll brought the water inboard and increased our danger, when I determined on a line of action which high-handed though it was, was our only chance of safety.

I resolved to hail the next passing fishing boat, make her heave to, with a shot if necessary; put my slaves on board, and my pistol at the captain's head, and compel him to take us and our dingy to our depot about twenty miles up the coast. I had hardly made this resolution when two things came into sight together, a fishing boat and our steam cutter. I soon got my cargo on board the cutter, and steamed off to the rendezvous, arriving at daylight. There were several fishing boats under sail hovering around us, so we loaded our rifles and awaited events in case of any attempt at rescue.

No attempt was made however, and the ship calling during the day, we transferred our woolly-headed fellow creatures on board her, to be taken to Muscat and put through the prize court; so that they might obtain their liberty, and we became entitled to five pounds apiece for their rescue. Another officer captured the fishing boat that had landed slaves at this place, the following day, for which we claimed five pounds for every ton burden, and so we thought we had cleared that matter up.

Imagine my disgust and chagrin about a week after, when the ship came back, and I was informed that the majority of the slaves I had captured were merely refugees, and had been in the country for several years, the least longer than two. We had only ten pounds to come for the lot, two being given in our favour; and this after such an experience! On closely questioning the Seedie I discovered that he had let the bona fide lot of slaves slip through his fingers the first night, and, being ashamed to say so, had employed himself for a couple of days in hunting up all his brothers and sisters in the place— nine brothers and five sisters—and had persuaded them to run away from their masters, and take refuge in the haven he had so cunningly prepared for them.

However successful or unsuccessful the Navy was in the capture of the slaving dhows, the key to the successful suppression of the trade itself lay in the closing of the slave market in Zanzibar. This was achieved in 1873 by a united blockade of the port which persuaded the Sultan, Barghash, to sign a treaty agreeing to the ending of the export of all slaves from the territory as well as the closing of the Market. This is how Humphreys described the matter.

Arriving at Colombo, we coaled ship and then started direct for Zanzibar instead of going by the Aden route. Under steam and sail, the journey took us about a month. We arrived there before the *Magpie* and remained just outside Zanzibar to get things in order and clean up the ship. When we arrived in harbour, we found the Admiral there with the fleet. The fleet had assembled to force the Sultan of Zanzibar to sign the treaty and had given him 24 hours in which to do it.

The signal was made to 'clear ship for action'. It did not take us long to do that. We had three guns on board, viz: 1–6½ Ton and 2– 40 Pounder breech loaders.

As time went on and the Sultan had not signed the treaty, we began to get excited and thought he would not sign it. Twenty-three hours passed and still he had not signed it and we were getting near fever heat with excitement.

Within twenty-three and a half hours we saw the Sultan going to the flagship in his barge with presents for the Admiral and he then signed the treaty. Our hopes were dashed to the ground when the signal was made 'The Sultan has signed a treaty to suppress the slave trade, and do away with the slave market.'

The closure of the market did not mark the end of the slave trade altogether. Barghash, though he kept faith within his dominions on the island, had no real authority over the sheiks on the mainland and the traffic continued, though much diminished.

As elsewhere, the slave trade could never be entirely extinguished until slavery itself was abolished. Though the specific anti-slavery squadron was disbanded in 1883, even as late as 1899 the last known slave ship to leave East African waters was wrecked near Mombassa and the District Officer arrested the master and the crew and sent the liberated slaves back to their homes. It was not until 1907 that slavery was abolished in the mainland domain of the Sultan of Zanzibar and not until 1922 that similar steps were taken in Tanganyika.

17

From Seaman to Coast Guard—
Charles Humphreys

Before I close, I must relate one or two narrow escapes I had. I was up aloft one day off the East Coast of Africa when the ship was rolling very hard. My mate, next to me, caught hold of the rope I was going to catch hold of, when it parted and down he went and was killed. He died within 20 minutes and the last words he said were 'Lay me on my left side.' Had I caught hold of that rope, it would have been me killed instead of him.

On another occasion, we were cruising in the boats, and had to board a dhow. While I was looking down the hold, an Arab rushed at me with a Scimitar. Had it not been for a pal I should have been killed instantly.

Another time, when cruising up a river to see if any slave dhows were about to run, we were about to land when a lot of natives rushed to the river bank and fired poisoned tipped arrows at us. We just managed to get to the middle of the river and by good Providence escaped, despite the fact that the natives rushed into the water after us. About 2 years previous, they had massacred a whole boat's crew.

Many minor escapes I had and in looking back I thank God for bringing me through them safely.

So Charles Humphreys ends his 'Reminiscence of Forty Years in the Royal Navy and Coast Guards'.
The only dramatic event in his Coast Guard service occurred at Mumbles.

I was promoted to Chief Boatman in Charge and sent to Mumbles, a very pretty place about 5 miles from Swansea, South Wales. During my stay there, several shipwrecks occurred. A very sad accident happened the first Sunday I was there.

The life boat was called out to a wreck. When she was going into Port Talbot, a heavy sea caught her and threw her on broadside. She capsized and 6 of her crew were drowned. This threw the whole of Mumbles into mourning and left about 30 children fatherless.

The duties of the Coast Guard were not very onerous or exciting. Raising and lowering the flag at sunrise and sunset (as Agnes Weston has recalled), was a major duty, and also, of course, keeping a general lookout on the shipping. It could be a very lonely life, as many of the stations were in remote areas. Humphreys spent some time in Ireland and there the Coast Guards were exceptionally cut off. Raghley, where he was stationed for nearly six years, was 17 miles from Sligo, and Teelin, to which he then moved, was 33 miles from the nearest town.

The stations themselves contained a fair size staff not simply for the duties they had to perform but also because the Coast Guard service was an important, if not the major, reserve of seamen for the Navy in time of war. The regular Navy had become extremely professional and the merchant seamen collected by the Press Gangs who had served the nation well in the Napoleonic Wars could no longer be expected to cope—and not simply because the Press Gang itself was unacceptable. The Crimean War showed the problem up very clearly. The Naval Coast Volunteers, founded in 1853, provided a reserve of sorts but though they received twenty-eight days training a year, they could only be expected to serve less than fifty leagues from the shore except in an emergency. This limitation was later removed but the organisation was disbanded in 1873 and replaced by the Royal Naval Artillery Reserve which in turn became the R.N.V.R.

For much of the nineteenth century the one fully trained reserve was the Coast Guard. There was also a Corps of Royal Naval Volunteers which was founded in 1859 and ultimately developed into the Royal Naval Reserve. By 1870 this consisted of nearly 20,000 men but even so it was the Coast Guard that at this period provided the leadership. One of the disadvantages of the Coast Guards tended to be their age, as the men entered after service in the Royal Navy but this was not as serious as might be thought. For example, Charles Humphreys having served eleven years in the Navy was still only twenty-four when he joined the Coast Guard service. How effective they might have been in time of war was, of course, never tested. The reserves were re-organised early this century and the Coast Guards disappeared. Nevertheless until then they did provide some measure of reserve strength for the Royal Navy.

Before joining the Coast Guard, Charles Humphreys had served in the Navy.

Leaving home at the age of 13½ years, I joined the Navy at Uxbridge on October 28th 1870. I was sent to the *Hebe* (then lying off Woolwich Dockyard) an old hulk, at that time tender to the *Fishguard*. My first impressions of sea life were very romantic, but I soon found that it was a very rough life. I was soon sorry that I had joined the Navy and wanted to go home. When I went on board the *Hebe* I was lost in wonder, although she had no guns on board. The dockyard was also a wonderful place to me.

I was drafted to Portsmouth to join the training ship H.M.S. *St. Vincent*. She had already too many boys on board, so I was sent to Portland to join the *Boscawen*.

His remarks on the *Boscawen* have already been recorded and after that he went to the *Excellent* for gunnery training. Again he was less happy with the service than contemporaries such as Noble.

I was then rated 1st Class Boy and entitled to 2/- per week, but as I was in debt to the Crown for my uniform, I had no money to come. At that time honesty was not the best policy in the navy, at least, not with the ship's stewards. Boys were robbed of their money; clothes were put down to them, which they never received, and as I suppose, I was a 'green horn', I was one of those who had to suffer. Of course, going to Portsmouth brought me nearer home and I thought I should be able to go home for Christmas. My chum (who lived at Staines) was better off than me. My parents sent me some money. It was not sufficient to take me home, but we trained to a place some miles from Staines and walked the rest, and I stayed the night with my chum. The next day I walked the ten miles from Staines to Uxbridge, as there was no train service in those days. Of course I had to walk back to my chum at the end of my holiday. After arriving at Portsmouth, I remained on board the *Excellent* until the end of January 1872.

His first fully commissioned ship was the *Vulture*, a small gun vessel with a crew of 96 officers and men, and he served in her for the full commission in the East. Some of their exploits have already been described in the chapter on the slave trade. It seems to have been a happy ship—at least the Captain was popular.

Our Captain travelled with us, and he was so much liked, that when we arrived at Victoria, some of the men took the horses out of the carriage that was waiting for him, and dragged it through the streets. This of course caused quite a sensation, but it was all taken in good part.

It was an eventful commission. Aside from their slaving exploits, some of which have already been recounted, and visits to unusual places they also acted as a funeral barge.

When we returned to Zanzibar in 1874, the mail boat arrived, with Mr. H. W. Stanley and two other Englishmen on board from England. They were going by dhow down the Zambesi river to find Dr. Livingstone who had been lost, nothing having been heard of him for some time. We had them on board for two days, and then gave them a good send off, wishing them good luck.

We then proceeded down the coast to Pemba to cruise. We sent two boats away to cruise. After boarding many dhows, they returned to the ship. Nothing eventful happened, so we returned to Zanzibar.

While lying there we received news that the body of Dr. Livingstone had arrived at 'Bagarnoyon' (the main land). We went across to bring the body to Zanzibar. When we arrived there, we found that the body had not arrived but was expected in about two days. After waiting that time, a party of 12 men, myself included, went ashore with a coffin our carpenters had made on board. We had to walk two miles inland to a French mission. When we arrived there we asked the priest where the body was and were directed to two chairs with a pole with a horse cloth wrapped round it and the body enclosed, on them. We were informed by Lieutenant Moffat that that was how the body was carried a thousand miles through jungle and desert. The journey took nine months. Their luggage was nearly worn through with age and rough wear.

We placed the body, pole and all in the coffin. The pole was sawn off at each end to allow the corpse to go into the coffin. These ends were afterwards sawn in 12 portions and one portion given to each of the bearers as a memento. We carried the body on board. This was a very trying job as the sun was pouring down and we had to walk two miles.

Dr. Livingstone's little black boy was with his master, so we took all on board and proceeded to Zanzibar and landed the body at the Consul's house to wait for the mail boat to take it to England.

The visit of the Prince of Wales, however, was more cheerful.

At this time we received orders to await the arrival of the Prince of Wales who was coming to India and would be out about November. Of course we had to make great preparations for him; at the same time, anxiously waiting for orders from home. They finally arrived by mail boat in September 1875. It seemed a long time to wait, but passed along as we had plenty of work to do to get ready for the Prince of Wales.

At last, about the 1st. November about 6 o'clock in the morning the *Osborne*, the Prince of Wales' yacht, arrived in advance of the *Seraphis* to see if all was ready. We were the only man-o'-war there, as the flying squadron had gone to Bombay to receive the Prince upon his arrival there.

The *Seraphis* arrived about 7 a.m. on 1st. November 1875 and we received him with honours. After the Prince landed and paid a visit to the governor he returned on board and gave a dinner to the officers. Early in the evening the homeward bound mail boat left for England before the Prince had got his dispatches ready. He heard that we were homeward bound but could not leave before our relief came out. He asked our captain if he could do anything for us. The captain wanted to be home by Christmas if he could. The Prince was good enough to order us to take his dispatches to Suez as soon as possible.

A signal was made at 10 o'clock at night 'Coal ship and prepare for home.' A great shout went up from the ship's company on learning the news. The *Seraphis* left the next morning and we left the same evening. Before we left we had to get some stores we had left at the Arsenal. The boat I belonged to was sent to fetch them and sailing up the river a squall came and capsized us. We were just out of sight of the ship, and but for some merchant ships we should have been drowned. As it was we were in the water four hours. The place was infested with sharks, but the natives also helped us, however, all's well that ends well. However, we arrived on board at last. The officers had wondered what had happened to us but were glad we were all safe. They were sorry some of the men suffered from the effects.

How different, too, was their homecoming from that of a ship seventy years earlier.

The port admiral inspected us the same day and was very pleased with what he saw and welcomed us home and hoped we would have a very happy New Year and well earned leave. We then went into the basin to strip and pay off.

The weather was so cold that we were unable to do anything, after coming from such a hot climate so the Admiral sent a working party to get our stores out while we went on leave for a few days.

After a time in the tender to the guardship at Harwich where he had his first contact with the Coast Guard Service. He then served for three years in an Indian troopship and having applied for the Coast Guard Service he was accepted and went to the station at Raghley in September 1881. He retired in 1909.

18

A Sailor of the Eighties—Michael Toman

Michael Toman, Engine Room Artificer, is a superb representative of the changes that had taken place in the Navy in seventy years. Unfortunately we know little of him beyond a diary he kept on board H.M.S. *Egeria* during a surveying voyage in the Far East between October 1886 and December 1889.

In one respect it is the similarities with the past which are the most noticeable. Here is Toman's entry for their first Christmas—which occurred while they were passing through the Suez Canal.

> December 25th. 1886. Christmas dinner not a bad one under the circumstances. Then the old routine was carried out of carrying some of the ship's company around the deck on a chair. And it is laughable to see a lot of blue jackets when they intend to have a bit of sport. They make up a strange band, and the day being fine (only rather warm) they were dancing and singing on the upper deck all afternoon. Then, after tea they formed a Nigger party on the quarter deck where all the officers came out to see them. There was dancing and singing until late at night when they finished up with the National Anthem.

But Toman's interests do show a marked difference from his predecessors.

> We tested the water for our information in the bitter lake and found 16 degrees of salt, that is 6 degrees more than our ordinary sea water at home.
>
> December 26th. Naturally disappointed because no leave at Port Suez. The First Lieutenant took the view of the ship's company in a group and afterwards took the C.P.O.'s and P.O.'s by themselves, he having an apparatus for taking Photos.

As his remarks about the bluejackets show, Toman obviously regarded himself as a cut above them, and indeed he did have the standing of a Petty Officer, having some control over the stokers' though he suffered with them.

April 14th. Through so many of our stokers being on the sick list we have had to put them in two watches. The weather is still very warm—average about 130 degrees in the Engine Room.

A great deal of their duties were somewhat monotonous. For example:

June 29. Arrived at and proclaimed the Island called Phoenix. This island is three miles by one with a lagoon in the centre, is uninhabited. The island is flat, the highest point being only 16 or 20 feet. There are no tall trees but is nearly covered with long grass and low bush. The island is noted for goane and is completely alive with birds. Two boats with officers and men landed to hoist the flag and had to keep waving a large stick left and right knocking the bush down as they went along. Nests were numerous in the grass, the parent bird not moving or offering to fly even when walked over. Sixteen different pairs were brought off to the ships and a few rabbits by our naturalist. Owing to depth of water, could not get anchorage. We left the island at 5.30, the colour pole and jack the only things to be seen standing out of the bush.

Toman had some opportunities himself of making boat trips but on one occasion such a trip almost ended in disaster.

Prepared to leave ship at 10 a.m. for a day's boating along with five others, with us provisions for the day, a gun, 2 axes, a saw, sails, oars and boat hook. We had not got very far away from the ship when we saw a signal hoisted to call us back, this being ordered by the captain on account of strong wind blowing. We turned around and as the wind caught the sail on the opposite tack the boat suddenly turned keel upwards throwing us all out in ten fathoms of water. As we all had our clothes on there was a lot of struggling to the upturned boat which sank beneath us and left us struggling again. My opposite number J. Mark grabbed at a small barrel containing fresh water; with this and an oar he had sufficient buoyance to keep him afloat as he could not swim well; they kept away from the boat which was left to three of us, Chief Artificer, myself and a stoker. The boat appeared again, this time stern upwards and I was the first to grab it, then the C.E.R.A., and as the stoker could not swim and it was a case of every man for himself, he just managed to get hold of the C.E.R.A. but as he himself was nearly exhausted I heard him shout 'Let go

Freethy', (this being the stoker's name). Freethy let go him and caught hold of me but as the boat was sinking again beneath us I had to shake him off. We were now about ten minutes in the water and as this place is noted for sharks I was expecting a visit all the time but fortunately they did not make their appearance. I was watching our lifeboat coming from the ship and unexpectedly I saw a boat coming up from behind me. I struck out for her and was the first to get in. Then I caught hold of the C.E.R.A. and hauled him in, while the boat's crew hauled Freethy in. By this time our life boat under the command of Lieutenant Munroe and ship's galley under command of Mr. Grant boatswain the others were picked up. There was a lot of excitement on board as the accident was watched by the whole ship's company and as they knew there was some who could not swim and could only see our black heads popping up occasionally they little thought we would all come back alive. Another boat arrived from our ship and took us all in and brought us on board while the life boat and galley turned our wrecked boat keel upwards alongside. When she was uprighted, the mast and sail were set but everything else was gone out of her and lost. The boat that arrived first and picked me and two others up belonged to a schooner lying at Anchor flying the Union Jack but manned by niggers.

Not all Toman's exploits were quite so hair-raising and his main interest lay in trips ashore, where inevitably drink was one of the main prerequisites. At Perim:

Went on shore this afternoon. There is not many inhabitants here and how they live I could not make out as there is no work of any description here and not a blade of grass to be seen or a tree either. I walked about the few huts here and there until I saw a white man. I asked him if I could get a drink. He told me there was not a pub in the place but he treated me to a bottle of whiskey. In our conversation he told me he came from Birkenhead so we had a long chat about home. He directed me which way to have a walk and I promised to call later on. In my travel I came to a small grave yard where a few English subjects are buried. Walking along the beach, I came to a fine oyster bed. Had a good feed and returned to see my towny. Stopped with him until late when I returned on board.

And at another port he noted:

Not much attraction for Jack on shore as things is pretty dear. A bottle of ale is 1 rupee (about 1/6).

Though there were other interests and at Colombo:

Went on shore this afternoon. Hired a cab and drove to Arabi Pasha's house about three miles. Also to the mad house; visited all the wards. There is 150 mad men all coloured; they seemed to be very quiet. I also visited the Temple. Saw Budha which they call God.

More appreciated still by the whole ship's company was a cricket match at Batticaloa.

May 24th. It being the birthday of the Queen we had bunting flying from stern to stern of our little craft and she looked very pretty lying two miles from shore by herself. We were all very glad to get here as soon as possible because we were going to play a game of cricket. It being the first since we commissioned so there was great debating about who would play and who would win however I was asked to play so I very soon accepted the invitation along with another of my mess mates Mr. Denton. The match was an invitation by some gentlemen on shore to the officers of our ship. There was leave given to the ship's company and all hands went, only part of the duty watch on duty. There was three boat loads towed by one of our steam cutters as we had to go up river about 4 miles inland. We reached the field about 3 p.m. where the resident gentlemen was waiting our arrival. Some were natives and others Englishmen. But unfortunately they were 4 short which was very good news for us as we soon made up the number, myself being one picked out to play against my own ship's company. The day being fine we very soon began the match the ship's club having their first innings, the last wicket falling to a score of 68. There was plenty of spectators who took a lively interest in watching the game. So after having a little refreshments at the tent during which time our first Lieutenant took our photo we commenced the game again. This time the numbers were reversed when the last wicket fell to a score of 86 after a very hard contested battle. We all gathered about the tent every player seeming quite pleased with the afternoon's sport. So after a song or two by our jolly tars we gave three good cheers for the gentlemen of the Batticaloa C.C. when the latter raised three good hearty cheers for the Captain and Men of H.M. Ship *Egeria* this time all the Natives joining in which made the air ring—finishing up by our Captain singing the National Anthem.

Their return journey was not without incident.

In coming back down the river we ran ashore on account of the tide being low. We soon got clear again and reached our ship about 7 p.m.

Batticaloa was a very popular place with the *Egeria* and on the Queen's Jubilee—28th June, 1887—they celebrated with the local inhabitants.

We had steam up early this morning. Raised anchor and steamed about 5 miles along the coast and anchored again opposite Fort. About 10 a.m. we spread our bunting rainbow style and fired 21 guns. The natives could be seen in hundreds in and about the fort trying to have a view of our ship. At 11:30 there was piped special leave for both watches, so every man in the ship felt inclined to celebrate the Queen's jubilee on shore, but as a certain number had to stay on board, they were lucky who got the opportunity of going on the 28th. However, I managed to be one of the party to land and about 12 noon the steam cutter with three boats in tow was ready for leaving the ship as we had to go about seven miles before landing. We had bunting flying from stem to stern of each boat. There was nothing of note until we reached a rounding point about half a mile from the village when to our surprise there was a volley of guns fired and so they kept it up until we landed. The place of landing was beautifully decorated with flags and flowers, the Bands playing so that we could not hear our ears. There were thousands of natives watching our arrival which lined each side of a long but narrow river. There was a beautiful Arch erected over our little landing stage. There was also Mr. Fisher the British Consul along with a number of other gentlemen and ladies awaiting our arrival and such a nice sight it was I shall never forget. When the party landed we fell in four deep myself being in the front rank under the charge of our Captain and officers. I felt my position rather awkward it being the first time for me, so I had to be attentive to the right about face quick march and so on. But we got over that all right and very shortly found ourselves in a field close by, where we were drawn up single line abreast so that we should see a native procession. The first part of it to appear was a very large sized elephant, which the keeper made kneel down to us when he was opposite. It was followed by a number of small ones each carrying three or four men on their backs and the men playing an instrument which made a horrid noise but I suppose they called it music. When this was over we marched to the Court House, a large building in the field which was already nearly filled with ladies, a great number of them seemed to be Europeans. So after a short speech by Mr. Fisher and our Captain, we all joined in the National Anthem. After that three cheers for the Queen three cheers for our noble Queen and so, which brought this meeting to a close. Then we marched to the fort and were shown a large room and a number of small ones. Mr. Fisher told us we would be provided with victuals during our stay on shore as we intended to make a four day visit of it, and no mistake we were very well provided for as only for this arrangement we could not get refreshments elsewhere. There was a programme of sports for the afternoon, which commenced about 2 p.m. There was running jumping etc. etc. and some very good prizes given for the winners and as it was open for natives as well as our ship's company there was plenty of entrys to make good sport. The sailors did not forget it was the Queen's jubilee and as they had permission to wear any clothing they wished there was some very curious rigs amongst them. They formed a nigger party of about a dozen, one being a very tall young sailor about seven feet; he wore a hat about three feet long, he came to the front of the party of ladies at a tent where there was a small platform laid. He sang a duet along with a little fellow about half his length which caused a deal of amusement and laughter. There was Long Sally three sticks for 5 cents which was pretty well patronized. And all together we spent a very pleasant afternoon. When 7:30 came around, we all went to the fort and had refreshments; after that a song or two. When we were informed that there would be a display of fireworks and at 9:30 it commenced. There was some very pretty illuminations amongst them being a model of the *Egeria*. This was kept up until a late hour, when we made our way to the fort for the night. Going on board the next day about noon to relieve our opposite numbers so that they could have a little amusement on shore.

Not that all went well for the *Egeria* all the time.

There has been an accident or two with our ship's company, one able seaman getting 42 days hard labour for using threatening language and another found in the store room forward suspended by the neck. He was cut down in time to save his life.

And some time later:

During our stay at Hobart, three marines and two blue jackets ran away and was not caught up to our time of starting for Sydney.

Yet, even on board there were diversions—fishing for instance.

Fresh fish being very acceptable, lines went to work early and fish was hauled pretty often. One man hooked one which he thought was a shark. The line not being very strong had to put a rope around him. On getting him to the surface he was hauled in board just in time as there were three sharks immediately underneath him to

14

devour him. He proved to be a fine rock cod measuring four feet
and weighing 48 pounds when dressed. No person in the ship had
ever seen one so large.

But they were not always so successful.

Good fishing being carried on by all, this afternoon, rock cod being
hauled in pretty freely. Saw a cod being hauled up followed by two
sharks. The cod which would weigh about 8 pounds was bit clean
off close to the head by one of the sharks. The head was alive a
considerable time after taken from the hook.

Nor did their pets prosper.

We have had poor luck with our domestic tribe. One goat from Ceylon
has died and two tortoises from Ceylon and one cat from England.

But there was always the ship's concerts to keep everyone amused.

Entertainment on board. A magic lantern by a Mr. Brown. It commenced about 8 p.m. by our glee party singing several songs. After
that we were in the dark and saw the views which consisted of
native life in these islands from photos which Mr. Brown himself
took. Some were very interesting, consisting chiefly of cannibalism,
one family cooking five bodies. Mr. Brown explaining how he saw
these things going on some years ago and the difficulty he had to get
the niggers to let him take their photo. Sometimes when he would be
adjusting his apparatus they would run away thinking he was going
to shoot them. The entertainment was very good the last view being
Queen Victoria. Nearly all the white folk from shore was on board.
At the conclusion Captain Aldridge thanked Mr. Brown; this was
taken up by a good clapping of hands amongst the tars and the glee
party sang the National Anthem.

Rather a different existence from the 'Old' Navy! But possibly the
best picture to end with is that of the celebration of the Queen's
birthday in Tongatabu.

Had bunting flying from stem to stern. Went on shore at noon, saw
about 200 natives gathered together in a field, a brass band in attendance, the centre of attraction being about two dozen of them
dressed something after the style of Mexican Joe's Wild West rig.
They looked very nice doing the war dance with guns, spears, etc.
keeping time to the band and Tom Jones. I was along with several
of my shipmates and we got to understand that they were gathered
to hold sports and subscribe to a collection for the loss of a fishing
boat belonging to a native. They came to us with the plate; all eyes

were turned on us and as each one put his small donation on they clapped hands and shouted Marlow at the top of their voices, Marlow meaning thanks or welcome. Afterwards they made signs to us to sit down. They brought us their native drink which tasted like soap suds, not a bit like Hobart hop liquid. We watched them nearly all the afternoon. There are very few houses here but hundreds of huts amongst the trees, mostly oranges and coconuts, the former at their best and lying on the grass in thousands. We came on board at 9:0 and at 9:30 a concert was held on the quarter-deck, a few European visitors being on board. Singing was kept up until 11 p.m. The song 'Green Lanes of England' being sung very well by S. Taylor, encore Benjamin Burns, finishing by Captain Aldridge. God save the Queen.

What could be a more appropriate end than the strains of the National Anthem floating across the lagoon at Tongatabu? Pax Britannica.

LIST OF NAUTICAL TERMS

Abaft: On the after side of. Further towards the stern.

Andrew, Andrew Miller: Colloquial name for the Navy. Andrew Miller was a zealous press-gang officer who impressed so many men into the King's Naval Service during the Napoleonic wars that he was said to own the Royal Navy.

Awnings: A canvas covering erected as a shelter against the weather or the sun.

Bidar: A paddling dugout canoe.

Boatswain's Call or Pipe: Whistle used to give orders to the crew. Generally used by a boatswain's mate.

Bollards: Large and firmly secured circular post used to secure ropes, etc.

Booby Hatch: A sliding cover that has to be pushed aside to allow passage to or from a cabin, etc.

Boom: Lower boom to which were secured the ship's boats when they were in the water.

Brig: Sailing vessel with two masts and square rigged on both of them.

Bunting: General term used for flags of all sorts.

Cable Length: A nautical unit of distance, about 200 yards.

Cable Laid: Referred to a rope, one that is made by laying up three ropes so that they make one large rope.

Canister: A missile consisting of small iron balls packed in a cylindrical tin.

Cat the Anchor: To carry the anchor to the Cat Head and so leaving the hawse hole clear.

Caulking: The oakum pressed into the seams between the 'planks' to make the ship watertight.

Circulars: Circular letters of instructions issued by the Admiralty.

Clear Lower Deck: Order given for all hands to fall in on the upper deck.

Clew: A lower corner of a square sail; the aftmost corner of a fore and aft sail.

Coamings: Vertical erection around hatches to prevent water passing down the opening.

Courses: Sails bent (attached) to the lower yard of a sailing ship.

Crosstrees: Thwart ship timbers on a mast, designed to increase the spread of the shrouds and form support for the tops.

Dabash: A gentoo agent—a pagan as opposed to a Mohammedan inhabitant of Hindistan in South India.

Dhow: Used to describe any Arab vessel. Generally low in the bows and high in the poop with a large triangular lateen-shaped sail and a dozen oars.

Ditty Bag: Small canvas bag in which a seaman kept his small personal belongings.

Divisions: Daily morning muster of ship's company. Men muster by divisions and proceed to prayers.

Earing: Certain small ropes employed to fasten the upper corner of a sail to its yard.

Epaulet: Mark of distinction worn by officers on their shoulders.

Forecastle: The upper deck from right forward to some line abaft (astern of) the cable holders.

Fore Cuddy: A cabin in the fore part of the boat.

Fearnought: Stout felt worsted cloth, used for port linings, hatchway fire screens, etc.

Flinch or Flench: The blubber of the whale laid out in long slices. Hence to cut into long strips.

Foul (of the Anchor): In general means the opposite of clear; here (p. 21), the rope round the anchor.

Frigate: A square rigged warship, used as a scout.

Fugleman: A specially expert and well drilled soldier.

Furl: To gather in a sail or awning and secure it in that position.

Gaff: Spar to which the head of a Spanker is attached.

Gig: A light narrow galley or ship's boat, either sailed or rowed.

Goane: Probably Goanna, any large lizard.

Grape: A Missile between Canister Shot and Round Shot. A number of small balls not normally placed in a container.

Grog: The mixture of rum and water issued to seamen.

Gunner's Wad: A kind of plug which is rammed home over the shot in the gun to hold it in place.

Gunroom: The mess of officers of subordinate rank especially midshipmen.

Halyards halliards: Ropes by which sails, yards, flogs, etc. are hoisted.

Handspike: Lever used to heave round the windlass.

Hawse: Here (p. 47), means the hawse hole through which the cable passes from the ship to the anchor.

Head: The latrine in a warship, situated right forward in a sailing ship.

Holystone: Small piece of soft white sandstone used for cleaning wooden decks by rubbing.

Hooker: Colloquial word for a ship—derived from the word for an anchor— a hook.

Hummock, 'hummocky': A pile or ridge or rock or ice, hence hummocky—uneven ground.

Hydrographer: One who surveys the ocean or sea, etc. for the purpose of navigation and commerce.

Indiaman: Any ship in the trade to India or the East Indies. More particularly one in the service of the East India Company.

Jack: Colloquial name for a naval rating.

Joey: Colloquial name for a marine.

Jury Rigged: Temporary makeshift rig in place of rigging carried away in a storm or a battle. Hence any old clothes.

Kedge, Kedging: Moving a vessel by laying out an anchor (usually the Kedge anchor) and then heaving her to it.

Lead: The weight at the end of the lead-line used to measure the depth of the sea.

Lee: The side opposite to that from which the wind is blowing (the weather side).

Lee Helmsman: Junior Rating who stands on the lee side of the helmsman learning the job of steering the ship.

Log: Used to ascertain the speed of the ship. The 'log' was dropped astern and line paid out to it as the ship went forward. The amount of line paid out gives the speed of the ship.

Lumping: Lumpers were labourers employed to load and unload merchant ships when in harbour—hence lumping, to load and unload.

Main Brace; Splice the: Issue an extra ration of rum. The Main Brace, one of the heaviest and thickest ropes in the ship was only spliced occasionally.

Main Deck: Principal deck next below the upper deck.

Master-at-Arms: The Petty Officer responsible for police duties on board.

Master, Master's Mate: The Navigating Lieutenant and his assistant.

Mizen: The after or sternmost of the three masts.

Necklace: A chain or stop round a mast.

Orlop Deck: The lowest deck in the ship immediately above the hold.

Pah, pa: A Maori fort.

Parrel: A band by which a yard is fastened to a mast.

Peak: After upper corner of a sail.

Pemmicen: Beef, dried, pounded and pressed into cakes, usually flavoured with currants or the like.

Pinnace: A ship's boat smaller than the barge, generally two masted.

Poop: Short deck raised above the upper deck right aft. Not found on steamships.

Plain Sail: Sail with no reef taken in.

Press, Press Gang: Gangs that were sent to 'impress' or compel seamen to join the Royal Navy.

Privateer: A private vessel commissioned to seize and plunder enemy ships.

Quarter-deck: The after part of the upper deck to right aft or to the poop if there was one.

Quartermaster: The Petty Officer who is responsible for seeing that the helmsman carries out his duties properly.

Rat Lines: Small lines that traverse the shrouds (q.v.) of a ship horizontally forming a series of steps.

Rattans: Lengths of stick tied together and used to beat the backs of seamen. Generally made of bamboo.

Redoubt: A field work, enclosed on all sides.

Reef: To reduce the sail area by rolling up and securing part of it.

Ring Bolt: Bolt secured to vessel and carrying a ring to which blocks, etc. can be attached.

R.M.A.: Royal Marine Artillery, sometimes known as Bullocks from their physique.

R.M.L.I.: Royal Marine Light Infantry, sometimes known as Turkeys because of the red tunics they wore.

Roster: A list kept of ratings or officers in order of promotion so that the next person to be promoted is the one at the head of the roster.

Royals: The sail set at the top of the three masts.

Seize: To bind two ropes together by means of a light line tightly turned round them. Here (p. 29), to tie the wrists and ankles to a grating.

Sheets: Ropes fastened to the lower corners of a sail to hold the bottom of the sail in a required position.

Shiners: Colloquial expression for coins.

Shroud: Rope or wire rigging that supports a mast or bowsprit.

Slops: Clothing provided by the service, carried for issue to the seamen.

Snug: Generally 'Snug Down'. To reduce sail.

Spanker: Fore and after sail spread on after side of mizen mast.

Spelloe: Strictly 'Spell ho!'—A call for relief.

Squeegees: Flat pieces of wood with a rubber strip at the lower end used to remove water from the deck.

Stays: Ropes that steady a mast in a fore and after direction, but a ship is said to be in stays when the head is being turned to windward for the purpose of tacking.

Stern Sheets: The space in the boat abaft the after thwart—i.e. the aftermost part of the boat.

Studding Sail, Stun' Sail: A narrow sail set at the outer edge of a square sail when the wind is light.

Swab: Seaman's mop for drying decks.

Swallow the Anchor: To give up going to sea.

Swing the Lead: To avoid duty by feigning illness, to malinger.

Swing the Monkey: This game probably consisted of a 'he' standing in a rope, which was attached from above. He swung round on the rope and attempted to touch the bystanders.

Tack: To change the course of a ship by turning the head through the wind.

Tacks: Ropes by which the weather, lower corner of a course is hauled down.

Taffrail: Originally the upper edge of the stern. More probably an ornamental rail going around the stern and above the original taffrail.

Thwart: Transverse seat in a boat. Hence athwart means across.

Top: Platform at head of lower mast (i.e. about half-way up).

Traps: Mess traps; The seaman's pots and pans.

Trice: To haul or lift by means of a lashing or line. Here means that the ports—openings in the ship's side—were lashed up.

Warrant-Officer: A subordinate officer whose authority was derived from a warrant issued by the Admiralty rather than a commission issued by the Queen.

Wear: To bring a vessel round on to the other tack by turning away from the wind. The opposite of tack.

Works: A ship is said to work when the timbers move and allow water to enter.

Yaw: To lurch or sway to either side of an intended course.

Yard: Spar fitted across a mast primarily to extend the head of the sail below the foot.

INDEX